STEWART BROWN

TOURIST, TRAVELLER, TROUBLEMAKER:

ESSAYS ON POETRY

PEEPAL TREE

First published in Great Britain in 2007
Peepal Tree Press Ltd
17 King's Avenue
Leeds LS6 1QS
UK

ISBN13: 9 781 84523 053 1

ARTS COUNCIL
ENGLAND

Peepal Tree gratefully acknowledges Arts Council support

ACKNOWLEDGMENTS

Acknowledgments are due to the editors of the following publications where versions of these essays first appeared: Journals –

Anglophonia: Journal of English Studies; BIM; Index on Censorship; Kunapipi; Kyk-over-al; New Literature Review; Planet; Poetry Review; Poetry Wales; The New Voices; The Works; Wasafiri; West Africa.

Edited books –

The Art of Derek Walcott, (1991); *Essays on African Writing 2: Contemporary Literature*, (1995); *Robinson Crusoe: Myths and Metamorphoses* (1996) *The Bardie Clan: Selected and New Poems of Don Burness*, (1998); *All are Involved: the Art of Martin Carter*, (2000); *Kiss & Quarrel: Yoruba/English: Strategies of Mediation*, (2000); *The People's Poet: Emerging perspectives on Niyi Osundare*, (2003); *Remembering the Sea: an introduction to Frank A. Collymore*, (2004); *The Oxford Book of Caribbean Verse* (2005); *Martin Carter: Poems* (2006); *Caribbean Dispatches: Beyond the Tourist Dream* (2006)

This book is dedicated to

(The) Ann_e_ Walmsley

CONTENTS

INTRODUCTION

This collection of essays is something of a *cohobblopot*, to use a rather wonderful Barbadian term – a mixed bag of talks, presentations, introductions to anthologies, academic and literary journal articles, all more or less reworked and loosely drawn together by a focus on poetry in English from parts of the world where I have lived and worked over thirty odd years – whether the calypso lyrics of Red Plastic Bag or the 'Yoruba poetry written in English' of Niyi Osundare or the radical Dub of Linton Kwesi Johnson. Or indeed my own work as a poet; I felt that it was important to include essays that relate to my own poetry in order to establish the ground from which these critical responses are made, that my claim – such as it is – to have anything to say about these other writer's work begins in my own practice as a poet rather than as an academic scholar. Which is not to equate my poetry with the work of Walcott, Brathwaite and Osundare or to in any way sleight the approaches and responses of non-poet critics but simply to establish that, as a critic, I have some practical and ongoing experience of what's involved in the making of a poem, and that I think that fact makes some sort of difference to the ways in which I respond to other poets' work.

The other biographical factor that informs my perspective as a reader of African and Caribbean writing is that as a young man I spent several years teaching in both West Africa and the Caribbean, and I have continued to travel and work in both regions through four decades now. So the collection begins with autobiographical essays that were written out of particular occasions when I was asked to speak or write about my own work as poet, in relation to travel writing or to contextualise a long poem, or to commemorate a particular occasion in which I was involved because of my poetry. Elsewhere in the collection there are essays that draw directly on my experience as an editor of Caribbean poetry anthologies or as a judge of the Guyana Prize, or as a member of the audience at the Barbados Crop Over Calypso Finals. I have not tried to distance myself from or to disguise the nature of my connection with the material that is the subject of these essays. Although the essays in this collection are primarily concerned with aspects of Caribbean and African poetry there are other discussions along the way of Welsh, English and American poets – most of them travellers of one kind or another – whose work I have encountered and admired and which seems to me to fit with the general thrust of the book.

For the most part, then, these are literary rather than strictly academic essays, many of them were written either to be read aloud at presentations of one kind or another or as essays in cultural rather than academic journals. That distinction is as much a matter of language and style as anything else. I have tried to write in such a way that a non-specialist reader can comfortably engage with these essays, indeed as several of them began life as 'Introductions' they assume an intellectually curious rather than a particularly well informed audience. Many of these pieces began as oral presentations and although they have been edited and changed in various ways for this collection I have not 'written out' that oral context altogether but rather tried to keep that sense of the audience and occasion that they were made for. That accounts for the occasional repetition of fragments of material across various essays – like any jobbing academic I have sometimes been guilty of recycling ideas in different contexts to different audiences. 'Spreading the word' about the work of a particular writer or indeed this whole body of writing which – until relatively recently – has not had much attention paid to it, seems to me a legitimate and important thing for a critic to do. I have felt, from the beginnings of my engagement with Caribbean and African poetry in English in the early 1970s, that I have been privileged to be allowed, as it were, to be part of that whole cultural enterprise and that insofar as I had a role to play, 'spreading the word' has been my primary contribution.

So *Tourist, Traveller, Troublemaker* isn't a conventional academic study in the sense that it has no great thesis to argue, it certainly doesn't follow any post-colonial theoretical line, except in a rather old fashioned way try to read the poems carefully and – however briefly – to set them in their social and cultural contexts, acknowledging especially that in almost every case the poem's primary intended reader/hearer was someone very different in all sorts of ways from this particular critic, a reader who might well take very different messages from the piece. Insofar as I have any kind of theoretical model in mind in any of this critic-work it is the one piece of fundamentalist structuralism I ever found useful and which I have imposed now on generations of students (on the basis that if I can get my head round it then they can!), that is Roman Jakobson's model of the event of communication, formulated back in the 1950s. The best and clearest discussion of this model that I have come across is in Terrence Hawkes' excellent, surprisingly reader-friendly book, *Structuralism and Semiotics*,[1] which I commend to anyone who doesn't know it. As I suggest my students do, whenever I set out to read or write about any piece of literature, but particularly anything that has come from 'elsewhere' as it were, I try and think through the elements of that model because it raises and reminds me to ask, of myself and of the text, all the essential questions about the wider cultural contexts that bear on my reading of – and taking some kind of meaning from/ making some kind of judgement of – that text at this particular time. Having acknowledged those issues however, in the end it is the engagement between the reader and the poem (wherever it's come from, whoever it's by, whoever the reader is, whatever the context of the encounter) that is 'meaningful' and inspires any kind of thoughtful critical response. My generalised gripe about much postcolonial literary criticism, which has become now the orthodox lens through which virtually any non-metropolitan writing is viewed, is that it tends to prioritise the theory over the primary texts and one way or another to stifle the excitement out of the encounter between the poem and the reader. It is the enabling or nurturing that excitement which seems to me the whole purpose of being a teacher of – or writer on – poetry, hence the anthologies, the 'Introductions', the reviews, the conferences and courses, all spreading the word in contexts where the poem is valued above the theory. And that, I suppose, is another relatively unfashionable attitude – at least in academic circles - that links these essays; a romantic belief in the power and value of poetry. I – still – think poems and poets are important, that some things can only be said in poetry, that some poets, sometimes, have access to ways of saying that, to adapt the advertising slogan, reach the places other forms of expression can't reach.

So the collection begins with an essay derived from a talk given to the Welsh Union of Writers conference, held in a hotel on the Pembrokeshire coast in 1989, on the theme of travel writing. I was invited to talk about my own poetry that responded to having lived for some years in Nigeria and before that in Jamaica. In the course of trying to find some way to frame or distinguish among those poems I came up with the categories, Tourist, Traveller and Troublemaker that might reflect the response of the poet/ poem to the place which was in some sense its subject. Those categories come back into play in the final essay in the collection, 'Imaginary continent: images of Africa in modern British poetry', a version of a talk given at the University of Ibadan in Nigeria on the occasion of the celebrations of Niyi Osundare's 60th birthday in 2007, which looks briefly at the interesting crew of contemporary British poets who have written out of their experience of Africa in the last half of the twentieth century. Those two talks and the places and occasions of their presentation, frame the collection in all sorts of ways. Between those two bookends then are essays that look at the work of Nigerian poets, particularly Niyi Osundare and Femi Oyebode, and in the context of a discussion of poetry as a form of cultural resistance which runs across several of the essays in the first part of the collection, the work of the Malawian poet Jack Mapanje. The focus then shifts to the Caribbean, with essays that discuss the cultural politics inscribed in the making of a poetry anthology, the homophobia of some Barbadian calypso lyrics and the trials and tribulations of judging the Guyana Prize. That Caribbean focus continues with essays considering the history of West Indian poetry and the work of individual poets from Frank Collymore, Martin Carter and Ian McDonald to Kamau Brathwaite,

Derek Walcott and Olive Senior. In the final section of the collection the essays focus on Caribbean writers who have settled elsewhere – James Berry, Linton Kwesi Johnson and Kwame Dawes – each of whom explores notions of exile and connection in their different ways. From a different perspective exile and connection are themes explored by the writers whose work is considered in the final essays in the book, the American poet Don Burness and then those British poets – from Kipling to Tony Harrison, Landeg White and John Haynes, who have engaged with explorations of their own 'imaginary continent'.

Stewart Brown

1. Terrence Hawkes, *Structuralism and Semiotics*, London, Methuen, 1977

TOURIST, TRAVELLER, TROUBLEMAKER

This essay is extracted and adapted from an address given to the Annual Conference of the Welsh Union of Writers at Druidstone Haven, in 1989 and subsequently published in *The Works*, the Union's journal.

The only real justification for my being here and speaking to the 'Travel Writing' theme of this conference is that I have, over the years, written poems in and about *strange places*. Trying to put that body of work in some kind of context for this presentation I came up with a package I've called 'Tourist, Traveller, Troublemaker' because it seemed to me that those three roles identified distinctive ways of seeing that might bear some exploration. I want to begin by reading from Jamaica Kincaid's nonfiction book, *A Small Place*. It's a kind of anti-travelogue that demonstrates the differing perspective of the traveller and the 'native'. It's a very uncomfortable book to read if you travel at all and certainly if you travel in the Caribbean. Let me read you the opening paragraphs of the book:

> If you go to Antigua as a tourist, this is what you will see. If you come by aeroplane, you will land at the V.C. Bird International Airport. Vere Cornwall (V.C.) Bird is the Prime Minister of Antigua. You may be the sort of tourist who would wonder why a prime minister would want an airport named after him – why not a school, why not a hospital, why not some great public monument? You are a tourist and you have not yet seen a school in Antigua, you have not seen the hospital in Antigua, you have not yet seen a public monument in Antigua. As your plane descends to land, you might say, What a beautiful island Antigua is – more beautiful than any of the other islands you have seen, and they were very beautiful, in their way but they were much too green, much too lush with vegetation, which indicated to you, the tourist, that they got quite a bit of rainfall, and rain is the very thing that you,

just now, do not want, for you are thinking of the hard and cold and dark and long days you spent working in North America (or, worse, Europe), earning some money so that you could stay in this place... and since you are a tourist, the thought of what it might be like for someone who has to live day in, day out in a place that suffers constantly from drought, and so has to watch carefully every drop of fresh water used. . . must never cross your mind. You disembark from your plane. You go through customs. Since you are a tourist, a North American or European – to be frank, white – and not a Antiguan black returning to Antigua from Europe or North America with cardboard boxes of much needed cheap clothes and food for relatives, you move through Customs swiftly, you move through Customs with ease. Your bags are not searched. You emerge from Customs into the hot, clean air; immediately you feel cleansed, immediately you feel blessed (which is to say special); you feel free.[1]

I think that extract very pointedly defines the essential attraction of being a tourist, that suddenly you are made free. When you arrive in a 'strange place' as a tourist your eyes – indeed all your senses – are unshackled, you can respond to things in ways that you aren't able to when you're at home, because you're not constrained by either the familiarity of the known or by worries about your own identity in terms of the life around you. In fact, as Jamaica Kincaid says, you really don't want to know about the realities of that life, you want to view the world you've dropped in to through the screen of your own expectations of the exotic, to maintain the romance of the strange that recognizing yourself as a tourist allows.

Tourist writing then, celebrates that kind of self-deluded freedom. It may celebrate the beauty of the place or the picturesqueness of the people, their charming rustic/native ways. Or it may even celebrate culture shock, the pain of the experience, the spoilt Edenic ugliness of the place. But essentially all it does is to present that experience to someone else, it says 'Look at me aren't I clever, I've been to this place. Isn't this a wild experience, let's relish it, let's, as it were, put it on a pedestal and walk around it.' And that, really, is the problem with tourist writing, that one of the essential challenges of making a poem – to make the familiar strange by the intensity of your attention to it – is done for you.

15

The imaginative energy that goes into that process of making strange, that provides a kind of spine to the poem, is replaced by the easy, sense-shocked observation of the exotic that comes with the plane ticket.

So, looking at my own writing to try and illustrate what I mean, there are some poems in which all I've done, really, is to try and recreate the picture, celebrate the experience of being in a strange place. And even if celebrate seems an odd word for the kind of passage I'm going to read now, what it is doing, really, is to manipulate sympathy for the 'picturesque' person who is the subject of the poem, while at the same time turning that person into an exotic object described for a reader who won't have access to the context – place, culture, history – that creates him. And the poem asks none of the uncomfortable questions that would explain the view the persona presents; who is he, how did he get there, how is he linked to the place, scene, person that he's describing? The passage is from 'Zinder', the title poem of my first Poetry Wales collection. Zinder is a town in the south of the Niger Republic in West Africa. It is a small, dusty, insignificant-seeming huddle of a place, apparently in the middle of nowhere. But in fact it's an ancient and important trading centre, the last place before the desert going east or north from Nigeria, and the first place you come to after the desert coming the other way on one of the immemorial caravan routes. And so it has a huge and famous market that's been there for thousands of years. It's only 'nowhere' as far as the brochure makers are concerned. When I lived in Kano in northern Nigeria I'd occasionally make trips north towards Zinder and the desert. Niger had been a French colony, so for us, making our own brochures, it was exotic, it had a different feel, you had to cross a border, change money, get your passport stamped, to get to Zinder. You had to speak a different language to get by. So I went there as a tourist and I think the poems I wrote about those visits to Niger have a different quality from those I wrote – or at least those I kept – about Kano, where I worked and had a life and identity for several years. If you settle somewhere you lose that touristic freedom Jamaica Kincaid writes about, your eyes see different things, you get involved.

This section of the poem 'Zinder', then, is really rather horrific; it's describing a badly deformed leper begging in the market. Looking at it now I see that essentially what I was doing was celebrating the horror of that encounter, recreating the spectacle, the frisson of our meeting:

> For the leper's embrace is a nightmare borne
> by multitudes, they hobble and scuff
> to the market like traders; arranging their wounds
> as others do fruit, (the ripest up front,
> raw, viscid) calling like any vendor
> summoning trade. . . songs old as affliction,
> tuneless as grief. Grinning gargoyles
> they beg just acknowledgement, the small
> tarnished change that clogs up your purse.
> 'Patron, Patron!' 'Merci Patron!'
> A woman without nose creases her head,
> the toothless Baba in Fulani sombrero,
> straddling a donkey, has no hands and no feet
> so waddles his stumps like a marionette
> as the dull coins chime in his plate[2]

In another circumstance I might defend that passage from my own charge, especially in the context of a long sequence, but there is something of that self-congratulatory cleverness in such selective reportage.

And even poems that are, as it were, self-consciously ironic about the position of the writer-as-tourist, are themselves part of this tourist writing category. I went last year to the Gambia in another part of West Africa. The Gambia is the only country in West Africa that has any kind of developed tourist industry and all the problems of Third World tourism – of deciding whether or not it's worth the cultural aggravation and economic distortions – are vividly apparent in that tiny country. Culturally it seems unarguable that tourism can only damage such a place, in terms of indigestible and arbitrary foreign influence, the trinketisation of local crafts into airport art and the gelding of music and dance styles into hotel amusements that only reinforce stereotypes of the primitive, savage, gyrating African. Economically the tourist industry demands all sorts of concessions from government and distortions of national priorities... water, electricity, road and communications infrastructure are all re-oriented towards the hotel fringe of coastline. Vast amounts are spent on imports of luxury goods that make the hotels brochurable in the terms of your local high street travel agent who has to sell them against more established 'destinations'... But on the other hand, the hope, the intention, is that tourisms may be an investment that will eventually create jobs and bring substantial foreign exchange into the economy to enable other things to be done... And what alternatives does a place like The Gambia have?

So anyway, someone like me, who has lived in West Africa and wants to think of himself as to some extent aware of the situation, who worries about issues bound up in the development of such an industry, but who also uses the very machinery of tourism – the cheap flights, the package deals in the hotels, the relative ease and comfort of travelling around in tourist buses, taxis etc. – for his own 'researching' purposes, is made particularly uncomfortable by the contradictions of his position. This poem, 'Tourist Guide, West Africa' is meant to be ironic, in the sense that although all it does is selectively reproduce words that were actually spoken by a Gambian woman who happened to be a tourist-guide, the cold words on the page become a critique of her deceived or self-deceiving duplicity, a critique of tourism in places like The Gambia, and also a critique of my own position, the knowing observer who is part of the problem, passively recording what she says just as the other tourists snap their cameras indiscriminately to record the views. She, the tourist-guide, was taking us, a bunch of visitors out on a 'safari' in the back of an open-top lorry round this little patch of jungle that happens to be left undeveloped, near enough to Banjul, the capital holiday area of the country, to be accessible for a day excursion. She was saying things that made me cringe but didn't seem to trouble either her or my fellow safariers, and that really is where the irony in this extract lies:

> Welcome to our *African Experience*
> where you will see jungle and monkeys
> and native village life.

As you know we Africans are full of energy,
and you see how rhythmically our women move,
even with buckets of water on their heads,
and we are very fertile, like the soil –
feel free to photograph
inside the compounds that we pass –
look, there are green monkeys
and here is Uncle John
who will climb a palm-nut tree
and let you try his *jungle juice*
and *fire water*... feel free,
feel free, remember, you are on holidays.
When the children shout 'Toubob' and wave
they mean 'Welcome, welcome...
We are very glad to see you here.'
But please don't throw them coins like that –
see how they're wrestling in the dust –
we don't want them to beg.[3]

The irony goes all sorts of ways in that poem. Just the act of noticing what was happening to that woman puts you, writer or even reader, in an invidious position. I think that recognition, that discomfort, moves us towards a definition of 'the traveller'.

So how do you become a traveller rather than just a tourist? Insofar as I can make the distinction, the traveller-as-writer is much more self-aware, much more aware of his own context, more aware of a heritage – both in terms of people who have been there before and, more particularly, those who have written about the place before. Their work becomes part of the cultural baggage the traveller inevitably carries with him. The best traveller-writers, I think, manage to convey both a sense of their own strangerness – recognising its consequences in terms of what they see – as well as a real sense of a place observed and 'tasted'. Life *there*, in the place you are travelling through, is measured against, is connected with, life *elsewhere*, your life, the life that fixes your identity beyond the role of the tourist or traveller. One of the elements of that identity for me is cricket. Despite oneself and despite what I know about the class and cultural implications of the way the first class game is played, the fundamental values and philosophy of the game are very much part of what I understand as home, as somehow representing whatever there is that was decent and admirable about England and being English. And wherever I have travelled – mostly in the former Empire – people have played cricket. It and the language of Empire are almost all that survived in some places. And all of that feeds into the poem 'Cricket at Kano'. Kano, again, is close to the desert, and as the Sahel moves further south more and more of that part of northern Nigeria becomes desertified. The conventional image of the desert is of rolling dunes of loose sand but it's not all like that, its fringes especially are hard-packed scrubland, 'becoming desert'. The ground, the cricket pitch, that this poem describes, was in fact just a big patch of this 'becoming desert' scrub, with a coconut-matting wicket in the middle and a few white painted stones around the edges as boundary markers. Certainly there was no grass to be seen; it was about as unlike a traditional English ground as could be. As the drought bit, the nomadic Tuareg people were being driven out of the desert into the cities on the fringe – Kano, Niamey, Sokoto – just to survive. And on this particular day I was playing cricket with all these other white folks – Australians and New Zealanders and Indian engineers and a few Africans who'd had that kind of colonial education, on that cricket pitch, that was hardly a pitch at all, which, it seemed, was actually set up across some ancient route out of the desert into Kano. We, the cricketers, didn't know that, and the Tuareg who came striding out of the desert had no idea what we were doing, dressed all in white, seeming to dance in the dust for no apparent reason:

> Cerulean and jet, the Tuareg
> From the Sahel with his bow and arrow
> stalks the dusty outfield
> which is his heritage, his history,
> like a wraith in some Gothic drama,
>
> squats at deep mid-wicket
> to watch the strange *baturé* ritual,
> the inexplicable dances
> of the white men in their bleached
> ceremonial robes.

20

Soon play continues,
the intruding spectator ignored,
merely a local hazard
like the gully-oak at Broadhurst
or the boundary stream at Brook,

and with eyes closed, behind
mosquito screens, the pavilion's
ceiling fans rustling an artificial breeze,
the sounds of leather on willow,
of 'Come one', 'No, wait!'

and 'How-was-that-umpire?'
appeal to racial memories,
recall the ancestors and holy places
of the tribe's formation...
Canterbury, Lords, the County Ground at York.

Such meditations would explain
our dancing to the nomad from Niger,
but neither he nor we will probe
beneath the fictions that our eyes create,
our shared humanity obscured

by vocabularies of such conflict
that their lexicon is silence.
So, at stumps, nomad and exile
pursue their disparate paths,
amicably separate, rooted in certainties

centuries old, our rootlessness
a fragile bond that will not bear embrace.[4]

There are all sorts of puns and ironies woven into that poem,
lots of cricket teams are called 'Exiles' or 'The Pembrokeshire
Nomads' or whatever, and of course most of the cricketers were
expatriates, exiles, nomads of a kind, engaged in something that
stood as a symbol for home. But the Tuareg, the real nomad,
was reluctantly moving towards a home that would be a kind of
exile... And all those issues of roots and rootlessness are focused
in that encounter. That seems to me a traveller's poetry because,
more than just a dip into the exotic, it suggests some awareness

21

of facts of travel in our time – exile, escape and expulsion: refugees, resources, and the remnants of Empire: walls and wars as well as wish-fulfilment and wanderlust.[5]

The traveller who stays, who settles, and so identifies him/herself with the place after a significant length of time, is distinguished from the traveller in that he gradually comes to see the place in a different way, and so writes about the place in a different way. Most of us have encountered a variant of the well-worn traveller's tale about a conversation between a tourist and a rather cynical resident of – wherever, let's say Jamaica – in which the tourist gushes about the abundance of exciting, exotic sights he's seen in his week's stay, to which the resident responds that if he stayed a little longer he'd soon be complaining that there was nothing in the place *to* see... However the traveller who stays, who settles and so identifies himself with a place after a significant length of time, is distinguished from the tourist and the traveller in that he gradually does come to see that place in a different way, and so – if he is a writer – writes about it in a different way. Gradually he sees beyond the glittering otherness to understand – to some extent at least – the contexts of what he's seeing, noticing the shit and the rubbish and the aggravation that's left behind after the colourful parade has gone by. The picturesque becomes *ordinary* and so the writer's imagination has to engage with it in more complicated ways to remake it strange. The settler, a kind of convert to the place, becomes sometimes and in some ways 'more native than the natives', feeling himself entitled to make public statements that local people might not – for various social, political or cultural reasons – feel able to make. The settler is both of the place and yet not really bound to accept the consequences of what he might say in terms of whoever he might offend. If push really comes to shove he can (almost) always go home. But the insights that he gains from staying allow him a kind of licence and gives what he says a measure of authority

The poem 'Whales' draws on that privileged experience, that troublemaking licence – it certainly stirred up a deal of trouble when it was first published in 1974. The poem dates back to the years I spent teaching in Jamaica in the 70s. The tourist season in

22

the Caribbean is around Christmas time and the tourists will come down, usually from the USA and Canada, to flop about on those beautiful brochure beaches which are consequently effectively closed to the local people except in their capacity as waiters or servants of various kinds in the hotels. I was teaching in a junior secondary school, a kind of comprehensive school, in St. Anne's Bay on the north coast, the main tourism area of Jamaica. It's difficult enough to motivate secondary school kids anywhere, in my experience, but when the best prospects of a fulfilling career you can hold out to those who 'behave' is that they can become latter-day house slaves for fat, rich and usually rude white folks, it was difficult to generate much enthusiasm oneself, as a teacher, let alone inspire it in the kids. So, anyway, as a VSO teacher on a local salary, I quickly began to identify much more with the people I taught and lived among than with the people who looked more like me – the strangers, the tourists. In those days I looked less like the kind of blubber-bound 'whale' that inspired the poem than I do now – and indeed one of the ironies of the poem now is that my only return to the island is as a sort of 'whale':

Whales

Each Christmas they come
white and blubbery from the frozen North,
strange bloated creatures pale as snow
cruising in vast, unnatural shoals.

Whales: the great white whales of myth
and history in all their spurious splendour.
Flopped ungainly along the sea's edge
or hiding, blistered, under a shadowed palm,

incredibly ugly, somehow, in their difference.
Designated a protected species
they are chauffeured around, pampered like babes
and generally kept in the shade.

Few stay long or leave anything behind
except litter and small hostilities.

'Peace an' Love' we tell them –
the government says we must show respect –

so we smile, sing, play Sambo:
secretly long for a black Ahab.[6]

'Whales' looks at tourism in the mid 70s and the troublemaker part of it stems from the response it generated when it was first published in the *Jamaica Sunday Gleaner* – the national newspaper which has a regular literary page and always publishes a poem or two. The poem was published just as I was about to leave Jamaica, at the end of my VSO stint, and I got back to Britain a couple of months later to find a telegram from the literary editor of the *Gleaner* saying that an international incident had ensued from the publication of the poem! Apparently it had been noticed by some Canadian tourists in the island and sent back to a newspaper in Toronto which had reprinted the poem under the headline 'Anti-White Racism in Jamaica' and presented it as the work of some black radical who was inciting his people to murder and revolt. Then, apparently, the government of Jamaica had issued a disclaimer to say that this Brown person wasn't a Jamaican at all, that his views were eccentric and nothing to do with them and that, basically, he'd better not try to come back…! I felt quite proud of this really. I received hate letters sent on to me from disgruntled Canadian tourists saying:

You have spoilt our holiday memories forever; I always took the happy smiling faces that greeted me to be of genuine friendship, but now, thanks to your disgusting poem, I know that those people really always resented me…

I felt quite proud of that too! I had become a 'troublemaker'.

'LUGARD'S BRIDGE'[1]: A CONTEXT

Extract from a talk given before a reading of the poem at The Centre of West African Studies, University of Birmingham, November 1988 and subsequently published in Poetry Wales.

I was interested to learn, from colleagues here at the Centre, that there is, apparently, a growing dissatisfaction within academic anthropology with the traditional ways of presenting the results of fieldwork, reflecting a sense that somehow those supposedly objective studies are inadequate to the experience they purport to represent. Several highly respected researchers – I am told – have produced 'anthropological fictions' as a way of getting closer to the things they wanted to record or represent. And there is of course, especially in Africa, a tradition of the historian-poet, giving back voices, smells and emotions – among other things – to the dry bones and bloated statistics of a thesis. Not that my poem 'Lugard's Bridge' aspires to the status of either anthropology or history, but it does try to focus and synthesize material drawn from many different sources, many conflicting cultural and emotional inputs, to say something that I couldn't find another way of saying about a particular time, place and experience.

The epigraph to the whole poem, and in a sense a key to it, is the phrase from Jean-Paul Sartre's Introduction to *Orphée Noir*, 'Africa beyond reach: Imaginary Continent'.[2] What I take Sartre to be saying is that for the European imagination, Africa is always a dark continent, impossible to encompass or fully understand. Even for those European individuals who – for wholly admirable reasons – attempt to know bits of it, indeed perhaps especially for them, it remains a symbol of something elemental that is ultimately inexplicable. This is not the *Heart of Darkness* otherness of an Africa full of savages and horror, though it perhaps shares the same tap-root, but it is much more positive, an acknowledgement of something indefinable which has been lost from 'our' civilization but persists in Africa. Whatever that something is, the lack of it disallows Europeans from ever becoming more than fellow travellers with the place and its peoples. The poem examines that idea in a particular instance. It has its roots in a fascination with Africa, the idea of Africa, the image of Africa that formed in my mind as a working-class English boy in the 1950s. It was an image composed of snippets of Tarzan films, 'native drums', Empire fiction, geography lessons with maps covered in pink patches that were *ours*, 'native drums', exhibitions of 'savage artefacts', newspaper cartoons of witch-doctors with bones through their noses and missionaries in cooking pots, 'native drums', 'Doctor Livingstone, I presume?', *Zulu*, Colonial Office films on development and locusts, TV and newspaper supplement images of drought, war, famine and emaciated African children pleading to be saved; all those among the other unrecalled but undeniable inputs that formed an image of West Africa in particular that was exotic, tragic and full of opportunities for self-aggrandisement.

That Africa is represented in many ways by the figure of Frederick Lugard, a character the historian George Woodcock describes as 'the Compleat Imperialist'[3]. An adventurer and professional soldier who had travelled widely before he came to West Africa, he was, in some senses, the founder of Nigeria. He began his work there at a time when that coast was still very much 'the white man's graveyard' and spent the best part of twenty years there. He worked initially for the Royal Niger Company but was subsequently High Commissioner for Northern Nigeria and then Governor of the whole territory from 1912 to 1919. Lugard was a figure I came to know about long after those schoolboy images had been absorbed and fed into my own imaginary Africa, but before I went to Nigeria.

I 'met' Lugard when I was a postgraduate student of African literature at Sussex University, an experience that generated its own fiction of Africa – albeit one which retained much of the earlier version but was sophisticated by some degree of self-consciousness about where those schooldays images came from and what they implied. But I became very interested in Lugard's life and personality, so that when I found myself going to northern Nigeria to teach, the sense I had of walking in his footmarks was quite eerie. But I donned Lugard's boots reluctantly; I was a very different kind of Englishman, wasn't I? A high-minded, well-intentioned friend of Africa, not an exploiter or agent of imperialism... And of course the Nigeria I walked into in 1980 was so very different from the imaginary Continent I had constructed – Islamic Africa, urban Africa, intellectual Africa, commercial Africa, political Africa... It was a dynamic and ingenious, but also a cruel and corrupt society, self-inventing, self-exploiting... Except on organised cultural occasions I don't think I heard a 'native drum' beaten in three years!

But looking at the reality of what I, and all the other expatriate Englishmen – consultant or publisher or teacher or engineer – were doing, the links between our roles and activities in contemporary Nigeria and Lugard's in his grew stronger in my mind. And that being so I had to confess – secretly, to myself – that the African reality I had stepped into was in many ways a *disappointment*... I had wanted the imaginary continent I'd constructed to be true. It was an unpleasant shock to discover how deeply embedded in me – but also in pretty well all my compatriots, despite any apparent commitment to Africa – was the fiction that Lugard stood symbol for, and shocking, too, to think what that said about the veils of prejudice through which we perceived 'our' Nigeria. But alongside that revelation – perhaps part of it – and almost more disturbing was the insistently absurd idea that Lugard seemed to prophecy Nigeria's contemporary leaders, that Lugocracy – a blend of graft and bullying – was a philosophy more appropriate to the realities of the society than the imposed ideal of Western-style democracy seemed to be.

While in Kano I played my allotted part, taught my classes, did my research, wrote occasional poems as they came along, but also kept a diary – not at all a literary diary but a very mundane and domestic diary, full of the kind of daily flux that one quickly forgets, the kinds of thing anthropologists are supposed to record about other people. And when I came back to the UK and wanted to make some kind of sense of the feeling that Lugard's shadow still stalked the Nigeria I had encountered, it was that diary, alongside Lugard's published diaries, that I referred to.

One strand of 'Lugard's Bridge', then, deals with that personal – but also, I suggest, representative – journey towards understanding the process of my own disillusion – and in this sense disillusion means a kind of awakening which, no matter how uncomfortable it may be, is a positive, enabling experience. But to make that journey real for a reader I had to try and establish both an historical and a contemporary context; to say something about Lugard and *his* illusions and about the kind of society Nigeria was in the time I was there. I needed an image to bridge the divide between Lugard and me, between his Nigeria and mine.

I had found that bridge, literally, in Kaduna, in a park by the river. Sometime in the 1950s, I suspect, the small iron suspension bridge that had been at Lugard's administrative headquarters at Zungeru was moved up to Kaduna as an historic relic and put across some tiny stream in this memorial park, with pleasantly English promenades among the shady trees and formally laid out gardens; there was even a paddling pool of sorts in the middle. There had been a sign there telling the story of the bridge; I found a photograph of it later in a history book, a sign saying that it had been erected 'in tribute to the founder of Nigeria'. But now, 'of course', the park has gone wild, reverted to bush; you can just make out the paths through it; the paddling pool has been raided for building more functional structures; and the bridge itself, when you come upon it, is totally unexpected and redundant. So you walk across Lugard's Bridge from nowhere to nowhere, and the only place to go is back across again... All this seemed too good a metaphor to resist, and the idea of the bridge, of linkages in time and space, is what structures the poem.

The first section of the poem looks at Lugard's activities and psychology, and tries to suggest echoes and parallels with contemporary events... the ways he manipulated truth to serve his own ends, for example. It begins with four lines from Kipling, who is another *Presence* hovering over this activity of an Englishman making a poem about African experience. The poem is dedicated to the Tanzanian novelist Abdulrazak Gurnah, who was a colleague of mine in the English Department at Bayero University in Kano. He was returning to a very different Africa from that he'd left in Zanzibar several years before, and his adjustment to – and accommodation of – those differences offset my own reactions and attitudes in (for me at least) very useful ways. He curbed my urge to romanticise the experience but was equally stern on my narrowly Eurocentric assumptions and value-judgments.

Part two of the poem tries to show the ways in which Lugard's shadow falls across events in contemporary Nigeria, both for expatriates like myself and the indigenous people. In fact, I met a very old man in 1982 who claimed to be able to recall Lugard's entry into Kano in 1903. It was quite possible. The ancient and imperturbable grandfathers outside the Post Office in Kano, slowly tying string and sealing wax round airmail packages because the postal regulations which survive from Colonial – maybe even from Lugard's – times, confer on them a power – which they relish – over seething, impatient expatriates, seemed another potent metaphor for this linkage of worlds.

The shock and guilt bound up in the recognition of so tangible a fellowship with a figure like Lugard whom, as students, we so easily dismissed as a comic colonial, excused only as a man of his times, is tempered by the story of the black American colleague, a former Black Panther who, returning to his African 'heartland', came up against his own distorted mythologies, his own identity crisis. To put that in context, there is what might be thought a rather selective and unfair portrait of life in Nigeria's Second Republic. But then this is fiction, even though it's all true!

The final section of the poem gestures towards that idea of 'Lugocracy' as a universal system of government – that MIGHT IS RIGHT and is, in the end, the way all diplomacy is underpinned. I was in Nigeria during the Falklands war and I was struck by the similarity between Lugard's justification of his actions and Mrs. Thatcher's – hence the Falklands reference. And that is coup philosophy too, as Nigeria discovered again the following year. Finally, that *Insha Allah* (God's Will be Done) fatalism, signalled in the slogans which decorate or insure the lorries and minibuses of the North: DESTINY UNCHANGEABLE, WHY WORRY, or NO

CONDITION IS PERMANENT. It is a fatalism that Lugard took for passivity and indifference on the part of the Northern Nigerian 'folk', but can better be understood as the kind of wry, seen-it-all-before wisdom the old men outside the Post Office embody and gummily preach.

LUGARD'S BRIDGE

'Africa beyond reach, imaginary continent'

(for Abdulrazak Gurnah)

I

'Take up the White Man's Burden —
*   and reap his old reward:*
The blame of those ye better,
*   the hate of those ye guard.'*

Austere amid the chaos
of a formal garden run to bush
(its ornate web of borders, beds
and secret ways laid out by some
despairing topee'd nurseryman,
his last barricade
against the fatal lethargy of exile)
the sturdy grey suspension bridge
commissioned for Zungeru
that dislocated elbow of the Empire
where pink, perspiring ADOs —
fit and spick but lacking means,
and not *too* bright, blues
and lower seconds were just right —
were disembarked and rested,
'to acclimatise' or so the Form Book said
but really to replace that pap
the desk boys and politicos
had stuffed them with in Blighty
by initiation
in those rugged, esoteric arts
that really kept the flag aloft
in Lugard's gritty Emirate.
And then the real set-off
with bearers, Bible and ammunition belts
across the bridge and north

towards those mud-walled towns
whose dusty trade routes stitched
the fraying hem of the Sahara –
Kano, Katsina, Sokoto.
Romantic names which veiled
a life too enervating for romance;
that savage, unforgiving sun
or bristling, fevered Harmattan –
the tropics' *cold* when painted lizards
slow to stones grey as sunlight
through the emery air, and boys
turn old, white-headed wise.
Oh how the pale 'first-timer' yearned
for green and frost and marmalade
but felt himself always on parade,
emissary of a culture
and exemplar of a creed
the natives were to judge by *him*,
for once across that bridge
he was the King and they his fickle
unenamoured folk, so many
and so far between the outposts
of gentility.
        So, as Lugard taught,
discretion proved the better part
of conquest; patronise the Emirs,
cultivate their tongues,
insinuate their ways with medicine
and education. Such coy
dissembling was a liberal art;
good men at heart
the DOs meant no harm,
were just the pages of a history
whose evil lay beyond
their honest understanding.
What could be wrong with Shakespeare
quinine and the Trinity?

Deceived by duty and a simple code
they were the heirs to a mythology
whose pantheon sustained
the grand delusions of a continent:
Livingstone, Barth, Rene Caillie,
'discoverers' of a geography
whose peoples had discovered Life
and named its fiercest mysteries,
but lacking rifles
and a sufficient greed
revealed themselves as
'helpless, childlike, inarticulate folk'
desperately in need
of decent – British – government.

So good Sir Fred
that 'mean and spiteful malcontent'
handy with mules and dervishes
was sent to bridge the great divide
between such cultured innocence
and *real* life
by demonstrations of the Maxim Gun
and smoky magic-lantern slides.
But first the fun;
to pacify those turbulent, ungrateful, few
who would not see the logic
of Colonial Rule. Emirs who swore
they'd perish with a slave
between their jaws before obey
some namby-pamby white man's law;
the Holy King of Sokoto
avowed, 'twixt Lugard and Mohammed's sons
no dealings except war!'

No fool, Lugard declared
he had no quarrel with the teeming folk,
only their *alien* Emirate.

Indeed, he came, he said,
to liberate the people from oppression
fear and slavery... and by such lights
proceeded to extinguish those
of any who demurred
as tyrants, rebels or fanatic fools.
All this, his modest wife could boast,
in service of 'The Great Ideal...
an Empire to secure the world,
ruled by its finest race.'

II

'leaning on an oilbean,
lost in your legend.'

And this less than a life ago:
the old man sprawling on his cardboard rug
outside the Post Office in Kano,
tying packages with wax and string
for, it might be, some pink, perspiring
expert from the University
as DC 10s scream overhead
and the roads choke on their daily bread
of Mammy Wagons, Five-Oh-Fours,
Vespas, 'Flying Pigeons', sheep,
camel trains and wailing armoured cars,
will sing of what he saw then
as a boy behind the blood-caked walls
of a fortress any fool could see
was quite impregnable,
of how they mocked at Lugard's crew
of wilting, whitening Yorubas
until his crude machine-guns slewed
the rearing rainbow wave
of legendary horsemen
to a bloodied and despairing spume

spattering the news of Kano's shame
to every dusty town between
the A and F in AFRICA.

And as he deftly twists and knots
the loose ends of his story
the old man bides his time and spits,
knows how the heresy *impatience*
chops at every white man's soul,
knows too, by heart, their still enforced
Strict Postal Regulations
and that notwithstanding sellotape
and satellite communications
no package leaves this office
he's not honoured with his thumb.

And true to type the expert squirms,
biting on his tongue;
he means no harm, a missionary
of technology or plain merchant
of the Word, enticed by curiosity
and a salaried compassion;
'An African experience'
and 'my dues to the Third World...'
Another plank in Lugard's Bridge
suspended now between
the pacotile of PROGRESS
and the trade in new antiques –
'See how this juju real, Masta,
you want buy dirty bronze...?'
between such arts of darkness
and the video elite.

He could not hide his disillusion;
where were the painted tribes, the drums,
the witchdoctors and gods
who cursed in elemental tongues?

35

No cosy camp-fire soirées
where Tradition's fables hummed?
Which steaming bush of ghosts
concealed Picasso's D'Avignon? Come on,
where were the cannibals, les
sauvages, the truly Africans?

Was Africa this stinking slum
of mud and rust and excrement
congealing between worlds?
This raucous brutal Limbo
where the lepers dodge Mercedes
and *Sweet Destiny's* unfurled
round every 'ghastly accident'.
Where Mammy Wagon lions roar
'NO CONDITION IS PERMANENT'
to the meek on Ayatolah Street
while children, blind or limbless,
scuff calloused stumps and hearts
among the charitable hub-caps, pleading 'Love'.
Where soaring glass-walled Ministries
encrust with clerks and bureaucrats
all polishing their vanities;
the Mallams Next-Tomorrow
and Alhajis Not-on-Seat.
Where cockroached *People's Clinics*
clot with every 'ten percent' machine
that flashes, hums or laser beams
but the sick must bring a mattress
and at least one change of blood.
Where bloated Marxcyst Governors
perform their Highlife antics
to the heart-beat of corruption
pulsed on empty oil drums.
Where God sold out to Mammon, so
InshaAllah: His will be done.

Of course the grey old-timers at the Club
are not surprised....
                              'Foresaw it all
dear boy, and told the clowns in Whitehall
at the time. The natives just weren't ready –
not their fault, really; though the country
is a shambles now, as you've observed.
Damn me, I'm *not* one of your Joberg Nazis
(though they at least maintain some order
still – things run to time – or so I've heard...)
but the plain fact is these jumped-up clerks
and messengers who rule the,
                              so-called, Ministries –
for all their *dash* and their chauffered Mercs –
they really couldn't organise a piss up
in a brewery, and that's the rub,
they just don't quite have what it takes, up top.'

So he'd kept clear of them at first
but as adventure shrivelled to frustration
he could feel the knowing nod, that cynic smirk
when some 'young innocent' fresh off the plane
unleashed another Guardian-smug outburst
against 'immoral multi-national corporations'
becoming just routine, a reflex,
like that dismissive shrug and wave aside
of beggars – cripples, sick, insane –
who festered, wailing round each parking car
alert for any token of contrition.

He was ashamed to face such shades of grey
within himself until that melancholy
Kano'd day his Alabama-black colleague –
a disenchanted Panther – leaving, swore
'Thank God for Slavery!' and he was freed,
forgiven the corruption of his own race memories,
the psycho-archaeology of *his* tribe.

37

He could concede the secret meaning
of his schizophrenic dream – that every
well intentioned Schweitzer nursed
his atavistic Kurtz beneath the skin.

III

'LEFT HAND, GO SLOW, OH GOD HELP US'

But old ways die hard:
'the Ibos still chop man'
our Hausa landlord warns
and so reveals the forbears
of the chef whose menu offers
'Lank Cashier Hotpot'.
'And I quote, though not quite
in the author's words...'
Language Rules, UK
the whispered codicil of Empire
still insinuates the deference
of tongue-tied natives
to the rhetoric of true born Englishmen.
Confirmed in *our* inheritance
we are invited, please,
to lecture *them* on 'English
as a Catalyst of National Unity'
and mock the patriotic upstart
who suggests a Federal Tongue
composed, so tactfully, of Hausa nouns
Ibo verbs and Yoruba adjectives,
'and all those little words
can come from all the other tribes...'
Our laughter is a creaking board
on Lugard's Bridge, that relic
of an arrogance the world thought

it outgrew, enshrined within
these formal gardens (which,
abandoned to their instincts,
have resumed that lush
impenetrable darkness
tradition has bequeathed on our
'Imaginary Continent')
by sycophantic been-tos
grateful for Colonial Scholarships:
'In tribute to the founder of Nigeria'.
A monument to WAWA's irony
it spans a backwater the sheep
who use it now – still none too bright –
could step across to reach those islands
where old Lugard's ghost –
polished whiskers, blood-stained boots –
was yomping like a born-again hussar.
From the revenge of Keffi to Goose Green
his Empirical philosophy won through...

But so much for history, time for a coup!

FOWL SELLER CAUGHT
WITH WELL DRESSED CROW
'Such initiative and enterprise go make this nation grow'
Mechanibals toss 'spare-part' in a *Flying Coffin* stew
while witch-doctors sell Valium, the chemist
'Toadsfootbrew'
THERE IS NO GOD BUT ALLAH, well,
        only one or two...
NEPA darkens all our lightness in the hot beer queue.
In the hospital the nurses will change dressings, at a price,
while the market mammies haggle over
        sacks of Oxfam rice...

Whali! Dis our Nijeeria goh dead on such Avar-i-i-i-ce!!

So sorry please de Mockracy done gone finish
we get indigenised Lugocracy; that is
the strong plot revolution while the weak
scrub voting fingers and turn another cheek
for HOPE again wears epaulettes and marches
      through the streets:
see how the Bar Beach vultures start to gather for a feast –
General or Statesman; murderer or thief
    TODAY IS ME, TOMORROW IS YOU
Rich man, poor man, beggarman, chief
      DESTINY UNCHANGEABLE, WHY WORRY?

FINDING THE RIGHT WORDS: A CANDLE FOR KEN SARO-WIWA

(1996. Published in *Poetry Wales*)

Among many other blessings and scars from the three years I spent teaching in northern Nigeria in the early 1980s there are two words that have entered my permanent personal vocabulary. One is the Hausa ejaculation of praise, surprise and congratulation 'Yaow-wah!' I'm sure that's not how you spell it but it gives you a sense of how it is said. It's a wonderful word that I find myself shouting at moments of excitement like – recently – at the end of a superb performance of 'The Rite of Spring' at Birmingham's Symphony Hall or when De Silva reached his hundred against – joy of joys – the Australians in the World Cup Final... What these examples suggest to me is that I don't consciously reach for the word because it's 'ethnically appropriate', its just in there in the word pile and emerges as the right word for the occasion. As does the other word – although it's technically a phrase I suppose, but it is always pronounced, at least by Hausa speakers, as if it were one word – the Arabic/Muslim 'InshaAllah'. Again that's not the way it would be spelt. Literally it means 'God's will be done' and is a statement of faith and humility. More mundanely though, it is also a declaration of a kind of passivity in the face of destiny and the fickleness of fate. So, for example, given the notorious nature of Nigeria's roads, anyone from the North setting out to make a journey of any distance will end their estimate of the length of time it might take with the cautionary verbal shrug that is 'InshaAllah.' Its commonplace usage combines the fatalistic and the pious associations to become a kind of talisman, an invocation of some divine insurance policy. I find myself saying it – to myself usually – when I'm pushed to promise to meet

41

some deadline or when confronted by some disappointment or even danger.

I found myself using both those words quite frequently when I was back in Nigeria last November. I felt genuinely honoured to be invited to speak at and read my poems to the Convention of the Association of Nigerian Authors (ANA) to be held at the University of Lagos, and the more so because ANA had persuaded the British Council that they should organise and meet the costs of the trip. Characteristically, however, the invitation came rather late, in the form of an almost illegible FAX and was followed by a period of ten days when telephone and FAX communication between the UK and Nigeria was impossible. This shouldn't have been too much of a problem except that the Nigerian High Commission in London won't grant visas on the strength of FAXed material but demand an official invitation on a genuine letterhead... So – InshaAllah – I really wasn't sure I would be flying until the evening before the morning I was due to leave, when a British Council motorbike courier delivered the visa. But anyway I was in two minds about whether I should go. Nigeria – and Lagos in particular – is not an easy or comfortable place to visit at the best of times, and given the way things have been in Nigeria under successive military governments, this was far from being the best of times. Not that the civilian regime which preceded the latest batch of coups and counter coups was much to write home about either but at least, I suppose, there was the notional prospect of democratic change, notwithstanding the fact that one of the more respectable reasons given to justify the overthrow of President Shagari back in '83 was the blatant corruption of the electoral process that had seen him returned to office earlier that year. But then what happens when you have fair elections, like those that took place in '94 which saw Chief Abiola elected... the military regime of General Sani Abacha steps in to annul them and indeed proceeds to imprison Abiola.

The tension engendered by the Abiola situation was one reason to be a little cautious about flying into Lagos for no good reason. But compounding that general mistrust of the political situation in Nigeria was the specific moral dilemma for me of the Ken

Saro-Wiwa affair. The convention was scheduled for the period just after his appeal against the death sentence was to be considered, and whatever happened there was bound to be a volatile atmosphere in Lagos and particularly – when you remember that Saro-Wiwa was the immediate past President of the Association of Nigerian Authors – at the ANA convention. And knowing how unsubtle Nigerian military regimes can be in putting down what they perceive as dissent, especially if it comes from a bunch of irreverent writers on a University campus... well, you had to think about it. But I had met Ken Saro-Wiwa only a year or so before, when we were both attending another conference in West Africa, and, wearing another hat as Series Editor of the Longman African & Caribbean Writers imprint, I had been responsible for the recent republication of two of his novels on an international stage.[1] So I felt somehow involved, implicated even.

There are many nuances to the issues around which Ken Saro-Wiwa was campaigning and few of the choices to be made are as straight forward as the accounts that followed his execution seemed to suggest. Saro-Wiwa was a complex man and far from being a saint – and indeed no one who actually knew him pretends that he was. But his international reputation as a writer (although I wonder how many people reading this article, for example, have actually read anything by Ken Saro-Wiwa?) his political background (dating back to his crucial stand *against* the secession of Biafra in the civil war) and his high profile cultural campaigning for some measure of justice for the people of Ogoni land whose territory has been so blighted by the way the oil reserves there have been exploited, made him a very visible opponent to the Abacha regime and one who could not easily be either ignored or quietly suppressed. He and his supporters made great play on the image of Saro-Wiwa as an oppressed writer on trial for the beliefs that informed his art, but as Odia Ofeimun, the Nigerian political poet *par excellence* argued in his address to the conference, in fact Saro-Wiwa's imaginative writing had nothing to do with his particular campaign in Ogoni land and indeed he had more or less given up writing in order to concentrate on his political ambitions[2]. Not that any of this is at all meant to try and excuse the horror and sheer wickedness of what Abacha and his thugs did to Saro-Wiwa (and, let us not forget, to his comrades) – a more corrupt and transparently rigged judicial process it is hard to conceive of. And the sheer brutality of the execution, compounded – insofar as it could be – by its timing, just confirms Abacha as the tyrant that his more outspoken opponents have long claimed.

Anyway I am jumping ahead of my story. Beyond simple cowardice and an increasing tendency to inertia, my hesitation about accepting the invitation to attend the ANA convention was reinforced by the campaign for a cultural boycott of Nigeria being led by one of the more distinguished of those outspoken opponents of the Abacha regime, the Nobel Prizewinning Nigerian playwright and poet Wole Soyinka. Effectively exiled himself, Soyinka was travelling around Europe demanding that South Africa style sanctions be imposed on Nigeria, including a withholding of cultural 'aid'. I have to say that I had never thought of myself or my poems in quite those terms before. Indeed I would have some sympathy with the proposition that the threat that I *would* come to Nigeria and that consequently some minion of the Abacha government would be obliged, out of characteristic African politeness and deference to my British Council credentials, to endure me reading the whole of 'Lugard's Bridge' to him at some public function, that such a prospect might be far more daunting to the regime than the threat that I might stay away! But as that scourge of woolly thinkers John Barnie asserted when I mentioned the dilemma to him, that kind of self justification was just a literary version of the Mike Gatting 'its only cricket' line of defence against accusations of South African sanction busting. So what to do? I had been invited by the ANA, itself vocally opposed to Abacha's government, and not only in relation to the Saro-Wiwa affair, so I could hardly be conniving with the regime, could I? The theme of the conference was 'Literature and Freedom Across Boundaries', hardly a neutral topic given the circumstances. I wouldn't have been at all surprised if the High Commission had refused to give me a visa to attend that convention, given the ANA's outspoken critique of the government. Also I suspected that at least two poets whose work I admire and whose friendship

I value, Odia Ofeimun the new President of ANA, and Niyi Osundare – perhaps the most distinguished of contemporary African poets writing in English – had both worked hard to get me the invitation, so to refuse to go would seem like some kind of slight to them. In fact Niyi Osundare was in Britain at that time on the Arts Council's African Writers Tour and speaking to him directly made up my mind that if I could go, I should. He was a little disdainful of Soyinka's boycott proposal, arguing that the broader writing community in Nigeria felt particularly isolated these days, what with the lack of imported books and journals and – because of the expense involved in travelling out and the reluctance of people in the arts to visit Nigeria – the relative dearth of real cultural exchange. And that, what's more, was precisely how the regime wanted them to feel. It was Ken Saro-Wiwa's international connections that made him such a thorn in their side. The writers at the ANA convention, he went on, would relish any kind of contact or news from outside, so to go would be an act of solidarity with them rather than any kind of tacit support for the regime.

So, InshaAllah, if the visa comes through I'll go. When it does arrive then, despite my sensible middle aged reluctance, I'm excited. Yaow-wah! This will, after all, be something of an adventure.

Writing it up in this way makes my visit to Lagos seem like some act of bravery on my part. To put it in context, there are at least five planes a day coming into Lagos from Europe and about half the passengers are Europeans, flying in to do some job or other, so this is hardly an occasion for self-aggrandisement. I was being looked after by the British Council, staying – for at least half the time I would be there – in one of the plushest hotels in Lagos. This is hardly heroic. All the same, I have to admit to being more than a little anxious as the plane landed in Lagos and I began the dreaded encounter with the immigration officials. 'Exercise patience' (another Nigerian phrase I find myself using more and more) and, InshaAllah, we will get through. In fact it was less of an ordeal than going through Immigration in Miami for example and certainly less fraught than the experience of many Nigerians trying to enter the UK. (Ask Niyi Osundare, a real literary VIP, accredited guest of the Arts Council, the British Council and several UK universities, about his struggle to get a visa and then to get through Heathrow last September!) And soon enough I was out of the airport and really in Lagos... Yaow-wah!

Of course the conference had been organised long before it became apparent that it would coincide with the awful climax of the Saro-Wiwa trial, although I'm sure the theme had been chosen to give the participants scope to comment on the issues his imprisonment raised. As it turned out the convention was dominated by Saro-Wiwa, initially in terms of a mixture of anger at what was happening to him and the hope that signals of support and solidarity with him by the ANA might somehow influence the military government to at least commute the death sentence. It sounds silly when I write it now, with hindsight, but at the time, despite what they knew of Abacha, I don't think anybody believed that he would actually carry out the executions. That first day and a half of the conference was strange; everything was dedicated to Ken Saro-Wiwa; all the delegates were issued with black ribbons to wear as a mark of protest against his treatment; we were issued candles, too, for a midnight vigil to proclaim our solidarity with his cause; there were petitions and plans mooted for more direct protest like a march on the local radio station... For me, though, nothing conveyed the tension and trauma of the situation as much as seeing Odia Ofeimun, one of the most outspoken and fearless of commentators on contemporary Nigeria, who has often been reckless with his own safety, to see him struggling to find words that would somehow convey his outrage and yet not sting the notoriously thin-skinned regime into precipitate action. To see him almost literally biting his tongue as he gave his Presidential address was indicative of a pervading sense of impotence in the face of the kind of tyranny that prevails in Nigeria now. It seems ridiculous; who did we think was listening? As it transpired, the direct representative of the regime who was supposed to attend the opening ceremonies didn't show up – perhaps he knew what else was to happen that day. For myself, speaking at the convention was a very disturbing experience.

Because I hadn't known if I was really going to get there or not, I didn't actually write my paper in advance. I thought about it and gathered together bits and pieces that I might stitch together to make the bones of a talk around the conference theme, but I didn't actually write it out until I was on the plane. I had decided to look at the way poetry has been a means by which individuals caught up in struggle or oppression have been able to express their irreducible freedom in a form that transcends boundaries of time and space. I would begin by talking a little about Derek Walcott and his image in 'Forest of Europe' of the anonymous 'prisoner of conscience' circling his cell or barbed wire compound sustained somehow by what he calls 'the bread that lasts.' Walcott is not referring to a religious or political faith but *a line of poetry* that has stuck in the back of the prisoner's mind somehow, from school days or just a chance reading, but which emerges into his consciousness now to feed the prisoner's spirit and sustain his intellect and imagination. But the body of the paper would take three very different poets from areas of the world with which I have some connection and look at the ways their differing approaches address that central idea. The poets I chose were Martin Carter – the Guyanese author of that classic text of colonial struggle *Poems of Resistance from British Guiana*, the long time 'exiled' Yoruba poet Femi Oyebode who is now based in Birmingham, and the Anglo-Welsh poet John Davies, whose work – particularly in *The Visitor's Book* – engages with those ideas of freedom, identity and the crossing of boundaries in very interesting ways. I wasn't sure how long the talk would be but, InshaAllah, I could cut or pad as the occasion demanded. So while the talk I prepared was perhaps a little 'close to the edge' as far as the immediate political context was concerned – and indeed I hoped some of the resonances and relevance *would* carry across to my audience – it was neither very original nor very daring.[3]

When I came to deliver my talk, however, I was very aware of the pressure to resist saying anything which might somehow offend those making the decisions about Ken Saro-Wiwa, but also I was personally scared that someone out there in the audience might be recording what I was saying and that before I was able to leave Nigeria I might be confronted by those words and have to defend them against some charge of sedition or contempt... Such paranoia in part reflects an inflated ego, I suppose, although such scenes are not at all unheard of, but it also taught me a little about the reality behind the concept of self-censorship that I have often bandied about in courses on South African literature. As it turned out I did have to cut chunks from my prepared talk for reasons of time, but I also found myself, in the moment before I said it, weighing the possible consequences of pronouncing that, for instance:

> the poetry that such prisoners of conscience write has a way of coming back to haunt and accuse those who seem to have all the power...

Of course my talk was politely received, and I was feeling a little smug about having dared to make my implicit critique of the regime when the news came through that they had executed Saro-Wiwa and the others that very morning. As Odia had been biting his tongue, as I had been trying to be witty and score ironic points, he was either already dead or was actually still writhing on the end of a rope. I still have nightmares about that. Words that were in any case pretty lame now seemed, at best, pathetic. It felt worse than that though, as if we had connived in some way. Odia, a man renown – even in a country full of outspoken commentators and powerful speakers – as a master of rhetoric and rage, was literally speechless. It was a terrible feeling, and again I must confess to being scared. Even as I joined the huddles of people who were tuning in to the BBC World Service to get confirmation of the event (until it was broadcast on the BBC people hoped it might just be malicious rumour) I wished I was out of there and was already dreading the process of trying to leave.

The rest of the convention pretty much turned into a wake. The planned events for the rest of the day were abandoned and people met in small groups to grieve for both Saro-Wiwa and the state of Nigeria. But the next day the ANA leaders decided to complete the business of the conference, 'in honour of Ken's memory and his personal commitment to the activities of the

ANA.' There was much sombre rhetoric and – now – many angry words spoken from the platform. Dirges were sung and prayers said. The official portraits of General Abacha that adorn all public buildings were ostentatiously – and probably treasonably – turned against the wall. The culmination of the convention is traditionally the awarding of major literary prizes that are administered by the ANA and it was determined that this should go ahead. Some joy amidst the despair and, symbolically, the pen's defiance of the sword. This was also the occasion that I was to read poems to the convention. I didn't feel much like performing, I must confess, but InshaAllah. It was probably the biggest audience I have ever read to, several hundred people, including many dignitaries of one kind and another, in a large theatre. That was nerve-wracking enough but I was also specifically invited to read from 'Lugard's Bridge', a long poem 'about' Nigeria, written out of my experience living there in the 80s. The poem begins by looking back to the days of Lord Lugard, colonist *par excellence,* who effectively invented the modern state of Nigeria and enforced his rule as Governor by means of some pretty crude sabre rattling. The middle section of the poem is a more-or-less autobiographical exploration of the role of the modern 'ex-pat' in Nigeria, walking – whether he wills it or not – in Lugard's shadow. The final section of the poem responded to the Nigerian army's seizing back of power in the 80s, suggesting that Lugard would well have recognised the modern General's attitudes in power. I had not reread that section of the poem for some time and, preparing my reading, I was surprised to see how pertinent some of that now seemed

So sorry please de Mockracy done gone finish
we get indiginised Lugocracy; that is
the strong plot revolution while the weak
scrub voting fingers and turn another cheek
for HOPE again wears epaulettes and marches
through the streets:
see how the Bar Beach vultures start to gather for a feast –

General or Statesman; murderer or thief
TODAY IS ME, TOMORROW IS YOU

Bar Beach is the site in Lagos where public executions were held under previous military regimes... Yaow-wah! But, dear reader, I chickened out and read from the middle section of the poem, which was hairy enough..

> Was Africa this stinking slum
> of mud and rust and excrement
> congealing between worlds...[4]

Of course my reading was politely received.

The rest of my stay in Lagos was pretty uneventful – I kept a low profile – you could see Bar Beach from my hotel balcony. I played tourist; found an amazing despite-it-all bookshop-cum jazz den; renewed my acquaintance with that most wonderful of capitalist exchanges – a West African market; spent a chilling/cheerful afternoon with Adewale Maja Pearce – the Africa editor of Index-on-Censorship – and some of his journalist comrades, who renewed my acquaintance with Star Beer and intoned, 'If they could do that to Ken then it could be any of us, any time'; I declined a late night drive across the armed robber district of the city to reach Fela's notorious/legendary 'cave'; was officially debriefed by the head of the British Council in West Africa. As almost everyone who visits it remarks, Lagos is an amazing city; awful poverty alongside awesome extravagance; long-suffering passivity and patience matched only by electric energy and inventiveness; crude brutality behind almost courtly civility. You have never driven until you have driven around Lagos... I have to say I was quite relieved to be leaving but was rather dreading the formalities. InshaAllah.

I wasn't disappointed. I made sure I was at the airport early. I had kept back enough money to pay any tax, *dash*, bribe or *gift* that might reasonably or unreasonably be required. I have been here before. I was worried that my luggage, swollen by the ton of books, manuscripts, letters and miscellaneous papers I had accumulated in what seemed like a very long week, would be over weight and so provide the first occasion for stress and 'negotiation'! However, as I should have anticipated, the weigh-scales were long broken and my bags were just hefted across to the

Customs desk. The Customs officials were reinforced by others in army and police uniforms as well as various baggage handlers and 'translators', so that this examination of my cases was a very public – and rather threatening – occasion. Over the years Nigerian Customs officials have acquired, rightly or wrongly, a notorious reputation for trying to extract *dash* from departing visitors, particularly nervous Europeans. There is, for example, a legitimate concern with the export of Nigerian antiquities, but this ban is regularly exploited by the officials who proclaim every knickknack and geejaw, even when the wood is still green, a protected item. However a few naira – or these days a few hundred naira – slipped to the right person will usually ensure that more reliable methods of dating such items can be found and the *objet d'art* returned to its suitcase! I had a few bits and pieces that I anticipated would attract such attention, but not a bit of it. These officials, four days after the Saro-Wiwa execution and wary now of the outside world's reaction, were much more interested in the books and papers. They were very suspicious of all those papers. Most of them, in fact, were things given to me by anxious and ambitious writers at the conference, desperate to submit material to UK publishers and magazines. Or letters that couldn't be trusted to the Nigerian postal system. And locally published books, to review, to promote, or just to distribute. What Niyi Osundare had said about the writers desperately wanting to make contacts outside was certainly true. Most of the soldiers and officials were barely literate but they took every piece of paper, every book, newspaper, magazine and envelope out of my bags and looked at them. A couple started to read, falteringly, from a manuscript of folk stories as it happened. I was grilled very suspiciously about why I had all these things. I explained about the conference, about teaching African literature, about research and being interested in Nigerian writers (whoops!) and no, I definitely wasn't a journalist. Ken who? I write this lightly now but at that moment I was seriously scared. Eventually, reluctantly, with a crowd of other passengers now forming behind me, I was waved away. The books and papers were disdainfully stuffed back in the case. No money changed hands nor was asked for; this was clearly a more serious occasion. Still, after a few more checks and having paid the legitimate departure taxes I was through, into the departure lounge area. Yaow-wah!

I now had several hours to kill and a lot of heavy, non-exchangeable naira to lose. Among the battered and rather dog-eared books on the back shelves of the little newsagents kiosk I found several copies of Ken Saro-Wiwa's play-scripts and poems. The lady who took my money frowned as she passed me the books, 'He was a good man,' she said, 'it is wicked what they do to him. God will punish them.' InshaAllah.

LITERATURE AND FREEDOM ACROSS BOUNDARIES

A talk given to the Association of Nigerian Authors' Conferences, University of Lagos, November 1995. The conference coincided with the date set for the execution of Ken Saro-Wiwa – see the essay 'Finding the Right Words' elsewhere in this collection.

The theme of this conference, 'Literature and Freedom Across Boundaries' is particularly resonant and apposite, given contemporary circumstances. The idea of literature and the idea of freedom are inextricably bound together. Writing is an expression of freedom, albeit one which those who live in relatively free societies tend to take for granted – as indeed they should. It is only when an individual's or a community's freedom is denied or threatened that we perhaps are made aware of the ways in which literature can be an agent of freedom, both in the sense of the writer who uses his work to campaign for a particular cause or set of values, and, perhaps more importantly, in the capacity of literature to free the imagination, to open doors and windows into regions that *cannot* be controlled by those who seem to have all the material power.

Over the centuries, writers who have been imprisoned or gagged in some way have found a means of escape through writing, and in recent times across Africa individual writers have had occasion to employ such tactics. One thinks of Ngugi wa Thiong'o's account in his prison memoir, *Detained*[1], of the way that setting out to write the novel which became – in subsequent translation – *Devil on the Cross*[2], effectively saved his sanity. Or the Malawian poet Jack Mapanje's lyrical resistance to the physical brutalities and mental tortures imposed on him for – as he said – "writing poems the Banda regime didn't like"[3]. It was certainly the writing of new poems – albeit that they had to be written in the head that gave Mapanje the psychological freedom to survive, and it was the fact that he was a poet, imprisoned for his poetry, that inspired friends across the globe to shout and scream and campaign for his release.

I think the most powerful and poignant image I know for the power of poetry to release the imagination of the prisoner and thus to release him or her from some of the horrors of their situation is in the work of the great West Indian poet Derek Walcott. Whilst he has never had to endure imprisonment for his art himself, (although he endured more than his fair share of censorship one way and another in his early days) Walcott did come to know the exiled Russian poet and Nobel Prize winner Joseph Brodsky very well. Through him he gained new insight into the horrors of Soviet 'silencing' over several decades of the twentieth century, so we find many references in Walcott's work of this period to writers such as Akhmatova, Pasternak and especially Mandelstam.

But it is in his poem 'Forest of Europe'[4], his imaginative entry into the mind of an anonymous prisoner of conscience', that Walcott writes most vividly of the power of the poem. The lines of this poem have become for me their own proof as it were, they are what they describe. He writes of the dangers of totalitarianism, even if the system of belief or ideology is fundamentally just or honourable, or if the tyrant feels himself to be benign, and worries that those who, in his words, 'lose sight of the single human' in their pursuit of a cause, have already compromised their vision. He then draws a vivid portrait of a lone, perhaps forgotten, individual circling his cell or barbed wire compound, sustained, Walcott says, in this wonderful image, by 'the bread that lasts'. Here he doesn't mean religion or faith in any political creed or ideology but rather a line of poetry, a line or fragment of a verse that has somehow stuck in the back of the prisoner's brain, from school days perhaps, or just a chance reading. It now emerges into his consciousness to feed his spirit and sustain his intellect and imagination. 'The bread that lasts' – that line, that image stays with me, becomes, as I say, what it describes.

We must hope that all such prisoners everywhere have access to at least a few crumbs from that miraculous loaf. At least writers who are prisoners, such as Ngugi and Mapanje, have the capacity to bake their own, even when denied writing materials. And it is amazing how often such writings, baked in the oven of the writer's imagination, come back to haunt and accuse those who would appear to have all the power and to be above any such retribution.

For another boundary that literature crosses, and in doing so defies those who would try to deny freedom of thought and speech and ideas, is the boundary of time. Poetry is 'the bread that lasts', it does not go stale even though it may, from time to time, perhaps for centuries, be hidden in some dingy corner of the larder! Poetry is by definition mysterious stuff; it works in unexpected ways and can have unexpected consequences. It is poetry that has brought me here today, not really to stand up here and talk about it in this generalised way, but rather a particular poem, 'Lugard's Bridge', which I wrote when I lived for several years in Kano in the early 80s. Or rather I wrote it just after I'd left, looking back on the experience. That poem was published in *Okike* and then became the title poem of my second book of poetry. In Britain its publication was met largely by incomprehension and indifference, but it has always enjoyed a more engaged attention and response from a few Nigerian poetic comrades who, while certainly critical of aspects of the poem, have offered it and its author encouragement and support – and were responsible, I guess, for my being invited to speak to this conference. I refer to this poem now as a demonstration of how poems work in unexpected ways. I certainly never thought it would be Lugard's Bridge which, literally, brought me back to Nigeria!

But I want to use the rest of my talk to address the theme of the conference by speaking very briefly about the work of three very different poets whose writing seems to me to address the notion of 'Literature and Freedom Across Boundaries' in very different but, I hope, relevant ways.

The writers whose work I would call to mind are, first of all, the great Guyanese poet of political struggle and, in his later years, intellectual freedom, Martin Carter – a man whose poetry has travelled the globe but who has not, personally, often ventured out of Guyana. Then the Anglo-Welsh poet, John Davies, a writer few in this audience, I would guess, have ever heard of before. His is a sensibility rooted in Wales but, having travelled for a season out of his native country, his sense of expanding horizons and the inter-connectedness of disparate peoples speaks to our theme in very pertinent ways. Finally I will mention the work of the emigré Nigerian poet, Femi Oyebode, a man who has lived in Birmingham in England for many years now and whose poetry is very much concerned with the crossing of boundaries in space and time and culture.

Martin Carter's work exemplifies the way that poems refuse to recognise boundaries of time or national/political borders. Carter's work would seem to speak particularly to the tradition of Nigerian poetry in English which has so foregrounded a determination to 'dare the beast' and confront political/military authority armed only with the weapon of the word. This verse is from his poem 'This is the Dark Time My Love', written in Guyana in 1953. It had a particular location and resonance there and then, but it speaks into many subsequent scenarios across the world, including perhaps some close to the concerns of this Association and this conference:

> Who comes walking in the dark night time?
> Whose boots of steel tramps down the slender grass?
> It is the man of death, my love, the strange invader
> Watching you sleep and aiming at my dream.[5]

Martin Carter is, I would argue, one of the major poets of the English language in this century. That his work as a whole – with the exception of a handful of those early poems of struggle – is hardly known outside the Caribbean is, to some degree at least, a consequence of the very success of those early political poems and the image of Carter they established. Carter had been imprisoned by the British colonial authorities in the early 1950s for his part in the 'subversive activities' of the first democratically elected, nonracial and idealistically socialist government in the Caribbean. His poems of that period – several of them written while he was in gaol – were published by the London-based socialist press Lawrence and Wishart as *Poems of Resistance from British Guiana* in 1954, and while poems like 'University of Hunger', 'I Come from the Nigger Yard' and 'On the Fourth Night of a Hunger Strike'[6] have become classics of socialist literature – translated into several Eastern European and Asian languages at the height of the cold war – and Carter's work constitutes one of the canon texts of Caribbean Literature – his later poems have hardly been acknowledged in more general accounts of poetry in English.

But the recent publication of Carter's *Selected Poems* make it possible for us to discuss his work as a whole for the first time. Previously, with the exception of *Poems of Resistance* which went quickly out of print, and a more substantial collection of Carter's work in *Poems of Succession*, published by New Beacon Books in London in the late 70s, all Carter's work was published in small literary journals and very limited edition/limited circulation pamphlets in Guyana. The *Selected Poems* offers us a kind of narrative of disillusion, charting Carter's early, essentially romantic, poems of identification with the broad mass of Guyanese people, through the public, declamatory poems of action like 'I Clench My Fist', on to poems which chronicle his growing disappointment and despair at the kind of society Guyana had become in his lifetime; poems that become increasingly private, inward and oblique. But I will concentrate here on the defiant early poems like 'I Clench My Fist' which was written in response to the British troops' 'invasion' of Guyana in 1953. This was a time of crisis in Guyana, but it was also a time when deeply entrenched class and race differences were subsumed in a genuinely shared popular outrage at the arrogance and hypocrisy of the colonial power's gunboat diplomacy which was so clearly designed to undermine the authority of the first government in the Caribbean to be elected under universal adult suffrage. The poem runs:

> Although you come in thousands from the sea
> Although you walk like locusts in the streets,
> Although you point your gun straight at my heart
> I clench my fist above my head and sing my song of FREEDOM.[7]

A bombastic and declamatory poem like 'I Clench My Fist' is

given an authority and licence by the particular circumstances of its composition and performance which the later poems never attained. Commentators recall that it was a poem chanted by striking workers on the sugar estates and at demonstrations and political rallies. That adoption by the uneducated and largely illiterate Guyanese proletariat, to use a word that has gone out of fashion, was possible because the poem uses few of the prized and sophisticated devices of literature; its language is straightforward and its intention unambiguous. Such qualities may be those of 'plain bad verse' as one critic remarked of the poem, but in the circumstances of Guyana at the time – when a whole society determined to 'dare the beast' – it was those very qualities which *allowed* the poem to move off the page and into the much broader arena of orality. Perhaps there are lessons here for Nigerian writers who would aspire to make such a revolutionary poetry, but if so they are not lessons that are easy for individual writers to put into practice. Certainly, they are not lessons reducible to those academic arguments over matters of form and literary language that seem to dominate most discussions of so-called protest poetry.

What is clear is that Carter's bold poems of struggle have not been rendered stale by the passing of time. The relevance of that early bravado and defiance shifts through time and place to regions of the world where notions of resistance and oppression and injustice are very much current concerns. One can well imagine political prisoners not so far from where we are gathered today being sustained on the 'bread' of some of Carter's early poetry. And the later poetry, too, will find its audience, albeit in unexpected and unlikely locations.

The work of the contemporary Anglo-Welsh poet John Davies would seem a long way, ideologically as well as geographically, from Carter's brave poems of freedom. But in fact one strand of Davies' work addresses the whole notion of cultural freedom and the crossing of boundaries – in a very different poetic language – with essentially the same mixture of outrage and despair. Well established as a poet of and in Wales, John Davies recently spent a year living and working in the Puget Sound area of Washington State in the USA. In 'All the Running'[8], an essay published not long after his return to Wales, Davies wrote with approval of poets he discovered there whose work is rich with a sense of what he calls 'the locative', of *belonging*, of having been written out of a profound understanding of a particular place, a poetry attuned to the subtler nuances of a region's landscapes, languages and lore. This notion of 'the locative' is something else that will be familiar to Nigerian writers who have expended so much energy in the last forty years struggling to establish the particularity of Nigeria as a *real* place, with its own histories, cultures and identities.

But while Davies might understand and applaud such ambition, what his own poems written out of that period of being away from home tell us is much more cautious, alert now to the dangers of too narrow a focus on the local – parochialism, simplistic nationalism, a distorted impression of one's own importance in the world. Such dangers are perhaps most clearly perceived by the reader who is also an outsider or who almost becomes one by virtue of his having travelled and returned. For although it seems almost axiomatic that a sensibility 'nurtured by immediate contact with felt life in a particular place' should be the foundation on which a poet's work is built and his identity understood, it is a familiar irony that the poet must travel in order to discover the real importance of roots and notions of *home*.

Returning to Wales from America, John Davies becomes again one who must sign 'The Visitor's Book'[9] – to quote the title poem of his second collection; he has become one who, with fresh eyes, may question the assumptions, the shibboleths of this now *strange* culture's present face.

Indeed, in 'The Visitor's Book' he asks the fundamental question: whether the idea of roots, of a particular attachment to the place of one's birth, one's culturally formative years, isn't, in fact, an intellectual illusion, a form of nostalgia for a time when identity was so easily established, so simply defined. Going back on a kind of pilgrimage to Cymmer, the village in the Afan Valley where he was born he finds:

> At journey's end, no surge but smoke, no sound
> from the deep except some lorry's threshing [10]

59

Again one is reminded of Derek Walcott discovering in an early poem that 'there can be homecomings without home'. But it is John Davies' American poems that are particularly relevant to our theme. They are almost all responses to *strangeness*, to differences of language, of elemental scale, of political perceptions between the life of the North West coast of America and that of the North West coast of Wales – the Prestatyn that is John Davies' present base. In the North West coast of America, place names seem exotic, the subterranean, domesticated Native American heritage is felt ghosting through cracks in the Coca-cola facade of today's 'real thing'. The visitor's sharp perception of such tensions, between past and pretence, is apparent in his sequence 'The White Buffalo'[11] which focuses on the tension between the destruction of the Native American culture and the contemporary rhetoric of 'the land of the free'. He senses connections of complicity between his own trek West to discover new worlds – his sense of being always the stranger on 'unsettled ground' where the laws and morality of the old world no longer apply – and the Europeans' ancestral betrayal of the Native American's trust. The poet watching the subdued, 'tamed', Native Americans, themselves watching the distorted survivals of their own culture at a *'pow-wow'* enacted for tourist consumption, is reminded of a similar process in the packaging of his own, Welsh, culture at certain eisteddfod-style occasions. He recognises a shared experience, (akin, of course to the simplistic ways in which African culture is so often promoted overseas) the experience of belonging to a people the world might judge to be living *on the edge*:

> This singing in another tongue old anthems
> in a shared redoubt, I've no part in.
> But am not apart. I have been here before
> elsewhere, just visiting from a century
> ageing faster than time that has said no
> to so much now there's just money,
> as though inside might be someone or
> something I'd half-known and lost.[12]

That 'singing in another tongue' and the emphasis on dislocation, the nagging consciousness of something 'half-known and lost' draws the poet and his readers back to a consideration of roots and realities in their own time and place. So John Davies' poetry is informed by that literal and metaphorical crossing of boundaries, looking inward in order to understand what he sees when he looks out and looking outward to measure his responses to issues closer to home.

That last sentence might well have been written about the work of Femi Oyebode. Certainly the dilemma of 'singing in another tongue' in order to address 'something half known and lost' is one that recurs throughout his poetry. In an early poem, entitled 'mastering the chaff', Femi Oyebode writes

> I have lived amongst the english
> in the genteel orderliness of their damp afternoons,
> surrounded by well-bred pink roses and lawns,
> terrified into my place by gestures and postures,
> largely by silence and the determined look.[13]

So he writes *in* England, *in* English, but with the consciousness always of his position as an outsider. He is both of and *apart from* the 'genteel orderliness' which he in some ways seems to cherish but in other ways seems to despise.

Born in Lagos on 1954, Femi Oyebode studied medicine at the University of Ibadan before coming to the UK to study psychiatry, and he has lived and practised there as a distinguished doctor, teacher and scientific scholar for almost two decades now. Yet he is also a prolific and accomplished poet – five collections now in the last six or seven years – whose reputation is steadily growing both in the UK, where his work is beginning to be seriously reviewed and anthologised and – I don't need to tell you – in Nigeria, where one literary journal is devoting a special issue to his work in the next few months. That crossing of boundaries and cultural worlds – Nigeria and England, poetry and science, English and Yoruba, past and present – as well as informing the manner of his writing has also become one of his major thematic preoccupations. As he puts it in 'An Abstracted Space':

I occupied several melodies, conspiring to win or lose
To grow between two worlds like hate and war. [14]

Although he writes through many voices, Oyebode's style is distinctive: a combination of lyrically imagistic song and a densely referential narrative surge that drives the reader along even when he or she is not quite sure where they are, or where the poem is taking them. Oyebode writes like no one else and, one feels, for no one in particular. Perhaps that says something about his sense of audience, that, because of his own travels and transitions, he assumes they will be so diverse in their cultural character and in a sense so fugitive as a reading community, that it is impossible to assume anything about them. Most poets can at least guess something about their readers' capacity to pick up on nuances and references. For Oyebode, there can at best be the hope that Yoruba references which elude the uninformed English reader will be balanced by the extent to which English readers will recognise and respond to the measured irony and nuanced precision of the description of England in the passage I quoted earlier – which might not be so apparent to readers in Nigeria who have not lived in England.

Often, the seeming 'difficulty' of Oyebode's work derives from the poet's apparent absorption in those two, more or less, closed vocabularies – closed at least to the general reader. These are the vocabularies of contemporary psychology and of Yoruba mythology. Not that those concerns are always intrusively foregrounded, but they are among the fundamental referents of Oyebode's experience which, however it is manipulated and disguised, is essentially the source these poems delve into and emerge from. His obsession with dream is the most obvious manifestation of his engagement with the language and symbols of psychiatry. Indeed his first collection, *Naked to your softness*, announces itself as a collection of dreams and is structured as a dream life-journey, from 'Dreambirth', through 'Dream-places' and 'Dreamdreaming', to the concluding 'Dreamaging and dying'. Dream, of course, is the ultimate visa, the ultimate agent of freedom as far as crossing boundaries is concerned, and Oyebode uses that visa to structure his readers' travels. But in Oyebode's work, dream is understood in the broadest sense, as if the life remembered, observed and anticipated can only be narrated – that is smoothed into approximately the kind of sequential linear story we can understand – through the license of dream. So the poet's childhood memory of Nigeria's Independence Day celebrations when his father showed him

> ...my first swarm of bees,
> they were british airforce jets
> with the sting in their tails [15]

becomes as much a dream as the exiled poet's imagined encounters with his ancestral ghosts, who appear to him '...like a dance of possessed spirits / in midnight forests' or like the malarial vision that is, I think, the tale told in the title poem of Oyebode's third collection, *Forest of Transformations*[16], which begins with the wonderful line: 'the corpse stood up!'

The dream device runs through all of Oyebode's collections, permitting various kinds of transition, juxtaposition and allusion, so that domestic family scenes set in the UK of the 1980s merge into horrific memories of the civil war in Nigeria in 1965 when '...death strayed into the courtyard' and 'crops failed in my dreams'.

Dream also permits entry into, and examination of, mythic and historical figures. In one sequence of poems Oyebode rewrites Johnson's *History of the Yorubas*[17], including a section on Gaha, the tyrant. At a recent reading of the poem in Birmingham, Oyebode suggested that anyone wanting to understand the mentality and behaviour of Nigeria's present military rulers should read of and understand Gaha, but also look to the responses his tyranny provoked. Clearly, for Oyebode, such an intense dream-entry into a figure of myth and history is a means of engaging with the issues of the present. This is not dream understood as an escape or withdrawal:

> he rose suddenly to power,
> he rose striking to death, four kings
> four kings foul and disposable

but four thousand others, firm
he slay, not foul, not disposable
just weak, just ordinary just souls [18]

But confronted by the kinds of brutality Oyebode recalls/envisions in 'Gaha', the oppression Carter addressed in 'I Clench My Fist', or even the cultural despoliation John Davies examines, how can poetry – for all its capacity to transcend boundaries of time and place and even culture – really make any kind of difference? Isn't this all so much hot air and wishful thinking? To answer that despairing question I am drawn back again to the qualities of Walcott's 'bread that lasts', for the power of poetry in such times lies not only in its ability to sustain the individual spirit but is also in its nurturing of collective memory and vision. As Femi Oyebode puts it in a line from his latest collection, *Master of the Leopard Hunt*[19], such poetry is 'a river of all our imaginations, brooding'. It is in that brooding that both the freedom and the threat of literature resides.

'ANOTHER MUSIC...' POETRY IN ENGLISH IN WEST AFRICA: A PREAMBLE

This essay is adapted from an introduction to a selection of West African poetry in a special issue of *Poetry Wales*, in 2005.

Poetry in English in West Africa is a problematic, hybrid – some would say anachronistic – form of elite culture. On the one hand, English is a global language, enabling contact, exchange of ideas, fellowship within the culture-of-the-language and even a degree of international fame that is just not available to the poet working in Igbo or Twi. But in societies where an indigenous language thrives and is widely used, (major languages such as Yoruba and Hausa are spoken by millions of people across several countries and support significant literary traditions) where the great majority of people still have little access to sustained formal education so that literacy levels (in whatever language) are low and where the primary vehicle for verbal art and artifice is the spoken rather than the written word, writing poetry in English seems a very strange and esoteric activity.

Despite such tensions there is probably more poetry being written in English across West Africa today than ever before. There are hundreds of younger poets managing, despite all the difficulties of life in West Africa, to find ways to publish their work. Though few literary magazines survive more than a few issues, sections of the Nigerian and Ghanaian press still maintain a commitment to the idea of poetry as a form of writing it is important to discuss and promote in its pages. There are many privately published slim volumes circulating and – in Lagos and Accra – established literary publishers[1] who have distinguished poetry lists – albeit that their books are notoriously limited in terms of their print runs and distribution. International publication is much more difficult these days, especially since the demise of the Heinemann and Longman African literature lists, although with the ever growing interest in 'authentic' African culture in the African American community, some established poets are finding more sympathetic publishers in the USA.

The history of poetry in English in West Africa is, of course, tied to colonialism and the gift or imposition – depending on your point of view – of the English language as the medium of education and social advancement in the major British colonies of Nigeria, the Gold Coast (now Ghana), Sierra Leone and The Gambia (not to mention Liberia and the Cameroons). As elsewhere in the colonial world, the capacity of 'a sound colonial education' to shape the consciousness and world-view of its most able and enthusiastic recipients was demonstrated in their efforts to prove that they too, whether in Bathurst, Bo, Obuasi or Ibadan, could create 'high culture' in the styles and forms approved by the colonial mother culture. So you find, in magazines and anthologies and even slim volumes published across West Africa in the early decades of the twentieth century, examples of pastiche English verse unashamedly modelled on Keats or Wordsworth or Tennyson, (the taste of colonial educators was always some decades behind the current fashions of London). Many of those literary efforts were penned by people with skill and wit and obvious intelligence but who were apparently unconscious of any incongruity between the literary models they were mimicking and the immediate cultural world outside their classroom/study windows. It is easy, from the perspective of today's situation of an established African literature in English, which is characterised by its oppositional radicalism, its wordy battle with the colonial legacy (even while acknowledging its own implication in the perpetuation of aspects of that legacy) to mock those high colonial sonnets and loyal odes. But what those poetic efforts tell us is just how powerful a force colonial education through the medium of a European language could be.

Whether the colonial administrators really understood the full implications or not, it's clear that the insertion of European languages into the cultural circumstances of a 'developing' West Africa, as the medium of education, the language of government and law and international commerce, was a profoundly political action. So while it is perhaps ironic, it should not be so surprising to discover that in the generations that succeeded those apparently culturally colonised pioneer poets, English (and indeed French) language poetry in West Africa has often been characterised as 'political'. And of course, those high colonial versifiers were only 'apparently' unaware of the tensions and incongruities of their situation; indeed it is among that generation of writers that – quite quickly – we see the first evidence of what has come to be understood as the 'postcolonial' perspective: that is to say writers who use the language of the coloniser to write back to their imperial masters. A poem protesting the injustices of colonialism was much harder for the powers that be to ignore or dismiss if it 'spoke our language' as it were. That privileged access to the cultural world of the colonisers was felt by many of the aspiring poets to give them licence to speak for the otherwise unheard peoples of the region, and in so doing to fulfil a traditional role of the oral poet in some West African societies – to literally voice the concerns of the powerless in the halls of the powerful. (There is a degree of self-deception in this, of course. By definition those beneficiaries of a colonial education were being taken away from the experience and values and views of the world of their less privileged contemporaries.) Across West Africa, poets, alongside the novelists and dramatists, began to use literature in English – in more or less radical ways – as a weapon in the struggle to create a climate for change, to inform a national consciousness and to argue the moral, political and social issues that troubled the intellectual classes. While this process began in the decades preceding the independence years of the 1960s, it has been in the post-independence era that the idea of the poet as agitator and social commentator – indeed of poetry-in-English as an alternative forum for political debate – has really taken root.

Another reason why West African poetry in English might generally be characterised as public and outspoken rather than private or intimate is the fact that for almost all of those who became poets, English was not their mother tongue. It was a language learned in school, and at best a second language (many West African people speak several regional languages). So no matter how successfully English was mastered, it would rarely be the language of the bedroom or the nursery, or that in which they dreamed; its use would always remains a self-conscious exercise. So it is not surprising that, on the whole, West African poets writing in English have used their poetry to argue and protest and inform – albeit in the ways that poetry does those things – rather than whisper sweet nothings. There are relatively few love poems in the corpus of West African poetry in English, few intimate confessional lyrics. These issues of the politics of language and identity, of the writer's responsibilities to him/her self and to the community, to the languages of Africa and to the crafts of poetry have been endlessly discussed by writers and critics across the continent (and indeed the whole postcolonial world). Most West African poets who choose to write in English take the pragmatic view of Chinua Achebe, the Nigerian novelist (and incidentally a much underrated poet) who famously declared that history had made English 'a Nigerian language' and as such he was entitled to use it. What is not so often remembered is that Achebe went on to say that *of course* his Ibo/Nigerian English usage would not be a simple echo of the ways English is used in the metropolitan centres but would be shaped by – and bear the evidence of – his distinctive and complex and sometimes paradoxical encounter with the language in West Africa.

It is those alternative ways of employing the language that makes so much West African poetry in English interesting from a formal and technical point of view. The most original poets use the whole range of literary tricks and devices available to any poet working in English but give them a distinctive cultural twist. Sometimes, because most of the poets are unaware of – and uninterested in – the swings and roundabouts of poetic taste in literary London or New York, their use of such devices (and even elements of their vocabulary) can seem strangely unselfconscious or old-fashioned to the metropolitan reader used only to the poetry of his or her own time and place. The great Nigerian poet Niyi Osundare's easy use of assonance and alliteration, for example, might sometimes seem 'overdone' in the context of the spare and informal styles of currently fashionable metropolitan verse. For an alert and open-minded reader, however, such mannerisms not only ask questions about the current metropolitan conventions but signal that Osundare isn't *trying* to sound like a contemporary English or American poet. His whole agenda is predicated on a very different audience, a very different cultural context in which, as Femi Oyebode has put it in a recent poem, 'another music, faint and masked from view' is understood to be shaping and energising this poetry. The reader who only knows English, or rather who lacks – in the case of reading Osundare – Yoruba, will not recognise that other music and so can only ever *overhear* the poem as it were, even though the poem is written in English and the words themselves are well understood.

West Africa is linguistically one of the richest regions on earth. Several hundred languages are spoken within it, and though the 'other music' may be different depending on the individual West African writer's particular cultural and linguistic roots, there is, in general, a creative tension between the 'background music', the dynamics of the English language and the individual writer's voice. And what do West African poets write about? Well, notwithstanding what I've said about an apparent dearth of love poems, they write about anything and everything, as writers everywhere do. They joke, they lament, they celebrate, they despair. However, in that predominantly public mode I have described, poets across West Africa have set out to address the issues that dominate people's lives across the region – the working out of history as the colonial legacies unfold, the hypocrisy and injustices of global capitalism, the inadequacies and corruptions of the postcolonial governments, the status and treatment of women, global warming and the destruction of the rainforest, the hostilities and wars that have so impacted on the life of the region through the second half of the twentieth century, tensions between traditional ways of life and the post-modern cyber-world, between brutal poverty and ostentatious affluence, between the rhetoric of the international agencies and the realities of life as it is lived out by the region's people's. Of course, each poet comes at such issues from his or her particular and distinctive angle, but the sense of the poem as an occasion for argument and confrontation is perhaps the attitude that distinguishes contemporary poetry-in-English-in-West-Africa from its more discreet and measured metropolitan cousins.

STILL DARING THE BEAST: NIYI OSUNDARE AND CONTEMPORARY NIGERIAN POETRY

This essay is a revised version of 'Daring the Beast: Contemporary Nigerian poetry' first published in *Essays on African Writing 2: Contemporary Literature*, edited by Abdulrazak Gurnah and published by Heinemann Educational Publishers, Oxford, in 1995.

Arguably the defining characteristic of Nigerian poetry in English has been its confrontational attitude to authority: from the poets of the high colonial period such as Dennis Osadebay who used his verse to oppose the deculturing practices of imperialism, most famously in his poem 'Africa's Plea':

> Don't preserve my customs
> As some fine curios
> To suit some white historian's tastes'[1]

through the labyrinth of Christopher Okigbo's mythologising to that strand of his work, in 'Path of Thunder', where – in no uncertain terms – he declares his opposition to a power-elite which is set on the destruction of the new Nigeria's potential for national fulfilment:

> parliament has gone on leave
> the members are now on bail
> parliament is now on sale
> the voters are lying in wait[2]

to J. P. Clarke's commentaries on the state of the nation in the 1970s. But it is among the generation of poets who began publishing in the 1970s and 1980s that the notion of the poet as being duty-bound to confront the political events of the times, or more particularly the antics of the country's rulers, has become axiomatic. Of course, across the continent writers have argued over the extent to which they should become, in Nadine Gordimer's phrase,

71

'more than writers',[3] and the arguments about *commitment* and *responsibility* are well rehearsed, not to say well worn, but in Nigeria – as with much else – the issues are felt and expressed in extreme terms. Several poets have incurred the wrath of the politicians or soldiers in power, victimised in one way or another for their outspoken criticism, although it is still hard to believe that Nigeria's presidents and generals spend much time reading poetry.

In 'The Emperor and the Poet', a lucid and passionate introductory essay to his book-length poem *A Song from Exile* (1992), the much-lauded young Nigerian poet and artist Olu Oguibe – compared by Chinua Achebe to the young Christopher Okigbo – describes the circumstances of his 'exile' from Nigeria and the strength of his feeling about the state of the country. He lists intellectuals, artists and writers who, like himself, have been effectively forced out. He is full of praise for those few, including Niyi Osundare and Tanure Ojaide, who stayed and risked speaking out, 'daring the beast' as he puts it.[4] His collection of poems *A Song from Exile* is a lyrical account in eight parts exploring feelings of anger, shame and despair at being away from the society which both abuses and yet feeds his creative spirit. Outside Nigeria, Oguibe's poetic persona feels that his

> tongue is blunt
> The songster has journeyed
> Without his voice.[5]

Oguibe acknowledges both anguish and a sense of guilt over his exile status, aware of the relative comfort of his situation as a doctoral student in London, considering himself, in one mood, 'A coward fled home and the battlefront'. He is unable to accept that there can be any 'peace away from home' and is tortured by a conscience that:

> makes my bed with a quilt of thorns
> Ah, conscience that leashes a man to his past
> Conscience that stakes a man in the open courtyard
> and pelts him with rain[6]

A Song from Exile is a moving expression of the author's dilemma and distress. If it reads as rather gauche and heart-on-sleeve in places that is to some extent proof of the authenticity of its sentiments. But what does such a poem do, beyond establishing Oguibe's sense of his own commitment to Nigeria and the pain of his exile? And why have so many Nigerian poets persisted in pitching their writing against successive regimes in this way? It can seem, after a while, like nothing more than a self-aggrandising *style,* a relatively safe way of asserting one's radicalism. In 'The Emperor and the Poet', Oguibe addresses the issue himself:

> It is arguable to what extent the artist can influence or turn the course of history, and we in Nigeria have had so long a history of battles between the artist and the state that we have even greater reason to be doubtful ... we are simply saying what we see, for it is seeing and not saying, our people say, that kills the elder. It is hearing and not heeding that will kill the child. That, for us, is the fate of the Emperor and the poet.[7]

That recourse to the oral tradition and its proverbial lore as validation for the poet's literary practice is another familiar assertion about contemporary Nigerian poetry in English, that there is a filial relationship between that body of writing and the oral traditions of the region. Quite how the influence of the one tradition is expressed in the other is not always clear. Oguibe, though, is calling up the notion of the oral poet as the literal spokesman for the common people in the courts of the powerful. In some West African traditions poets were indeed 'licensed' to air grievances or criticisms of the rulers in praise-song or at communal gatherings when those being criticised were obliged to hear and to react. Perhaps, as Odia Ofeimun has suggested, by their responses to the poets' critiques the generals have just been acting out their part in the cultural transition![8]

Certainly in claiming that traditional duty to speak out and in challenging the politicians' contempt for the alter-native[9] poetic licence so openly, Oguibe joins a throng of contemporary Nigerian poets[10] who have often seemed more concerned with that public role, and with the political content and effects of their poems, than they have been with the techniques of their craft. Their engagement with this role has perhaps resulted in neglect of the wider implications of writing a hybrid 'English poetry', or of ways in which that borrowed role might be more effectively underpinned by an adaptation of the oral poets' techniques.

One defence against that charge has been the urgency of their situation. For Tanure Ojaide, confronting the desecration of Nigeria's civil society by successive corrupt governments is a sacred duty, and words, given appropriate poetic shape by the very pressure of the circumstances, are the only weapon available to him. As he writes in 'Before Our God':

> Neither bullets nor other savageries can arrest words
> that have already been aired –
> paper is witness to the lone mind.
> ......
> These words file out on the dirt road
> to stop nerve-wrecking waves of despots;
> they are the charms worn before battle[11]

That poem answers the question of 'why write at all' and in terms of Oguibe's presentation of the necessary opposition between the Emperor and the poet in Nigeria, Ojaide's poem 'What poets do our leaders read' is unequivocal in its condemnation of poets who take a less critical, less forthright stand than his own. They are, he says:

> Perjurers of the Word,
> drummers of bloated drums,
> carriers of offensive sacrifice;
> fanners of vanities.[12]

Over six collections now Tanure Ojaide has practised what he preaches, using his poetry to expose the perceived evils in his society and imply the necessity of a different morality. His poetry is much admired and has won prestigious Nigerian and international prizes. His work has been compared with that of David Diop, Pablo Neruda and Mayakovsky, and certainly he shares their socialist commitment and values. In plain-spoken, interventionist poems like 'When soldiers are diplomats', 'The levelling rule' and 'Song for my Land', he chronicles the destitution and despoliation of Nigeria in recent times:

> More and more the land mocks my heart.
> Where are the evergreens of my palm;

why is the sun of salvation eclipsed
by coups and intolerable riots?

Wherever I pass, mockery of the land;
naked trees flaunt sterile bodies at me[13]

There are other, gentler, strands in Ojaide's poetry – he has
written some fine love poems for example – but for the most
part his poems are blunt 'messages from the front', sacrificing
imagistic complexity or formal musicality for a rhetorical outrage
that – arguably – overwhelms the 'poetry' – insofar as we equate
poetry with subtlety, ambiguity and linguistic cunning.

That is a charge which might be levelled at the work of many
of Nigeria's contemporary poets, particularly when their work
is read *en masse*. While there can be no doubting these poets' sincerity
or the depth of their anguish, the unending self-righteousness
of the narrative voice, the artless predictability of the sentiments
and the clichéd language of protest undermine, at least for this
reader, the force of so many of these poems, *as poems*. But that
'at least' is, of course, an immense qualification. Where, in cultural
and ideological as well as in geographical terms, is such a response
coming from?

Nigerian poets and critics – not noted for their reticence or
the gentleness of their own critical judgements – have been loud
in their assertion of the particularity of African and especially
Nigerian circumstances which have aesthetic and cultural as well
as economic and social aspects. Indeed another explanation of
the younger Nigerian poets' obsession with social and political
commentary, advanced most eloquently by Funso Aiyejima,[14] is
that it stems precisely from their engagement with – and continuing
reaction to – that most cataclysmic event in recent Nigerian history,
the Biafran war. This is the generation of writers who, as children
or young men (they are almost entirely men), saw both the horror
and the passion that went into that war and understood most
vividly what it cost their peers who were caught up in it. Their
collective vision of a better society is, Aiyejima argues, as much
a consequence of that historical experience, that memory, as it
is a reaction to the reality of the corrupt and ineffectual governments

that their country has since endured. So that 'alter-native' aesthetic, informed both by that sense of an historical duty and notions of poetic function in some way derived from the oral tradition, seems largely to foreground content over form, to value accessibility above linguistic or imagistic subtlety and to prefer 'statement' to 'song'.

And yet the poet who was effectively the founder of that alter-native tradition, Odia Ofeimun, whose poems are as uncompromising as Ojaide's, as outraged as Oguibe's, is very much concerned with both form and the power of wit and startling imagery as poetry's most effective agents. Ofeimun is set apart from many of his contemporaries too in the grounded experience that underlies his political vision. He was not always part of the society's educated elite. For several years after leaving school he worked at a variety of manual and petty clerical jobs, including three years as a factory labourer with the West African Thread Company in Apapa. Then after studying political science at university and a spell spent teaching and working as a civil servant he was Chief Awolowo's private secretary for several years. That broad working experience clearly shapes the moral agenda that drives all his poetry.

Paradoxically the withdrawal of the original 1980 edition of Ofeimun's *The Poet Lied* (published by Longman) when J. P. Clarke decided that the title poem pointed a finger too uncomfortably at him and threatened to sue for libel – that 'scandal' ensured that Odia Ofeimun's name would be well remembered even though few people, even in Nigeria, had had the opportunity to read much of his work. 'It put my name on the literary map in a way that I find intimidating,' Ofeimun has remarked.[15] Several poems were well known, of course, from journal and anthology publications, and his reputation as a powerful performer of his own work was well established from his days at the University of Ibadan. That original edition of *The Poet Lied* was a very slim volume indeed and it was clear that the selection of poems included there represented a very thin trawl of Ofeimun's work up to that point. His second collection, *A Handle for the Flutist*, came out in Nigeria in 1986 to wide critical acclaim – if to some political discomfort – and quickly sold out. In 1989 a new, much expanded edition of *The Poet Lied* appeared in Nigeria (Update Communications Ltd, Lagos). It was effectively a provisional Collected Poems, including all that was in the Longman collection, plus many of the poems of that period which were edited out of that volume, all the poems in *A Handle for the Flutist,* and, significantly, a long interview with Onwuchekwu Jemie, which explores many of the philosophical and political ideas that underpin Ofeimun's poetry.

The interview provides a very useful context for a reading of the poems, establishing that the heart of the book is indeed the poet's consideration of the events and ramifications of the Civil War, or rather, as Aiyejima suggests, what that dreadful experience meant for the artists of the society in terms of their understanding of the roles and functions of art. Ofeimun's ambition in 'The Poet Lied' was to establish – by parodying its opposite – a moral position for the 'committed' poet of the postwar Nigeria into which he spoke. So the lying poet asked only:

> to be left alone
> with his blank sheet on his lap
> in some dug-out damp corner
> with a view of the streets and the battlefields
> watching the throngs of calloused lives,
> the many many lives stung by living.
> He would put them in his fables
> sandwich them between his lions and eagles,
> between his elephants and crocodiles.[16]

Ofeimun weaves echoes, half-quotations and some well-known literary positions into the ironic fabric of his poem, and for those who felt themselves thus identified it must have been a painful experience. But as Ofeimun makes clear in the interview, that was not the main intention of the piece. It was rather to construct a manifesto for himself and his generation of writers against which their own integrity might be measured.

Clearly Ofeimun takes the business of writing seriously; this is no therapeutic, leisure-time activity. His ambition is to make a poetry that is both committed and crafted, relevant and resonant. He cites Salvatore Quasimodo, Rilke and Martin Carter among his formative influences and his work does read – in a way that much contemporary Nigerian poetry in English pointedly doesn't – as if it, too, acknowledged a notion of art that transcends regional and even cultural boundaries. You feel that the language, not just the writer, is under pressure:

> She whose tongue could coil
> a rig of pythons to break oaks
> She whose fire could raze
> palaces to dust in rainstorms
> She whose hands could wield pestles
> to make miscreants footloose with dread
> She was always the first
> to call the doves to witness[17]

Robert Fraser in his book *West African Poetry* characterises Ofeimun as 'a manic harlequin' in the courts of post-independence Nigeria's corrupt leaders. Fraser reads the poems in the 1980 edition of *The Poet Lied* as seething against 'the pure absurdity of injustice it (the poetry) knows itself powerless to redress'[18]. But Ofeimun sees himself rather as a literary guerrilla and, certainly with the later poems, he clearly feels that such poetry *can* make things happen. In societies where the written word is still regarded with some suspicion and where the formalised spoken word has long been one of the accoutrements of power, such poetry must resonate and will be attended to. As he puts it in 'A Handle for the Flutist', a poem rich in literary allusions and yet located very precisely in contemporary Nigeria:

> the worshipped word is enough
> to expiate crimes and to lay honour
> upon whom the pleaded grace of song has fallen.[19]

Indeed Ofeimun argues that it is the Generals' fear of poetry's loaded words – more potent than the loaded guns of more familiar kinds of guerrillas – that has lent poets such authority as they have in Nigeria. Echoing that image of the oral poet able to make 'gods crumble to their knees/questioned by simple images', Ofeimun declares with characteristic irony, and with an awareness of the paradox in what he, the scourge of the tyrant, is saying:

so let us praise those who will track down
folksongs with police dogs

They will not live with poets
in the Peoples' Republic[20]

If Ofeimun is the voice of the harlequin, the goad, the wit
puncturing the pomposities of Nigeria's rulers with his ironic
barbs and bells, then Niyi Osundare is the high priest of the
'alter-native' vision. Perhaps it is significant that, like Ofeimun,
he is not from a traditional elite background – 'farmer born peasant
bred' he asserts in an early poem. He is the one poet whose lyrical
and critical intelligence seems to offer both an alternative politics
and a notion of poetics which suggests a real way forward for
Nigerian – indeed African – poetry in English. Osundare's work
is at once both aware of the cultural traditions that feed its roots
and of the potential for a unique flowering in the fertile hybridities
of an 'African English'. Much of his poetry addresses issues of
global significance, although his poetry speaks directly into the
topical debates of modern Nigeria. There is a gravitas and weight
about Osundare's poetry that, while the reader is aware of the
characteristic quality of anger that is so prized in this 'alter-native'
tradition, makes his arguments seem the more considered, the
more measured. And indeed they are measured, for the other
quality of Osundare's poetry, which might seem at odds with
the notion of gravitas and weight, is its musicality, its lightness
of touch. One never feels that Osundare is preaching, nor that
– as reader – one is being harangued, yet the effect of much of
his poetry is both to teach and to inspire a critical rage against
the global inanities that are the targets of much of his own wit
and anger.

These general comments are true of Osundare's work as a
whole, from his first collection, *Songs of the Marketplace* (1983),
through to his most recent book, *Horses of Memory* (1997),[21] but
I would like to look at the two volumes that to me best exemplify,
on the one hand, the philosophical and political ideas that underpin
his work, and on the other, the techniques and cultural resources
that so distinctively shape his poetry.

The Eye of the Earth (1986), his third collection, is as much a celebration of the natural world and the peasant traditions of his Ikere people, as it is a critique of the geo-political and economic forces which he feels threaten the earth's very existence. Osundare's commitment is not exclusively to one race or to one nation but rather to an ecological vision of an ideal harmony between Man and Nature. But despite the urgent passion of his concerns, Osundare seems always conscious of the priorities of his craft. *The Eye of the Earth* is by turns lyrical and declamatory, carefully structured and yet rich in bold, original imagery. The sequence is broken into three movements. It begins autobiographically by delving into Osundare's childhood memory of peasant life in Ikere, and then, by contrasting that seemingly idyllic past with the present circumstances of his people and their land he draws out the political criticisms that are the heart of his concern.

The sequence opens with 'Forest Echoes', an extended praise-song to the Nigerian forest, drawing vivid portraits of its trees and creatures. The poet's intention here is more than just to celebrate the landscape of his childhood: it is to demonstrate the balance in nature, the reliance of each element on the others in maintaining the ecological harmony. So the Iroko, the ironwood tree that defies the 'sweating sawyer' and 'champion machet' is king of the forest, but even he will fall eventually to the 'block-headed termites' and the 'scalpel-toothed' squirrel, that 'adzeman of the forest'.

The poem goes on then to consider the land itself, and the balance Osundare's ancestors understood between harvesting its mineral and vegetable wealth and paying due respect to the earth mother as the provider of such riches. He contrasts that traditional honouring with the cynical and short-sighted way today's entrepreneurs exploit the earth's gifts. Addressing Olusunta, one of the gold-bearing rocks sacred to his Ikere people, he asks, 'how dig the gold/without breaking the rock?'[22] Of course the rock is not just the mountain itself, it is the community, the whole social system that has developed around it. For the poet recognises as perhaps only a modern Nigerian could, how easily sudden wealth, if not carefully managed, can turn from a blessing into a curse.

In 'Rainsongs', the second movement of the sequence, the poet celebrates the gift of rain as nature's 'arbiter between plenty and famine, life and death'. The seven poems in this movement focus on different aspects of the experience of the rainy season. First comes a prayer for rain, 'Let Earth's Pain be Soothed' but soon enough, looking at the lush transformation of the countryside after the first rains, the poet can ask 'Who says that drought was here?'

'Homecall', the final movement of the sequence, brings Osundare's political argument into focus. The decline of his people from that balanced lifestyle he remembers as the world of his childhood is used as a metaphor for the experience of the whole nation, indeed of the whole Third World. The life of the child who was 'Farmer born and peasant bred' was rich in spiritual experience that helped sustain his community, in material as well as religious terms. But the culture was not strong enough, the poem argues, to resist 'alien' ideas and values, unadapted to local circumstances, that began in school and ultimately produced a national culture of materialism, envy and corruption. The result is a whole society reduced to dependence on imported food for its very subsistence:

> Farmer-born peasant-bred
> classroom-bled
> I have thrown open my kitchen doors
> and asked hunger to take a seat,
> my stomach a howling dump
> for Carolina rice[23]

That decline inspires Osundare's rage, not only in *The Eye of the Earth* but throughout his work, and in essence, is the source of Osundare's political vision. As I've described it, Osundare may seem something of a romantic, a reactionary figure even, lamenting the passing of a golden age. Rather his poetic and political vision spring from a profound awareness of African history and the debilitating effects of the long-term contact with Europe which has disrupted the mechanisms of balance he sees in the experience of his own people. What, in human terms, most disrupted that balance was the Atlantic slave trade, and Osundare's bleak, passionate but restrained poem 'Goree', responding to a visit he made to the notorious Senegalese slaving station in 1989, establishes the force of his historical imagination. Elsewhere in his work, and in common with the other poets of the alter-native tradition, he is not averse to pointing out the injustices of 'traditional' as well as contemporary governments. So he is no reactionary. And while the notion of a balance, in nature and in political structure, that sustains the community, may be idealistic, as one critic has remarked,[24] it does represent an *imaginable* alternative to both the brutalising crude capitalism of post-independence Nigerian governments and the crude ideological socialism of the intellectual 'opposition'. Osundare's alternative political vision, as it is enmeshed and expressed in his poetry, is both pragmatic and practical, informed by an essentially optimistic view of humanity's ability to change and a belief in the fundamental instinct of mankind to both respect and nurture the earth and its resources.

That pragmatic optimism is evident, too, in *Waiting Laughters,* which won the 1991 NOMA award for poetry. It is this collection – and Osundare's books usually seem to have been conceived as extended poems – which seems to me to best represent Osundare's notion of poetic craft and his relationship to the oral tradition. Subtitled 'a long song in many voices', it is broken into six sections, each of them announced by a different musical setting. For example the opening, 'Some laughters are very significant', has the instruction *flute and/or clarinet; medley of voices.* As a mere reader one has to try and 'hear' the poem in that performance context in order to get a sense of how effective the words off the page might be. As straight text, sections of the poem occasionally seem over-ornamented, particularly in the first section where there is an almost baroque quality to the language, *every* noun encrusted with adjectives, *every* line an image. But it is clear Osundare knows what he's doing, and knows what effect he is striving for. A note to the poem explains that the sequence:

> is about waiting in different and often contrasting circumstances, and the behaviour of time in the waiting process. But more than anything else, it is a poetic response to the gloom and despair which seems to have gripped contemporary African society.[25]

The opening section of the poem establishes various 'levels' of waiting; from the political:

> Every tadpole is a frog-in-waiting
> In the wasted waters of my greed en-tided land

through the elemental:

> Oh teach us the patience of the Rain
> Which eats the rock in toothless silence

to the cosmic:

> Waiting
>   on the stairs of the moon
>   creaking up and down
>   the milkyways of fastidious comets[26]

In such contexts, the poet seems to imply, there *is* time to indulge in the playfulness of a language rich in puns, alliteration and the mannered laughter of literary wit. In section two of the poem, 'The freedom of any society varies proportionately with the volume of its laughter', the social and historical context of African, particularly Nigerian, history is drawn, and issues like those he explores in *The Eye of the Earth* are considered. So is the fundamental question, for a poet, of language:

> The tongue is parrot
> Of another forest
> ...
> A white white tongue
> In a black black mouth
> ...
> And the tongue hangs out its blade
> blunted
> by the labyrinthine syntax of ghostly histories
> ...
> History's stammerer
> when will your memory master
> the vowels of your father's name?[27]

It is in his brilliant use of that 'borrowed tongue' – as he calls it elsewhere – breaking and remaking English, capitalising on the tension set up by that confrontation of language and culture, that

Osundare answers, for his generation, the question of authenticity-in-English that dogged the previous generation of African writers. Osundare is doing for African poetry what Derek Walcott did for Caribbean poetry, claiming and maiming the language for his own ends. No English poet *could* use the English language in the way Osundare does. He uses it to confront the same outrage and distress that Oguibe and Ojaide lament, but with an understanding of the power of wit, of mockery, of laughter, to both discomfort its targets and revitalise its users.

Aderimi Baniikule has usefully pointed to the close relationship between Osundare's techniques and the devices of the Yoruba oral tradition – from the more or less literal 'translation' of certain poems of occasion[28] to the more subtle adaptation of forms and functions and, as with *Waiting Laughters,* the incorporation of music into the fabric of the poem's 'event'. The notion of the poet *speaking for* a community is as important to Osundare as to the other poets of the 'alter-native' tradition, but this need not be the overt assertion of that right and duty that Oguibe and Ojaide claim, but can be expressed rather in that nuanced adaptation of the oral poets' devices which signal his awareness of the responsibility that accompanies those forms. This is apparent in the ways he has used both aspects of the praise-song tradition, on the one hand to genuinely praise the person or even object that is its subject, as in 'Sowing':

> When a long-awaited shower
> has softened the pilgrimage of the dibble,
> corn-grains sing their way to germinal roots
>
> of lying ridges. Seedlings dream truant tendrils
> in the moistening bed of unpunctual heaps;
> the tuber is one patience away,
>
> climbing through stalks
> through pinna-leaved groves
> through vines which twine the moons
>
> like wayward pythons[29]

or to be bitterly ironic in debunking its subject's hypocrisies:

Waiting,
like the corpulent clergy
for his tithes

like the white-wigged judge
        for his turkey

like the hard-faced don
        for his chair

like the policeman
        for his bribe

waiting[29]

Neither of those examples takes praisesong forms as a literal template for the English-language poem, but the effect, within the sequence as a whole, is to recall that dual function of praisesong in Osundare's tradition, and the risks that the praise-singer who was more than just a sycophant always took.

Similarly his use of proverbs – and by all accounts his poems are rich in echoes of Yoruba proverbs – is a matter of subtle adaptation rather than a simplistic translation. Even for the reader without knowledge of Yoruba proverbs, much of Osundare's work bears the cast of proverbial utterance. Indeed some of the more obvious echoes are from proverbs that exist in English:

The plough has no share in
the malady of running swords[31]

And in a sense it doesn't matter about such origins. Osundare's sources, his technique, like his language, are hybrid, and his poetry is inevitably *about* crossing boundaries. 'Peasant born and farmer bred' but, in Walcott's words, 'with a sound colonial education', Osundare's genius is in welding his several inheritances into a unique and appropriate voice for his times. That quality is evident at the conclusion of *Waiting Laughters* where Osundare uses the traditional techniques of poetry, traditional across boundaries of culture and race: unusual imagery, a rhythmic surge, a concise, considered use of a language crafted to produce more of a sense of threat to the status quo than any number of ranting, breast-beating statements of the kind he satirises in the opening couplets of this quotation:

> Our laughter these several seasons is the simper-
> ing sadness of the ox which adores its yoke,
>
> The toothless guffaw of empty thunders
> In epochs of unnatural drought
>
> The season calls for the lyric of other laughters
>
>> New chicks breaking the fragile tyranny
>> of hallowed shells
>
> A million fists, up,
> In the glaring face of complacent skies
>
> A machet waiting, waiting
> In the whetting shadows of stubborn shrubs
>
> A boil, time-tempered,
> About to burst.[32]

Unlike some of his more outspoken contemporaries, Osundare 'dares the beast' not only at the level of rhetoric but also in terms of ideas. If the generals would object to his poetry they must first *read* it; they cannot skim the surface for the obviously offensive word but must explore the metaphor, understand the irony, consider the ambiguities, discover its measured 'beauty'. Beauty and the Beast! Now that would be, in Oguibe's words, for a poet to 'turn the course of history'.

NIYI OSUNDARE – CROSSING THE THRESHOLD
BETWEEN YORUBA AND ENGLISH

This essay began as a presentation given at the International Colloquium, 'Thresholds: Anglophone African Literatures' on the occasion of Niyi Osundare being awarded an Honorary Doctorate at the University of Toulouse-Le Mirail, in 1999.

When I actually came to write this paper, long after committing myself to the title, I realised that there were several problematic elements to what it was promising. In the first place, I wouldn't now argue that Osundare's poetry *does* cross those thresholds, rather that it is, precisely, a poetry *of* the threshold. Although, perhaps even more seriously, I want to query whether there can be a 'threshold' in any meaningful sense, between two such discrete languages and poetries. And as for identifying the relationship between Yoruba poetics and English verse in Osundare's work – well, that challenge has already been taken up by critics who were certainly far better able to comment on the Yoruba influence than I would be.[1] The whole question of the relationship between Yoruba poetics and English verse, particularly in relation to notions of form, verse architecture and patternings that function in Yoruba but hardly translate into English, was brilliantly examined in an essay by another Nigerian poet, Femi Oyebode, in 1995.[2] What is more, Osundare has himself discussed in detail his sense of the creative tension between these two linguistic empires and two poetic traditions, in his essay 'Caliban's Gamble', published in 1995[3] and in a currently unpublished essay 'Yoruba Thought, English Words: A Poet's Journey through the tunnel of two tongues' which is included in a volume I have edited in the Birmingham African Studies Series entitled *Yoruba/English: Strategies of Mediation,* currently in press.[4]

I will be quoting from that essay later, but given such a

distinguished and authoritative body of discussion, what can an Englishman with only a very tangential knowledge of Yoruba language and culture actually have to say on this topic? It would be particularly presumptuous for me to attempt any such analysis before an audience that includes so many Yoruba speakers, many of whom are daily moving between Yoruba and English in a variety of contexts. My own sense of that journey is somewhat perverse. I live in a peculiar relationship to Yoruba in that, while I hardly understand more than a few words, it is a language I have heard almost every day for much of the last two decades. I lived in Kano, in northern Nigeria, for several years in the early 1980s and both in the university and in the part of the city where I lived, hearing Yoruba spoken was an everyday experience. Then, since 1988, I have worked in the Centre of West African Studies, University of Birmingham, where courses in Yoruba are taught by Professor Karin Barber. Consequently we have many Yoruba-speaking visitors passing through the Centre as visiting scholars and/or language teachers. So, as I say, I am very used to hearing the language. But what I hear is a choral music really, just tones and cadences, a particular sound pattern that I recognise as 'Yoruba'. That would not seem – in terms of the apparent argument of this paper – a very useful relationship with the language. In fact, I want to suggest that my lazy perception of Yoruba *as music* might prove to be a fortuitous aid to my recognition of the music-of-Yoruba in the English language poems of Niyi Osundare.

What my experience of Yoruba also suggests is that there can be no 'threshold' between English and Yoruba in a practical sense – you either understand the languages or you don't. There are degrees of comprehension and competence, of course, and versions of pidgin that may incorporate elements from both languages at various levels, but they wouldn't really constitute a threshold, in the sense that we are using the term. Even for the Yoruba speakers who daily move between the two languages, insofar as they may be translating from one language into the other, while that conceptual space 'between' the two languages at that moment of translation perhaps constitutes a threshold, it is a pretty rarefied space! The term threshold implies 'common ground', a shared liminal space, not a no-man's land between competing linguistic and cultural worlds. So what to make of a written poetry by a Yoruba poet using English as his primary medium of literary expression? I have argued, controversially, elsewhere[5] that – for reasons at least in part to do with the purposes to which it has been put – much modern Nigerian poetry written in English lacks many of the qualities of wit, ambiguity and metaphorical wordplay that we associate with 'poetry' as a genre. But with a great poet–intellectual like Niyi Osundare, what he contrives is an original, hybrid form, very precisely defined by Steven Arnold as 'Yoruba poetry written in English'. That formulation allows me, for the moment, to cling on to the title of this paper but to understand it as inviting a discussion of issues around a view of Niyi Osundare's work as operating on the threshold between '(Yoruba) poetry in English'[6] as distinct from 'English poetry'. There clearly is a threshold – common ground – between those two categories and as a native speaker of English I will inevitably have a notion, or prejudice, as to where the thresholds of the language might be situated in terms of conventional contemporary usages. And as an English poet who has been struggling for twenty years to find a language and forms appropriate to a discussion of the African issues with which my work has engaged,[7] I can perhaps speak about these matters from a position somewhere on the other side of *that* threshold.

Just recently I was again teaching the broad outlines of the debate over which language an African writer chooses to use, and why, to my first year African literature students. Knowing I had to give this paper but hadn't written it up yet, I was trying to work out where Niyi's work fits in terms of that debate. Not simply to ask why he chooses to write in English at all, but given that he does, where would he situate himself in relation to the English language as his primary poetic medium? Professor Irele has helped clarify that situation to some extent, in so far as Niyi's work would fit into his discussion of the distinction between monoglot native speakers of a language and what he called the 'L2' category of non-native speakers who nonetheless master and use the language in their daily life.[8] Such people will use – in this case – English, not as a foreign language, (nor as instrumentally as the notion of a wilfully employed *lingua franca* would suggest), but to engage in a creative, expressive relationship with the language. Their version of English is informed by, is indeed enriched by, the knowledge of and continued usage of that other, mother-tongue – in Niyi's case Yoruba. It was interesting though that just about all the examples of authors who have written in a language other than their mother tongue that Prof. Irele gave were novelists – Conrad, Joyce, Achebe. Interesting because although a writer of fiction clearly has to be completely confident and competent in his command of the language in which he tells his tale there is a sense that – and perhaps it is my romance or claiming a particular privilege for poetry – but I would say that most poets would argue that the relationship between the poet and his language *has to be* more intense, more intimate, more instinctive than the novelist's relationship *has to be*. Which is not to say that novelists don't or can't have such an intimate and intense relationship with the language in which they write, only that they *needn't* have. Nor is it to suggest that all poetry, in Keats's phrase, 'falls like the leave from the trees'. I know well enough how hard-worked, worked-out – indeed sometimes worked-over – poetry can be. But nevertheless I would want to argue the *necessary* intensity of the relationship between the poet and his language of self-expression.

There is an interesting case relevant to this discussion in contemporary British poetry in the situation of the great Anglo-Welsh poet, R.S. Thomas. Thomas did not learn Welsh as his mother tongue but learnt it as a young man for both emotional and practical reasons. Practically, he needed to be able to speak, at a fundamental level, with his parishioners in North Wales – he was a priest for most of his life – and emotionally he felt that – as a Welshman – he *needed* to be able to speak Welsh. In his later years, R.S. Thomas has lived his life almost entirely through the medium of the Welsh language; he will speak only Welsh in conversation or interview, he writes prose essays and letters in Welsh, but he continues – reluctantly – to write his poetry in English. He continues to write his poetry in English because, he has said, although he has been fluent in Welsh for more than half a century, he still does not feel that he can be true to that poetic instinct in anything other than his 'mother tongue'.

Thomas's situation is not quite the same as that which pertains for a poet like Niyi Osundare who has, more or less, always lived in full knowledge of the two languages – although he certainly ascribes Yoruba the status of his mother tongue – but the comparison does make the point about the intensity of that relationship between poetry and the language of its expression. Osundare obviously *feels* himself to be in a close enough relationship with English to be able to compose poetry in that language. And let me be clear here, I am not in any way seeking to deny or denigrate his achievement in making what seems to me some of the most moving and important poetry in English in our time. Indeed, one of the things I want to argue is that it is precisely because of his unique relationship to the English language that he is able to make such poetry.

As a scholar of linguistics Osundare has a better technical understanding of how language works, how English works, than most monoglot English speakers, indeed than most contemporary British poets writing in English. But that technical knowledge cannot compensate – insofar as compensate is an appropriate word – in terms of his literary usage of English, for his not being a 'native speaker'. In a sense 'compensate' would imply that Osundare might or even should aspire to use English as a native speaker would, but of course culturally the implications of such an ambition are fraught with contradictions. Osundare would not, in any case, claim that instinctive, natural relationship with the English language that – by definition – everyone has with their mother tongue, but *as poet* he must convince himself and his readers that he can fully explore the emotional range and expressive power of the language. Perhaps that is the fundamental distinction between 'English poetry' and 'poetry in English', that the former is not simply a matter of nationality but signifies a poetry that draws on the English language as a 'primary source' as it were, while that the latter (Yoruba or otherwise) signifies, rather, a self-conscious tension between the poet and the language in which his poetry-in-English is written.

91

I am sure that the last thing Osundare would aspire to is that anyone should think him an 'English poet', but the distinction between 'poetry in English' and 'English poetry' is revealing and provocative in several ways. First of all, to move the context to France, it is interesting to contrast the relationship of a poet like Senghor to the French language – his medium of literary expression – with Osundare's relationship with English. I don't have the linguistic expertise to judge for myself, but I understand that Senghor's French is very much the 'correct' French of a member of a linguistic elite and that his work is often included in anthologies of French verse, as if his poetry were – notwithstanding his race, nationality, colour or subject matter – French poetry.[9] That would not happen with Niyi Osundare's work and current notions of what 'English poetry' might be, both for literary and political reasons.

I won't go off on a tangent into a discussion of contrasting colonial policies, the French notion of *assimilation* as against the British policy of indirect rule, though those attitudes do still cast their shadows. But the position of someone like Senghor and the distinction between 'poetry in English' and 'English poetry' both come to mind in relation to the current discussion, in Britain, around the appointment of the new Poet Laureate. You will probably know that Ted Hughes, who had been the laureate for the last decade or so, died a couple of months ago and his successor is yet to be announced. In a certain narrow and hierarchical view of English poetry, the laureateship should go to the greatest living exponent of English poetry. In the past that definition might just have extended to a Scotsman – though I don't know if it ever did – and in theory could have been held by a woman, though it never has been. What is interesting about the current discussion over the new appointment, in our terms, is that one of the front runners for the position, apparently, is the West Indian poet Derek Walcott. Now I don't know how Walcott feels about that and I would be very surprised if he was either offered it or would accept it if it was offered.[10] However the fact of his being seriously discussed[11] is revealing in several ways. First of all it says something about the way that Britain has changed in the last few decades

92

that this black West Indian who has never lived in England can be regarded by so many in the British cultural establishment and literary media as a serious and acceptable candidate for the Laureateship. Kipling, who once turned the offer of the laureateship down, is probably turning in his grave! But more to the point it tells us something about Walcott's poetry and, indirectly, about Niyi Osundare's poetry.

Walcott and Osundare seem to me to be very similar poets in many ways: both master technicians, both poets who live in metaphor, both with a great love of and respect for the English language and English literature, both profound thinkers about poetry and contemporary poetics, both wryly sceptical about the state of criticism and literary theory now. Most significantly, both work in a creative literary space designated by the tension between – or among – different linguistic codes. Walcott's relationship to English is not at all straightforward, St. Lucia is linguistically very complex with French and English creoles crossing over and rubbing up against a formal English. But crucially it was more-or-less formal English that was the language of Walcott's home life, his childhood and his education. Walcott *thinks* in English, albeit that it is an English aware of those other linguistic dimensions of St. Lucian life. Osundare, on the other hand, has said that his most profound challenge as a poet is 'to express Yoruba thought, Yoruba ideas, in English.'[12]

The difference that makes is revealed, I think, in the fact that as a young man Walcott could declare, without irony, and not simply in terms of a colonial cringe, that he aspired 'to prolong the mighty line of Marlowe and Milton,'[13] to enrich English poetry with his West Indian inflections. In that sense it would not be so surprising if he were made Poet Laureate: his poetry does belong to, or at least can sit quite comfortably in, the cannon of English poetry. Indeed, it is quite frightening to see how his poetry has been *domesticated* into both the British and American poetic mainstream, especially since he won the Nobel prize. That process is possible because of his fundamental relationship to the English language as his language of thought and feeling, which is – as we have seen – very different from Niyi Osundare's relationship to English. That difference explains – I think, why Walcott's poetry might indeed cross that threshold into the domain of 'English poetry' and why Osundare's can't. Osundare's (Yoruba) poetry-in-English refuses to be 'domesticated'. It is in essence a poetry *of* the threshold – continuously reminding his readers/hearers that it is mediating the two traditions.

I can't imagine that Osundare would ever have made a statement like Walcott's, expressing an ambition to become part of the line of the great English poets. Wide-ranging and diverse as his reading and references are, his mentors, in terms of a poetic pantheon, are more obviously in the Yoruba oral traditions he so skilfully draws on. In the as yet unpublished essay I referred to earlier he remarks:

> Yoruba is my mother tongue, English my acquired language. The former brings warm intimations of the cradle and the homestead, the latter stern memories of the classroom and the blackboard. In Yoruba, poetry is song and chant, a performed or performable *event* throbbing with human breath, with a robust sense of audience and participation. Accomplishment in the art is still largely natural, a matter of talent, or lineage inheritance; it is still demotic, if not democratic. Illiterate village women chant *oriki* (praise poetry, panegyric) (Barber, 1991)[14] with a virtuosity that would make a university professor of poetry go blank with envy; traditional hunters regale one another with *ijala* (hunters' song) from sundown till the last cock at dawn has crowed. At the personal level, I grew up admiring my father's performance of *alamo* (a long, colourful, episodic song popular among the Ekiti-Yoruba) [15]

Excuse the long quotation, but it does lead me to look back at that seemingly negative formulation I made earlier when I remarked that Osundare never uses English in quite the same way that a monoglot English speaker or writer would. It is not just the obvious use of Yoruba words and phrases to enrich his English resource that really sets his poetry apart from standard English texts, nor is it the musicality of his wordplay or even the distinctive verse patterning. If we look at a few passages of his poetry that contains none of those linguistic referents to Yoruba, that are not obviously located in a Nigerian context (that is, to adapt Stephen Arnold's wonderful metaphor, to remove the Yoruba watermark from the banknote of Osundare's verse) then we can see how non-standard his 'straight' English actually is and how significant a contribution that daring reformulation of English makes to the overall texture of his poetry.

Lines and phrases like these few, taken almost at random from his collection *Midlife*[16] could not conceivably have been written by a British-based poet used to the contemporary conventions of English usage, notwithstanding that the regional and multicultural variations of English now commonly employed in all sorts of British literature gives poets plenty of leeway:

> I am the luminous covenant
> Of short and tall spaces (p.3)
>
> Waiting noons are auricles of radiant blessings   (p.7)
>
> The loam-fattened yam put a bounce on my biceps (p.38)
>
> Toe marks embrace the streets, toe
> Marks which find their name
> In the clayey book of lettering gallops (p.84)

As is apparent from these examples, Osundare's poetry 'verbalises' the English language in ways that a contemporary English poet would hardly dare. His English does things that the grammatical conventions suggest cannot be done, he uses devices like onomatopoeia and alliteration without any sense of literary affectation or concern for poetic fashion. He invents and remakes words to suit his expressive purposes and there is a *seeming* unselfconsciousness about the range of his poetic vocabulary, often employing words and expressions which would seem anachronistic to a contemporary English writer. He will twist conventional English syntax to accommodate the inflections of a very nonstandard English voice rather than force that voice to sing an 'English' song. Indeed the music of much of Osundare's poetry can be difficult for an ear trained to the traditional measures or even the contemporary dissonances of English versification to hear or appreciate. Quite often, while it is obvious that this is measured verse, the phrasing, line breaks and sound units jar with conventional expectations. This is where my sense of the music of spoken Yoruba comes into play, for it is an echo of that music I hear playing beneath the surface of his English constructions.

In a similar way there are other linguistic features in Osundare's verse that strike a reader of mainstream English poetry as unusual, if not problematic, which even a passing knowledge of Yoruba helps to contextualise. The accretion of verbs and adjectives, the metaphors piled one on another and developed over so long a span make for a rather florid, ornamented style which is certainly at odds with the "lean and competent verse"[17] that has become so fashionable in the last half of the twentieth century.[18] Reading Niyi's poetry in the context of modern English poetry I am reminded of lines by perhaps the most self-consciously English of the poets of that period, Philip Larkin:

> Too much confectionery, too rich:
> I choke on such nutritious images.[19]

But from my work with Karin Barber[20], I understand enough about the difficulties of translating Yoruba into English to know that Yoruba is an intensely metaphorical and proverbial language. Meaning and metaphor can hardly be disentangled in much 'ordinary' Yoruba speech – still less in its poetics. So it is that innately Yoruba valorisation of metaphor which informs this aspect of Osundare's technique as a poet writing in English. One might almost say that Osundare's work is only masquerading as English poetry, dressed in borrowed clothes, so that Stephen Arnold's designation of his work as 'Yoruba poetry written in English' seems more and more to be the only adequate description of this unique body of work.

I would invoke again the authority of the poet/linguist himself, again from that unpublished essay, in a passage that reveals how little about his use of English is in fact unselfconscious; this is a very thoughtful and *considering* poet:

> I am painfully aware of the difference between the Yoruba in my mind, and the English poem that is born after laborious midwifing,

of the long journey between a song summoned from memory by the urgency of the human voice and a poem committed to cold print with its scribal rigidity. I am aware of the liberty I am taking with English syntax, of the expansion and liberalisation that must take place before a structural space now almost completely given to the lean and competent verse can concede some room to the vibrant lyricism of the song of the marketplace and the village square. Most times the innate flexibility of the English language rallies to my assistance, but I have tried not to push it beyond its elastic limits.[21]

So no one will mistake this body of work for English poetry. No one, I suspect, will ever nominate Niyi Osundare to be the British Poet Laureate. Which returns me to the apparent foolishness of my title – it seems to me now that Niyi Osundare's poetry is emphatically *not* a poetry that dances across 'the threshold between Yoruba and English' nor even that threshold between Yoruba poetry written in English and English poetry. This is a poetry which celebrates that liminal space, that teases and tantalises and threatens but will not conform, will not bow its head to enter the compound of English poetry. Rather it dances at the doorway, daring the owner of the house to come outside and listen to a different song.

BREAKING OUT OF THE DREAM:
FEMI OYEBODE'S 'BLACK KITES CIRCLING'

Femi Oyebode's poetry, perhaps more than that of any other contemporary Nigerian poet, negotiates its music and its meanings in that liminal Yoruba/English realm between two cultures profoundly known and understood but never quite owned. I suggest his consciousness of working in a poetic space circumscribed by this sense of both belonging and not belonging to those two linguistic and cultural worlds is particularly intense because while he has chosen – with all the caveats that accrete around that word – to live most of his adult life in Britain, living in and through the English language in his professional and domestic life, his poetic imagination – as other commentators on his work have remarked – appears preoccupied with a notion of 'home', of rootedness, in that other, Yoruba, domain of his childhood and personal cultural formation.[1] This is not to say that he does not write about his life and concerns in England, but taking the body of his work as a whole – running through six collections now[2] – his focus is overwhelmingly on Nigeria and in particular the Yoruba world from which he is physically distanced.

Most Nigerian poets writing in English[3] have, in a sense, chosen to endure that dilemma of cultural allegiance to some degree or other but, while they stay in Nigeria or spend only brief periods away from Africa with the certainty always of return, the dislocation is manageable, may even be creative. For the writer permanently 'exiled', however, his lived life remote from the sounds and rhythms of his mother tongue and the cultural life with which it is inextricably bound, the strategies of mediation are so much more complex. Two remarks made by Femi Oyebode at a recent poetry reading in the Centre of West African Studies – in response to questions from the audience – provide a measure of that cultural dislocation:

Asked the inevitable student question as to why he chooses to write in English, Oyebode replied that, having lived so long away from that other linguistic source, he no longer felt fully competent or comfortable in his use of Yoruba, not able to use its resources, resonances and complex musics in the ways that he felt a poet writing in any language must be able to. The deep sense of loss that underpins this confession perhaps helps to explain why Oyebode holds so tenaciously to those elements of Yoruba culture which remain for him as touchstones of his identity.

Asked who he thought of as the audience for his poetry, Oyebode confessed that, despite the fact that his work has gained a considerable critical following and is included in several recent anthologies, he really couldn't envisage a readership or audience, either in Britain or Nigeria, which would really be able to 'make sense' of the poems in regard to their cultural referents and the complexity of the individual experience that is – one way or another – reflected through them. Oyebode writes like nobody else and, it seems, for nobody in particular, perhaps because he knows that his readers will be so diverse in terms of what they bring to any response to the poems.

That sense of a double isolation has not, in general, driven Oyebode to make many concessions to his potential readers. The seeming difficulty of much of his work for the non-Yoruba/non-Yoruba-speaking reader resides in part in the intensity of his engagement with a Yoruba mythos which he takes for granted, as a given intellectual hinterland to his poetry. Unlike some other African writers who have been criticised for simplifying or distorting their texts in English to accommodate the understanding of a foreign audience, Oyebode is not often inclined to explain those references for the benefit of possible uninformed or lazy readers. If 'we' would engage with this poetry, we must either do the contextual/intellectual spadework necessary to come to some understanding of the ground from which Oyebode writes, or we must be content to accept the intriguing cultural *otherness* of the poems as part of their distinctive quality and make what we can of them as poems-in-English, working in all the ways that poems can.

Oyebode has argued persuasively regarding the importance of the relationship between the formal devices of oral Yoruba poetry and the techniques of Yoruba/Nigerian poets writing in English.[4] Although he did not refer to his own practice in the essay in which that argument is made, those observations must also apply to any informed reading of Oyebode's poetry. Certainly, the uninformed reader of this poetry in English will sense that much is happening between the lines as it were. One of the factors tensioning Oyebode's poetry is that sense of, as he puts it in a recent poem, 'another music, faint and masked from view,'[5] which is nevertheless a tangible presence in the English language poem, whether or not the reader can identify its Yoruba origins. The language of Oyebode's poems on the page, however, is essentially a rather formal, grammatically correct literary English. The Yoruba dimension in his poetry is a matter of reference and cultural assumption– and perhaps an echo of that 'other music' – but these are not linguistically 'difficult' poems for a reader used to contemporary British or American poetry. Indeed, while there is a lyric strand and a distinctive music about Oyebode's work, his poetry is essentially a poetry of stories: weaving a narrative through sequences and extended poems[6] that engage in various ways with aspects of history: personal, Yoruba, Nigerian.

Insofar as there is a difficulty in engaging with Oyebode's poetry at that more prosaic level of a paraphrasable understanding, it derives from the ambiguities – self-consciously employed – of what is in effect the *medium*, the structuring device that he most commonly employs to tell and colour those stories, that of the dream. The dream is a trope which allows Oyebode further licence – in terms of the ways the stories unfold – within the larger licence of poetry, to address that very mix of memories, oral histories, researched 'facts' and received opinions (as well as the contradictions they inevitably throw up) which is the *stuff* of his writing. It may be, too, that the notion of dream can accommodate and contain the consequences of the process of his engagement with those contradictions – psychological and imagistic – in ways that more naturalistic modes of narration could not. Oyebode is seemingly mistrustful of a poetry that does not foreground its ambiguities;

his life's experience as well as his professional expertise confirm him in the view that stories are always more complicated than they appear on the surface. He sees history, in particular, as being subject to 'the fitful Muse' of memory[7]. As a professor of psychiatry in a British university, working in a post-Freudian / post-Jungian context, the notions of dream and dreaming obviously carry particular significance. The Nigerian critic Oshita O. Oshita suggests that Oyebode's work not only draws on European-derived theories about the meaning and significance of dreams but also refers to ideas on dreams derived from Yoruba tradition.[8] Whatever the source of inspiration, the overall effect of the repeated recourse to dream as a structuring device is to suggest that dream is to some extent the subject of as well as the vehicle for Oyebode's poetic enterprise. What this means for the reader is that to engage with the poems s/he must be willing to enter not so much an artfully contrived version of the cultural reality the poems draw from, reflect or imply, but rather be willing to enter the dream narrative which that place/time/event inspired in Oyebode.

In the earlier books dream was used in its broadest sense, as if the life remembered, observed and anticipated could only be narrated – smoothed into the kind of story that we understand as realism – through the agency of dream. So the childhood memory of Nigeria's Independence Day celebrations recalled in 'Dreamdreaming' from his first collection *Naked to Your Softness and other dreams*:

> My father showed me my first swarm of bees
> They were british airforce jets,
> With the sting in their tails,
>
> I remember
> The hungry, patient crowds, the talakawa,
> How the dust clung to their feet and rose
> With alexandra, her hat and gloves, pale and bored.
>
> My father's silence was heavy
> You were making a gift of our land to us [9]

has become as much dream as the meeting between the exiled

persona's encounter with his familial and ancestral 'ghosts' in 'Dreamtime':

> my ghosts arrive at the stairs, the current peak
> heading upwards, by steps to another century, to logic
> arrive, through secret passages, from another country
> with laughter, like a dance of possessed spirits
> in midnight forests, tempests inhaled and embraced [10]

Over the course of the next five books Oyebode employs ever more sophisticated and precise version of poetry-as-dream to explore the range of his concerns, both in terms of offering a vehicle for a personal, inward journey:

> I have withdrawn far, farther, further
> Crawled into my shell, into the tunnel,
> The disturbed nest [11]

and as a means of discussing the complexities and ambiguities of public, historical and contemporary issues. In his third collection, *Forest of Transformation*, the sequence 'This Sense of My Being', a poetic retelling of Samuel Johnson's *History of the Yoruba* (1921), is a series of portraits that are powerful individual poems in their own right, but in a dream-linked structure create an awesome pantheon of Yoruba mytho-history. Oyebode uses metaphor and allegory to discuss issues of power, corruption and human nature, implying that the horrors of successive tyrannical regimes in contemporary Nigeria can best be understood in the context of a knowledge of the Nigerian past and its legends, including, for example, the methods of the notorious dictator, Karan:

> Karan, unmitigated in his tyranny
> killed his own subjects
> basked in the red of their expiration
> guilty, he executed others for his sins,
> remorseless, his scourge drained
> the store of our patience,
> he purged us of our tolerance. [12]

In *Adagio for Oblong Mirrors* and *Master of the Leopard Hunt* Oyebode again uses the dream-vehicle to explore aspects of his concern that lie outside the range of a realistic framework. At one point in *Adagio* he seems to offer a definition of both dream and his – rather sceptical – sense of his own practice:

> this tension is the necessary premise of all dreams,
> the balance of hunger and need, of expressive song
>
> robed, ribbed and notated in a haunting script
> and then filed dead in a ledger like a sum,
>
> a tune which lives in the structures of knowing [13]

In *Master of the Leopard Hunt*, a book celebrating the skill and – more importantly, the vision – of the anonymous artist/craftsman of Benin's most important classical sculpture, Oyebode presents a more positive account of his ambition for the dream-narrator, the creative process which is a kind of dream:

> I will have no shape, no visible fabric
>
> I will merely enclose an abstracted space
> But meaning will flow from me, a river
>
> A river of all our imaginations, brooding [14]

The dynamic of Oyebode's poetic expression then, over the course of his first five collections, is increasingly to engage the mythos and licence of dream to confront the ambiguities of history, exile and identity. This dream-perspective is arguably a function of the complex and uncomfortable relationship to that history that Oyebode's 'exile' status confers. Initially this pattern seems to be maintained in his most recent collection *Indigo Camwood and Mahogany Red*. Of the three sequences that make up the collection, two – 'Seize the Lords' and 'This Square Land' – are very much in the style of his earlier work. The former is in part a meditation on the cultural, social and mythic history of the River Niger, '..the river a dream against the banks and flowing/ The juice which oils and rigs our soul, our myth.' The sequence 'This Square Land' evokes another kind of dream journeying, 'In these dreams some moaned aroused by the caress of phantoms'.

However, the final sequence in the book, 'Black Kites Circling' has a very different tenor and tone.

'Black Kites Circling' is a sequence of seven poems written in response to a visit Oyebode made to Lagos in 1998, when the Abacha 'terror' was most intense and the material circumstances of many of the peoples of Lagos at a particularly low point. Rather than translate the observations, feelings, personal and historical perceptions that his visit generated into the heightened mythic dramas of the dream poems of the first two sections, (distancing and also 'fictionalising' the experience in that process), the poems in 'Black Kites Circling' are much closer to raw reportage.

In 'The names of the principal houses in Ikole' the sequence begins calmly enough, almost nostalgically, with the meilifluous and elegiac roll-call of the names of Yoruba families attending the poet's uncle's funeral:

> Ajayi, Olatawura, Filani, Bamgboye, Ojo,
> Ogundana, Babalola, Odupaiye and so on [15]

That gathering of the great and the good of his childhood and the sight of 'the king's staff silent and beaded in his pew' establishes the reality of a rooted and enduring life fixed in that place and reconnects the long-exiled poet to a sense of 'home' that he has not been able to establish in quite the same way elsewhere. This cultural world is:

> The place where I never need to explain
> The colour, the shape, the broody
> All too blue melody, the meaning of ruling
> This place where I too can just be
> Like any hill justly hilly in its place. [16]

So the poem constitutes a declaration of belonging, a celebration by one who knows it intimately of the place and its people and its ways. That assertion then gives licence to the very critical and disappointed commentaries that follow which draw stark and brutal pictures of other aspects of the contemporary reality of that place.

The second poem in the sequence, 'Lagos at night, is like a cluster of gems' immediately contrasts the comforting images of the previous poem with a very different portrait of the city, which is now a place of menace and danger, a place where, 'Any innocence of spirit is vulnerable to rape', where the sight of a naked pauper woman washing herself in 'a puddle of filthy water' has become so commonplace as not to draw any comment from passing motorists. Worse still, where the dead body of a young man can be left to rot on the roadside, attended only by:

> ...flies, like priests in an ancient ritual
> Black cassocks and hoods, susurrating in prayer [17]

The final line of the poem repeats the title, which has plainly become now ironic, a tone reinforced by the addition of the phrase 'fake gems' at the end of the line.

That impression of shocked sensibility is made explicit in the title of the third poem in the sequence 'The poverty, here, wraps and pulls the facial bones'. The distorted and disfigured bodies of the urban poor remind him of 'tin cans squashed and battered'. Initially the poet finds only cause for deepening despair in the material poverty of the mass of the people of Lagos:

> But the ugliness which is a scar, the cheapened
> Rough and pustulant geography of living
> Weighs down the shoulders and jaws [18]

However this grim, dehumanising vision is ameliorated by two moments of revelation. The first is the appearance of a young woman whose physical beauty 'would capture the breath' and reminds those around her of their humanity despite 'the lethal cocktail of ash and benzene' which constitutes the air they have become accustomed to breathe. She is described as 'a jewel... an elegant chiselled light,' which echoes back to the imagery of the previous poem in the sequence.

Her appearance in some way reminds or enables the poet to identify the spirit of the people[19] which survives, despite the depredations of their material circumstances, and the poem ends as a celebration of the people's determination to 'make life', not least with words:

> The soul refuses to gather dust, to gather dust
> The people employ the varied tones of language
> To soothe, to tickle, to tease, to cry at night

An undeniable world of fellowship, like sap, rising
Through language and custom to create
No, to nurture the indefinable but real princely estate. [20]

In 'the lagoon has become even more populated', the central poem in the sequence, Oyebode again presents a harrowing portrait of the material conditions of the masses of people living around the Lagos lagoon, so many cramped into slums and 'these impoverished crevices/These microscopic valleys, embankments and peninsulas.' Again he notices and praises the determination of many people here to try and resist the degradation, 'To be better than the obvious ruin, the moral decay.' But poverty and the corruption of the society overwhelms that ambition. It is the squalid circumstances of the children that most disturbs the poet, 'Handicapped and ailing from the lack of tenderness.' Even here he sees, in the weary compassion of their long-suffering mothers, 'teasing love from the parched throat', signs of that spirit to resist the ultimate despair.

The poet begins to ascribe, in fairly direct terms, blame and responsibility for the terrible decline in the living standards and quality of life of so many Lagosians – and by inference the general population of Nigeria – in 'The lagoon is being claimed for land', the fifth poem in the sequence. He begins by pointing up the contrast between the lifestyles of the business people and government appointees in the affluent suburbs of Lagos – grandiose houses with manicured gardens of 'Hibiscus and jacaranda, Canna and bird of paradise lilies' – and the lives endured by that 'undercity of the dispossessed'. The poem asserts that a 'concentric ring of terror rules' over this unjust and corrupt scenario. The ruler is not named but unmistakably evoked in powerfully damning imagery recalling the style of the praise singer – who does not always, of course, indulge in simple praises:

A ruler whose silence advances like a sullen cloud
......
The ruler absent from view but yet a burdensome silence
Compresses the air, depresses the soul of the dead
......

The ruler overflowing like a stagnant pool of green algae
......
An incomparable destitution of spirit is dressed
In starch and cap, green algae uniform overflowing [21]

The penultimate poem in the sequence, 'I am yet to write about the agama lizard' contains some of the harshest, most shocked and shocking descriptions of Lagos:

A diseased city sunbathed in filth accumulated like wealth
And stored in heaps, gold bullion in gutters and pavements [22]

Images of the natural world that have somehow adapted to the city, like the lizard, the starling and the cattle egret, are 'symbols of the possible, of hope in the realm of the hopeless.' The exception is the black kite, a predator and scavenger, that becomes, in 'the road is lined by cocoa trees' – the final poem in the sequence – emblematic of General Abacha's regime; a regime characterised by theft, extortion and cold-hearted brutality. The General himself, 'isolated and alien, immersed in the gluttony of power' is described as, 'A hippopotamus, mud bathing, in its own excrement' – a fairly unambiguous critique.

'I am yet to write about the agama lizard' ends with the image of Christ on the cross as a figure of suffering passivity, offering hope to the downtrodden people of Nigeria but only in another life to come. However the sequence as a whole ends on a slightly more assertive note, invoking the Yoruba creator god Obatala, a deity with particular responsibility for the deformed and disabled – terms Oyebode has repeatedly used through the sequence to describe the oppressed people of Lagos. Obatala is credited with the power to avenge the evil done by his human creations when his patience is finally exhausted. Opposing the black of the scavenger kite, Obatala's colour is white and his creative energies, the final line of the poem asserts, 'Electrify and embolden the dispirited.'

So the poem-sequence as a whole shifts between the poet's rage and despair, on the one hand, as he surveys the conditions of his homeland and an assertion of hope, in the idea of deep spiritual resources embedded in the 'traditional' Yoruba understanding of the divine and its relationship with the people in times of distress and suffering. While it is written in a relatively direct style that distinguishes it from most of Oyebode's work it is certainly not bald protest or polemic; this is a poetry that draws on symbol and metaphor as well as a realistic and vivid account of the material conditions the poet observes on this visit to Lagos. With this sequence, Oyebode's work becomes much more characteristic of Nigerian poetry in English over the last forty years, for the most part directly engaged in the socio-political-cultural debate about the state of Nigerian society and the direction of development should take. In terms of that national debate, English can be presented as the appropriate language for such a discussion, whether as directly political rhetoric or a more obliquely poetic discourse.

Oyebode's more contemplative dream-poems on the other hand – written out of memory, a physically distanced relationship to place and events, and scholarly research – sit somewhat uncomfortably with that corpus of Nigerian poetry in English. 'Black Kites Circling' is unusual for Oyebode in that the events and images that inspire the poems are more or less contemporary with the occasion of writing, which has generally been the case with most of the poetry in English produced by Nigerian writers living in Nigeria in recent times. The sense of anger, despair and personal engagement in an ongoing struggle is part of what sets the sequence apart from much of Oyebode's other work. There is no need to filter this experience through dream, the response is immediate, is visceral, is *real*.

But even in this poem-sequence Oyebode writes as if he is not able to identify completely with the people whose suffering he chronicles. This is a world known and understood by the poet, but it is no longer *his* world. Recalling Oyebode's remarks about his relationship to the Yoruba language quoted at the beginning of this essay, it is pertinent to notice the importance he puts on language – invariably in this context the Yoruba language – as the agent of identity, community and, by implication, as the expression/conduit of the spirit. Insofar as it makes any sense to ask the question what language does any God speak, can one imagine

Obatala speaking English? Throughout the sequence, Oyebode's observations of people speaking to each other are located in occasions of celebration and resistance, occasions from which he – as exile, been-to, only temporary resident in the country – is to some extent excluded. When, for example, in the opening poem of the sequence, the calling of Yoruba names serves to 'locate' the poem and the poet, it also emphasises that the life this poem responds to goes on in another language than that in which the poem is written. Those Yoruba names recall to the 'English' returnee:

> A darker, veiled and dramatic ritual
> Incantations rubbed in blood, disrobed
> And elemental like thunder wedded the nobility
> Like the tongue to words, cursing the tribal enemy [23]

That deep, elemental – oral – connection to the life of that place is contrasted with the dry, deracinated record of 'words in a book' –

> black shapes on vellum light
> Spoken in the guttural silence, the unheard language
> And inflection of an unseen tribe,[24]

– words which are the exiled poet's practice.

So while the evident commitment of 'Black Kite's Circling' suggests that Oyebode is reasserting his connection to the contemporary Nigerian world, the poet's negotiation of the Yoruba/English 'translation' which must take place before those words can reach the page reminds him – and his readers – of the *distance* such a process of mediation imposes between the subject of description and its representation on the page. In much of Oyebode's work that distance is blurred by the dream trope which legitimates the slippage between time, place and linguistic 'states of being'. In 'Black Kite's Circling' the absence of that dream device emphasises both the force of the poet's connection to the people, places and events he describes and the simultaneous remoteness from them that his *necessary* use of the English language implies.

RESISTING THE CHAMELEON: THE POETRY OF JACK MAPANJE

In his introduction to the first major collection of his poems, *Of Chameleons and Gods* (1981) Jack Mapanje wrote

> The verse in this volume spans some ten turbulent years in which I have been attempting to find a voice or voices as a way of preserving some sanity. Obviously where personal voices are too easily muffled, this is a difficult task; one is tempted like the chameleon, who failed to deliver Chiuta's message of life, to bask in one's brilliant camouflage...[1]

Preserving sanity, voices muffled... where can this be? Surely, if we rely for our perception of the world on the establishment press of the time, this Jack Mapanje must have been a Soviet dissident or, if an African, a victim of one of those Marxist states the then US President was so fond of telling us about... or maybe just a bolshie black South African in too much of a hurry. He's from Malawi? Where is Malawi...? Oh yes, it used to be Nyasaland. Well what's he going on about, isn't Malawi one of the *safe* African countries, like Kenya, where some semblance of order has been maintained and tourists may safely graze? In fact His Excellency the Life President Ngwazi Dr Hastings Kamusu Banda, who ruled Malawi for the thirty-one years from Independence in 1963 to the first free elections in 1994, was one of the more consistently repressive rulers of the old pink-for-British African colonies. Although many other countries have endured periodic dictators, wars and economic hard times, Malawi's ordeal was among the most sustained.

Jack Mapanje's early work – collected in *Of Chameleons and Gods* – was rooted in the landscapes and manscapes of Malawi, its history and its traditions, but also looked forward to the emergence of a different kind of society, a democratic meritocracy that might replace the prevailing 'political, social and cultural structures that imprison(ed) the human spirit and erase(d) creative endeavour and energy' – as he says in the introduction to his volume of new and selected poems, *The Last of the Sweet Bananas* (2005)[2]. Like so much African poetry in English, this is work committed to the notion of verse as a kind of interventionist social commentary, a poetry of satire and irony intended to expose hypocrisy and undermine the pomposity of those in power. All the same, it is hard to see how it could represent any real threat to an entrenched and all powerful regime like that which Banda had established in Malawi by the mid 1980s. It is not clear, even now, who exactly Mapanje had offended or why the response to *Of Chameleons and Gods* should lead first to the book being banned in Malawi and then to his arrest and imprisonment for almost four years in the notorious Mikuyu Prison in Zomba. Engaged and edgy as his poetry has always been, Jack Mapanje, as poet, never struck simplistic moral or political poses. Rather, insofar as he was a critic of the state of his country's government, it was to lament the waste of such opportunities that existed for the development of a humane society by individuals obsessed with the trappings of power. Like many other African poets writing in English (still the language of power in much of postcolonial Africa) Mapanje has always felt himself bound to take on the role of the 'spokesperson for the so-called 'dregs of society",[3] a dangerous role to play under a repressive and elitist dictatorship.

For example, in his poem 'Out of Bounds (or our Maternity Asylum)' Mapanje draws a harrowing picture of the state of a rural maternity hospital:

> Sixty inmates of spasming women top and tail
> On the thirty beds; ninety others with infants
>
> Scramble over the cracked cold cement floor –
> A family under each bed, most in between.

But the heart of the poem is his despair that twenty years after the nationalists – who are now the political leaders – condemned the colonial authorities for allowing similar conditions to prevail, they still manipulate the truth to pretend – to themselves, to the world – that substantial progress has been made:

> Yet *this* was the rallying cry of the dais
>
> Once upon a time. And when the powers visit
> The sick at Christmas, some caesareans will be
>
> Prematurely discharged; others jostled into
> Neat lines, clapping their praises. The windows
>
> Will have been glazed, the blood-bespattered
> Walls painted. They'll borrow beds and canvases
>
> From the nearby hospital so Father Christmas
> Sees one patient per bed: another dream done!
>
> But I hear, I am out of bounds.[4]

That last line sums up Jack Mapanje's dilemma; not only as a man is he 'out of bounds' in the maternity hospital but more pointedly as a poet, he is not permitted to *see*, to make such observations. And of course the maternity hospital is a particular symbolic location from which to relate the stillborn promises of the politicians. That kind of muted dissent runs through *Of Chameleons and Gods*, with intriguingly coded observations of the way things are that might just have embarrassed the regime's thin-skinned leaders, if they understood them. So an apparently 'innocent' poem like 'Song of Chicken' in the 'Cycles' sequence perhaps carries a subversive meaning for those who recognise the context and have the wit to see through the verbal camouflage:

> Master, you talked with bows,
> Arrows and catapults once
> Your hands steaming with hawk blood
> To protect your chicken.
>
> Why do you talk with knives now,
> Your hands teeming with eggshells
> And hot blood from your own chicken?
> Is it to impress your visitors?[5]

Some poems in that first collection reflect the poet's disillusion more plainly, but generally the poems are remarkable for their crafted restraint. Irony is the political poet's most potent weapon and Mapanje uses it to great effect in poems like 'The House that Florrie Intended', which laments the detention (worse maybe) of a strong, hard-working mother, whose only crime was to 'witness in protest', and 'On his Royal Blindness Paramount Chief Kwangala', a mock praise-song. There is one *dread*-ful poem in the collection, 'Waiting for the Electric Forceps', dedicated to Felix (I assume Felix Mnthali, a fellow poet detained in 1975) that is particularly searing given what subsequently happened to Mapanje. Developing the classical image of power corrupted – the butterfly broken on a wheel – in his local circumstances, the poem ends with this awful picture:

> ...your handcuffed butterfly sprawls
> in the freezing dark walls – waiting
> for the electronic pins and forceps. [6]

Given *that* prospective reward for writing poems about what the regime thought 'out of bounds', it's no wonder that Mapanje acknowledged the temptation to 'bask in one's brilliant camouflage', to settle for a safe life and write – or at least publish – only those poems the authorities would not find objectionable. In a poem he wrote shortly after returning to Malawi after a period spent studying in the UK, 'Another Fools' Day touches down: shush'[7], the word that dominates the poem is that 'shush'. Shush is what you say to naughty children to stop their whining, it's the chameleon's whisper, it's what Florrie and Felix Mnthali and the poet 'out of bounds' should have remembered to do, it's the instinct to cringe that Jack Mapanje's poems are written against. It was all too appropriate, then, that the teasing, inscrutable chameleon should become the image presiding over Mapanje's early poetry.

A poet whose early work is tagged with the label 'political' – especially if he is subsequently imprisoned as a consequence – has a hard job escaping that designation throughout his career, no matter what direction his poetry may take. And while there are several poems in the 'New Poems' section of *The Last of the*

Sweet Bananas that suggest he may want to focus on other concerns and other aspects of his life, it may be the fate of Jack Mapanje always to carry that 'political' tag. Perhaps inevitably the cruelties and injustices of the years of his imprisonment haunt Mapanje's imagination still, almost two decades after his release and settled as he is on another continent. The three collections he has published since the Banda regime released him into exile in the UK[8], have been dominated by a writing-out of the demons of that prison experience. He has spoken and written movingly of the discomfort and distress – although the words are hardly strong enough – of the day-to-day routine in the prison, the ritual humiliations and blatant contempt of Banda's regime for issues of justice or human rights. 'The Streak-Tease At Mikuyu Prison, 25 Sept. 1987', describing his strip-search induction into the prison regime on the night of his arrest is characteristically wry, beginning in a post-grad student memory of 'the striptease at The Bird's Nest / London Street, Paddington in the seventies' and ends with the cruel realisation of his new reality:

> Now the stinking shit-bucket tripped over drowns
>
> The news about the lights being left over night for
> You to scare night creepers, as the putrid *bwezi*
>
> Blanket-rag enters the single cell & staggers on to
> The cracked cold cement floor of Mikuyu Prison.[9]

That poem was included in the first collection Mapanje published after his release, *The Chattering Wagtails of Mikuyu Prison* (1993)[10] a book which bristles with indignation and outrage, but also retains an ability to laugh at the black farce that was life inside the prison and at the ridiculousness of the regime's self-aggrandising pomposities. The spirit of resistance bound up in that mocking laughter is explored in greater depth in the next collection Mapanje published, *Skipping Without Ropes* (1998)[11]. The brilliant title poem is a powerful declaration of that human spirit of resistance and, in its re-enactment through the process of rewriting after his release, of the poet's resilience when confronted by the regimes's cruelty and weasel words. So, denied skipping ropes to exercise with on the grounds that he might try to harm himself, the poet rhymes 'rope' with 'hope' to generate a skipping aid as he defies this latest attempt to break his spirit:

> Watch, watch me skip without your
> Rope; watch me skip with my hope –
> a-one, a-two, a-three, a-four, a-five
> I will, a-seven, I do, will skip, a-ten
>
> Eleven, I will skip without, will skip
> Within and skip I do without your
> rope but with my hope; and I will,
> Will always skip you dull, will skip
>
> Your silly rules, skip your filthy walls [12]

Like that imagined rope, the real thing that distinguishes Mapanje's work from the political and prison verse of many other African writers is his apparent belief in – and understanding of – the ways *poetry* works. This is not the familiar poetry of statement and protest, simply reflecting back the horror of injustice, cruelty or oppression – shocking and worthy as some of that writing can be. But such work dates and very quickly becomes more interesting to the historian and social scientist than to readers of poetry. Mapanje's measured and crafted poems depend for their authority and their most memorable effects on metaphor and literary cunning. These are poems that speak far beyond the immediate context of the grim events that inspired their making.

THE POWER TO EXCLUDE: ANTHOLOGISING WEST INDIAN POETRY

This essay is adapted from a talk given to the annual conference of The Welsh Academy, at Gregynog Hall, University of Wales, 1991.

I got into Caribbean poetry as a consequence of finding myself, more or less by chance, a teacher in a secondary school in Jamaica, back in the early 1970s. I knew absolutely nothing about West Indian literature, and finding these new writers – Walcott, Brathwaite, Louise Bennett – writing so vividly, so vigorously, about a life I was discovering at the same time as I was discovering their poetry was really exciting. Not that it was so easy to get hold of Caribbean poetry then, especially in a rural market-town on the north coast of the island. The Public Library was stocked with sun-foxed, brittle-leaved slim volumes by Dylan Thomas and T.S. Eliot, hardly read, but no anthologies of Caribbean poetry. (To be fair, there were hardly any at that time that they could have stocked). The school library, such as it was – the World Bank built all these concrete shells of schools but put nothing inside them – did provide a way in though. There I found a pristine copy of John Figueroa's slightly stuffy, but all the same invaluable, anthology *Caribbean Voices*,[1] a selection from poems included in the BBC radio programme of the 1950s, and Anne Walmsley's superb lower-school anthology of poems, stories and extracts from novels, *The Sun's Eye*,[2] which included fascinating autobiographical notes provided by the authors. I vividly remember reading Walcott for the first time, and thinking that he, at least on the evidence of his poem lamenting 'A City's Death by Fire', had read his Dylan Thomas.

The next step, and a piece of cultural arrogance I'm rather

appalled by now, was to write to as many of these poets as I could discover addresses for announcing that I intended to start up a Caribbean literary magazine and inviting contributions in the form of new writing and subscriptions. The magazine, *NOW*,[3] was a rather scruffy production, duplicated through the night in the back room of the local betting shop, trimmed on the school metalwork guillotine and distributed more or less at random. The magazine was taken vastly more seriously than it deserved; positively reviewed in the national papers and on radio, partly financed, though they didn't know it, by Harvard University – persuaded to take out a 'lifetime' subscription, even though I knew the magazine could hardly survive more than half a dozen issues. More significantly, though, a number of important figures in Caribbean poetry actually sent in material – Kamau Brathwaite, Dennis Scott, Andrew Salkey, A.L Hendricks, Harold Telemaque, Wayne Brown, Anson Gonzalez, Philip Sherlock, Gloria Escoffery, Neville Dawes, Anthony McNeill, Victor Questel, Maria Arrillaga. And the magazine allowed me an entrée to their world, it was intoxicating.

Teaching English in the secondary school, though, I hardly came across West Indian poetry, certainly not at exam level. That gap between the study of serious literature (ie. the English canon) and the Jamaican education system's indifference towards the literature of the life that people were living around me, was what prompted me to try and make an anthology. I wanted *Caribbean Poetry Now* to serve both as an upper-school text in the Caribbean and as a vehicle to 'spread the word' about this exciting *new* poetry among potential readers in the UK. But it was ten years between my leaving Jamaica and the appearance of *Caribbean Poetry Now*. The key to the book's appearance, finally, was the establishment of the Caribbean Examinations Council to gradually replace the British GCE boards and their 'tropical papers'. At the same time there was a growing interest in the UK in Caribbean culture, partly generated by the success of literary figures such as Walcott and Brathwaite but more generally to do with Bob Marley, reggae and Rastafarian style.

In the meanwhile I'd been living in Africa for several years, then – daring the wilds of Mid Wales – getting myself 'Doctored' at UW Aberystwyth and so had become academically respectable enough to be trusted to edit such a book. All the same though my approach to Caribbean Literature continued (and continues) to be that of the enthusiastic amateur rather than the scholarly academic – the would-be fellow-poet rather than the authoritative editor. But such special pleading doesn't allow me to duck the critical, cultural and theoretical issues which hedge the production of anthologies like *Caribbean Poetry Now* and, later, *Voiceprint* and the collection of stories *Caribbean New Wave* and, presently, *The Heinemann Book of Caribbean Poetry*. A lot of these issues are familiar in the context of debates about Anglo-Welsh literature, beginning of course with language. What language(s) should a West Indian poetry be written in? Should it be in the received language of the poetry that students studied in their English classes – the standard English that hardly anyone there (or here!) speaks? Or could it be written – and/or spoken – in versions of dialect/Creole/nation language – even the terminology was fraught – which demand forms that inevitably challenge received notions of poetic craft and also have distinct social and political overtones?

How far do you, as anthologist, with the power and responsibility to 'represent the best regional writing' to a generation of students – in effect to construct a counter canon – how far do you try and represent – and so to some extent legitimise – the whole language continuum? And how does that need for linguistic balance square with the need to represent a *fair* range of voices in terms of gender, race, nationality, generation, religion or political views? The issues around language meld into questions of form and worth in terms of the orality/literary struggle that is a vital element of West Indian culture; are Mikey Smith's dub *texts for performance,* poems? Is a Bob Marley lyric a poem? Do we misrepresent Louise Bennett either by calling her a poet or by consigning her work to some special oral category? Should we have a poem by each of them at the expense of three more poems by Derek Walcott, unquestionably one of the great poets of our time but whose language, ideas of form and craft, cultural references and associations with a notion of European high culture will perhaps exclude or alienate the readers we are trying to reach? And alongside those problematic issues are questions of cultural traditions, cultural directions, attitudes to history, issues of self-definition and national allegiance, and so on. All those questions are raised in the making of an anthology, and heightened by the fact that the anthologist is a foreign, white, male academic who inevitably makes his selection, in the end, on the basis of his own cultural conditioning. All this is compounded by an increasingly tortured understanding that the anthologist's only power, really, is the power to exclude.

I tend not to push too hard at these things though; most readers or reviewers assume that Stewart Brown is a Jamaican and the issue of cultural imposition doesn't come up at all. But maybe that's worse. Pragmatically, I tell myself that in terms of engaging with the poetry, I've immersed myself in it over the last few decades in a way that few others – West Indians or not – have been able to. (It's still easier to get hold of books produced in Tunapuna or Castries in Birmingham or Cardiff than it is in Bridgetown, Barbados or Brownstown, Jamaica.) I convince myself that, after all, I have worked in and travelled widely through the region and that so long as I'm alert to the issues outlined above, and West Indian readers think I've done a good job, then "No problem". (In fact the only published concern over the cultural identity of the anthologists of Caribbean literature that I've seen has been in a thoughtful essay on canon formation by another white British anthologist, Anne Walmsley.[4]) And then there's all that stuff about the importance of an 'outsider' perspective and my immunity – pretty much – from the accusation of regional or racial bias that has beset so many selectors of the West Indian cricket team over the years... However, notwithstanding that comfortable self-deception, in an ideal world it would *obviously* make more sense for these anthologies to be made by West Indians rather than a Brown of the wrong colour. But, to (mis)quote my all time favourite West Indian poem, Mervyn Morris's 'Valley Prince': 'the world don't go so'. Part of the reason I'm able/asked to make these anthologies is that I'm *on seat* as it were, in the place where the books are published. Heinemann, Longman, Hodder & Stoughton between them dominate Caribbean publishing[5], especially in literature and education, and it's easier to work with someone to hand than to keep trying to make telephone contact with Kingston or Georgetown [note: this is before the days of email!]. Perhaps, too, there is an element of race in it – most of the publishers in the multinationals are white middle class British people, who are, maybe, *at ease* dealing with someone like me in ways they perhaps can't be with (real) West Indians in Britain who might have done the editorial jobs I've done, although I'm sure they wouldn't recognise that as a reason for the decisions they've made. And, obviously, I'm not innocent in such transactions. But that said, I honestly don't think that any of the poetry anthologies I've edited would have been made at all if I hadn't pushed and harassed and cajoled the publishers into doing them, and surely what's important is that the Caribbean poets whose work was selected for the collections should have the advantage of an international platform. And anyway, in the end, who remembers the names of the editors of poetry anthologies?

The publishing houses themselves represent the other pressures that bear on the anthologist, for no matter how enlightened individual publishers might be, the overriding motive for book production as far as the companies are concerned is the idea of profit. And in publishing terms, poetry anthologies are really quite expensive books to make as so many – albeit small – permissions fees have to be paid up front to the individual poets. So pressures of cost, of scale, of imprint tradition, of taste, of expertise,* all these considerations bear on the book that is finally produced and on the freedom of the anthologist. It's certainly not a simple process of just picking a bunch of one's favourite poems.

* for example, despite accepting the intellectual/educational, even financial, argument for producing a cassette to accompany these anthologies, none of the publishers I've worked with have been able to overcome the logistical difficulties of making and distributing such a tape.

Anthologies referred to include:

Caribbean Poetry Now, ed. Stewart Brown (Hodder and Staunton, 1986)
Voiceprint: Caribbean Oral and Related Poetries, eds. Stewart Brown, Mervyn Morris and Gordon Rohlehr (Longman 1989)
Heinemann Book of Caribbean Poetry, eds. Stewart Brown and Ian McDonald (Heinemann, 1991).

INCEST, ASSASSINATION AND 'THE RED FLAG':
JUDGING THE GUYANA PRIZE

Guyana is one of the poorest countries in the world. I can't remember what the 'per capita' income is, and anyway those numbers always seem to me to disguise the reality of the kinds of poverty endured by most people in the Third World rather than illuminate it, but as someone who has been to quite a lot of poor countries one way and another I would put Guyana pretty near the bottom of the list.[1]

The first time I visited Guyana, in 1988, things were worse. That was just after Forbes Burnham had died. Burnham was the idealist-turned-despot who ruled over Guyana for almost thirty years, overseeing – and I use the word advisedly – the transition from colony to self-styled Co-operative Republic. He is still a hero to many Afro-Guyanese, including some intellectuals who regard the isolation his mock-socialist policies forced on the country – ostracised by the US and so, for example, out of range of the ubiquitous CNN and Jerry Springer type neo-colonisation by satellite TV that is so pervasive now all across the Caribbean – to have been a period of creative opportunity for the country. 'What we have we have made ourselves,' I remember the painter and scholar Denis Williams remarking enthusiastically to me on that first visit. But in material terms at least, what they had was not much to boast about. Georgetown was – and indeed if you are prepared to be just a little selective in your gaze – still is, a beautiful city; architecturally, the many fine wooden buildings, both public and private, are remarkable while the broad, tree-lined streets and generous parks suggest a society that appreciated its richness, at least in terms of space, especially when compared with the cramped clutter of many other Caribbean cities. But many of those beautiful buildings were in a terrible state of disrepair, the parks were overgrown and the increase in 'choke and rob' attacks meant the broad thoroughfares were dangerous places to walk. The education system, once the envy of the Caribbean, had crumbled. Teachers – like most other public servants – could no longer live on the meagre government salaries and those who could find a way, migrated. The university campus was a ruin: no books, no chairs to sit on in the classrooms, no prospects for the students. Crime and corruption of one kind or another was rife, and understandable; how else amass the money to escape? Everyone who has anything that anyone else might conceivably want to steal lives behind burglar-barred doors and windows in Guyana. And beyond Georgetown? On the one side the Atlantic – held back ever more precariously by the battered and cracked concrete of the sea wall – threatens impatiently it seems to reclaim that narrow coastal strip of cultivated land given over mostly to sugar-cane and rice that is 'developed' Guyana. And on the other side the great brooding presence of *the interior*, the seemingly endless forest stretching all the way to Brazil in the west, traversed by those great rivers with their exotic sounding names: Essequibo, Demerara, Mazaruni, Potaro, Pomeroon… The jungle, too, seems threatening, waiting there on the edge of cultivation to move back into those too neat acres when the time comes. In the elemental timescale that seems appropriate to those two great natural forces, the ocean and the rain forest, the five hundred years or so of occupation by Europeans, Africans and Indians hardly signifies. The Amerindian peoples who live, for the most part, in the interior, though they have their own representatives in the government now, are still second-class citizens in many ways. But they too seem to know how to 'exercise patience', to understand things in a different time frame.

As I say, things are a bit better in Guyana now than they were in the final years of Burnham's reign and those immediately following his death. But not much; children still die every day in Georgetown's Mercy Hospital of diseases and ailments that would cost so little to treat elsewhere. It is nothing short of criminal that they should have to suffer and die as they do. Mad people walk naked in the streets, old people can't afford to live but can't afford to die either. The announcement of an increase in the charges for a grave plot in a municipal cemetery caused a huge outcry the last time I was there. Beggars fester outside every shop doorway and around every parked car. Of course there are cars, there is a substantial middle class which enjoys all the trappings of civilization, there are some very grand houses indeed around and beyond Georgetown, and enough chauffeur-driven, body-guarded, executive and entrepreneurial folk to justify the imports-stocked department stores, the gold and diamond jewellery dealers, the private hospitals and clinics, the restaurants and night-clubs of what is – at this level – an exciting and cultured city. Guyana is potentially a relatively rich country; it has reserves of gold and many other minerals; it could better exploit and sustain its forests, and not least it has great potential as an eco/green tourism destination if the infrastructure and ethos could be developed. But for now, and the foreseeable future, Guyana is, as I say, a very poor country.

Which makes it the more surprising in some ways that Guyana's governments, of both major political parties now, should initiate and continue to sponsor – with significant amounts of hard currency – a major literary prize. The Guyana Prize for Literature, which has been awarded in alternate years for a decade now, is intended to acknowledge the achievement of Guyanese authors, both at home and overseas, and encourage aspiring writers to develop their talents. Over the years Guyana has produced – for a small, poor country – an amazing number of artists and writers who have made major international reputations. The work of the painters like Aubrey Williams, Stanley Greaves, Denis Williams, Frank Bowling and the sculptor Philip Moore, for example, is represented in public and private collections around the world. The novelists Edgar Mittelholzer, Wilson Harris, Jan Carew, Roy Heath, and more recently figures like David Dabydeen, Fred D'Aguiar, Jan Shinebourne and Pauline Melville have all made an impact overseas while the poets A.J. Seymour, Martin Carter and Ian McDonald, who stayed in Guyana through the lean years, produced work which is only now gaining the kind of international readership it deserves. Younger poets who joined the mass migration of

Guyanese talent include John Agard and Grace Nichols, both of whom have enriched the cultural life of Britain to the extent that their work is now regularly represented on the English GCSE and A Level syllabus.

So the Guyanese people can justly be proud of their writers and the waves they make overseas; they are in a real sense ambassadors for the country. Apart from Clive Lloyd and a few other outstanding cricketers, and maybe Sonny Ramphal, the former Secretary General of the Commonwealth, which other Guyanese could you name? But the prize is much more than a means for the Guyanese government to bask in the reflected glory of its writers' achievements. The continued support for the prize is understood, especially by that easily alienated intellectual middle class, as an acknowledgement by the government of the place and importance of culture in the development of a genuinely free and civilised society in Guyana. Guyanese writers, whether at home or abroad, have not been shy to air their political views, views which have often enough been critical of the incumbent regime. Martin Carter, the great poet of Guyana who won the Guyana Prize in 1990, used poetry as a powerful tool of political protest and analysis all his life. Yet if anything could symbolise the implicit determination of Guyana's governments to save the country from the fate Carter long feared – that it be reduced to a 'community of degraded citizens' worn down by the crude barbarities of economic exploitation, political corruption and second hand cultural cynicism – it is the maintenance of the Guyana Prize for Literature as an independent and high level literary award. In terms of the quality of the winning books, the Guyana Prize is on a par with international literary awards like the Commonwealth Writers Prize, The Booker Prize and the Noma Award in Africa. To maintain that standard, and, though it is unspoken, in tacit recognition of the political and ethnic/cultural pressures that bear on locally based Guyanese judges, the Guyana Prize committee has always invited two or three of the five judges from the wider Caribbean and usually one from Britain. There is a suggestion in some quarters that this inclusion of a British judge is some kind of colonial hangover, that Guyanese writers and academics should be trusted to judge their own national prize. It's true that one can't imagine, say, a Jamaica Prize for Literature inviting, as a matter of course, an Englishman to come and help with the judging. But the Prize Committee has always maintained that the presence of such 'outsiders' helps to ensure that international perspective and to guard against any kind of parochialism. The judges are regularly reminded that the committee would far rather no prize were awarded in any of the categories than that prizes were awarded just to 'the best of the bunch', whether or not they were of the standard set by previous winners.

The prize is in several categories, with major prizes of US $5,000 in fiction, poetry and drama, and first book prizes (which can include unpublished manuscripts) of US $3,000 in poetry and fiction. (For Guyanese-based winners $5,000 was a very considerable sum, then more than a university lecturer's annual salary.) When you add on the administration costs inc. the judges airfares etc. then I would estimate the total comes to about US $40,000, more than half a million Guyanese dollars, most of which comes from the government, though some other contributions come from the University of Guyana, the Guyana Sugar Corporation and other business sponsors. It is a significant sum for a country like Guyana to devote to literature, especially as it is in addition to the provision made through the Ministry of Culture for more general support of literature at local level. I don't know that anyone seriously objects to this money being used this way, although there is always some muttered resentment from locally based writers about so many of the prizes going to Guyanese writers based overseas and the suggestion that the prize is somehow stitched up between the clique of writers and academics who seem to be judges one year and prizewinners another – but that is more sour grapes than real unhappiness with the institution of the Guyana Prize itself. As far as I can judge, there is a genuine sense of national pride around the achievements of the country's writers, even though in reality few Guyanese read – and fewer still buy – contemporary fiction or poetry. (The book that won the prize this year costs fifteen pounds or so in the UK, that's about 4,000 Guyanese dollars, serious money for most people in Guyana.)

Although there were more than seventy books entered, the judging this year was pretty straightforward. It seemed to me – and as it turned out to the other judges as well – that the books which should win the main prizes stood out clearly from the rest and that in the first book poetry category only one poetry collection – an unpublished manuscript – was really of the necessary standard. I have judged the prize three times now and it has always been the drama award that has caused the most aggravation. Not only are we asked to judge the plays on the basis of scripts alone, but we are also confronted most starkly by those difficult questions over what we mean by 'quality' and 'originality and 'accomplishment' which are somehow easier to fudge when talking about poetry or fiction. The issue really comes down to some notional line between popular and literary theatre, for while there is not much more interest in Guyana in Drama, with a Shakespearean D, than there is in fiction or poetry, there is a strong and vibrant tradition of popular, topical, vernacular theatre. Al Creighton, secretary to the Guyana Prize Committee and an authority on Caribbean popular culture, remarked that in Guyana you can tell what kind of play is on without entering the theatre; if it is a high brow, usually dead-white-European's play, then the car park will be full, but the theatre half empty and silent. If it is a popular play by a local playwright then the car park will be empty but the roar of the crowd overflowing the theatre can be heard streets away. Obviously playwrights working that tradition have different concerns and write with a different notion of 'quality' and 'success' than playwrights writing in more conventional ways. Not least of the differences is the relationship between the audience and the players that is understood by both and becomes part of the performance but can't be easily be indicated on a script. Every time I have been involved, the panel of judges has worried this issue at considerable length but, over the years the drama award has usually gone to more literary, conventionally stage-crafted scripts which, just to rub salt in the wounds, have often been written by authors based outside of Guyana. Insofar as there has been serious criticism and resentment of the Guyana Prize it has been around this issue, with a cohort of disgruntled playwrights crying foul, fix and foreigners!

Partly in response to that criticism the Guyana Prize judges now have to attend an open forum, during the week in which the judging takes place but before the short lists are announced, when suspicious or merely curious members of the public can air their grievances, ask difficult questions and generally make sure the judges understand the context within which all this literary *flim flam* takes place. For the judges it is quite a gruelling experience, one way and another. Can you imagine the Booker Prize judges opening themselves up to that kind of public and unmediated debate? As Chairman of the Judges this time I had to both field the questions and move the meeting along, not always so easy when an old man from West Coast Demerara – a journey of some hours away – is determined to have his say *and*, this being his moment in the limelight, to read us his poem in case we missed it in our careless dismissal, as he anticipates, of all things local and *authentic*. As everywhere people take what they perceive to be the rejection of their writing very personally. A previous Chairman of the judges was threatened with a bottle after the announcement of the winners, and this year, while no violence was offered me, several people came and quizzed me quite aggressively about the qualities of their particular entries... Did I understand enough about Hinduism to comprehend the range and subtlety of the references in her poems... No, obviously not. Did I understand the significance of December the 15th in recent Guyanese political life? Did I recognise that such and such a number in the title of this play that didn't win was a reference to the number of square acres of land that comprised Guyana? No? And you call yourself a judge! Ho Hum.

In truth the incongruity of my being there in that capacity did strike me from time to time. The award ceremony takes place in early December and I had to be there to deliver the Judges Report and announce the winners. The hotel where I was staying was across the street from the main department store in Georgetown, which, as its contribution to the festive spirit, was broadcasting at incredible volume and rather too slowly some terrible old tape-loop of Christmas Carols played on a Melatron or some such half-tuned electronic organ. This dreadful noise went on for several hours every evening and try as I might I couldn't ignore it. In the middle of the sequence, between 'Good King Wenceslas' and - ironically - 'Silent Night', was a version of 'The Red Flag'. This may have been the 'Oh Christmas Tree, Oh Christmas Tree' variant but I suspect the tape dated back to Co-operative Republic days and the socialist anthem was in there to assuage the comrades. Either way, even as I tried to concentrate on writing my report and ignoring the 'music', the tune grated. I fear I will always think of Guyana Stores now when I hear 'The Red Flag'. To escape that noise, on the afternoon of the award ceremony I found myself standing on the sea-wall, on the shoulder blade of South America, relishing the breeze and watching the Atlantic roll in from Africa. But I was worrying about how to address the President and ex-President of the country, sworn enemies, in the preamble to my report at the ceremony that evening, worrying how much I would sweat if I had to wear a jacket and tie because I knew the air conditioning in the National Cultural Centre hadn't worked for a decade, worrying most of all about how to accommodate the need to describe the winning novel – which revolved around issues of incest and infidelity – when the novelist herself had implored me not to mention either of those words because her aged Amerindian aunts would be there in the audience and would be scandalised to know she had written about such family secrets... But this was small beer really, other people had more serious worries. When Al Creighton went to collect the cheques for the prizes, the Guyana Central Bank said they couldn't issue them because there weren't sufficient reserves of hard currency to cover them just at present. Fortunately that problem was resolved later in the day. And worse, the previous day I had ventured into Bourda Market to look for souvenirs and had noticed some commotion in the distance. In the morning paper was a report that a young man had been stabbed in the incident, the report read:

> ... there was some difficulty in getting transportation to take the man to the Georgetown Hospital. Arrangements were made to convey him in a donkey cart... but he died on the way.

The ceremony itself was a surreal occasion one way and another. I was standing in the foyer, waiting on the Presidential party, talking to the poet Ian McDonald, a member of the Guyana Prize Committee. A stout, middle-aged Afro-Guyanese man in a grey shirtjac suit came and hovered near by us, but as I didn't know him and Ian didn't stop talking I thought nothing of it. After a little while the conversation paused and the grey suited man stepped forward, Ian turned to him and nodded, 'Mr Prime Minister'. So, I'd failed to recognise the Prime Minister of Guyana. The President, Mrs Janet Jagan, the diminutive, white-haired, American-born widow of the former President Cheddi Jagan, arrived and the assembled dignitaries – to the accompaniment of a steel pan – processed along a red carpet onto the stage. There a semicircle of hardwood thrones – there is no other word for them – awaited us. There were maybe three hundred people in the audience, but as the hall can hold more than a thousand it looked rather empty. As I anticipated, the air conditioning was long gone and under the glare of TV lights in that airless concrete bunker, it wasn't only me who began to sweat. Still, the event seemed to be going well enough. There were tributes to Martin Carter and Denis Williams who had both died in the last year, a special award to the Guyanese lexicographer Richard Allsop who had recently published his monumental *Oxford Dictionary of Caribbean English Usage*. Then I made my report and the prizes were awarded, and we were into the readings by the winners when, suddenly, all the lights went out. A major power cut across that side of Georgetown it transpired, but just for a moment, before the emergency generator cut in, I was expecting a shot to ring out, the perfect scenario for an assassination. And I was in the throne next to the President! Indeed, given the resentment of some slighted writers, who might the target really have been? I thought this was my paranoia but when the lights came back on it transpired that such thoughts had gone through several people's minds, though I didn't dare ask Mrs Jagan! After that, although the writers kept on reading, the generator drowned them out and most of the audience drifted away.

Oh, and the winners, well Pauline Melville won the fiction

prize with *The Ventriloquist's Tale*[2], a wonderfully complex and cunningly tangled novel, drawing on her intimate knowledge of Amerindian life and mythology. This was combined with a real gift for storytelling and a sharp sense of the ways history works itself out over generations, with consequences that could never be predicted nor hardly imagined. As I remarked at the award ceremony, the novel turns around two linked love stories, both in different ways forbidden by social norms and taboos, but each too intense for the lovers to care much about such conventional barriers. Rather than look out to a hostile world, Melville's Amerindian characters turn inwards to explore and understand their deepest feelings. She plays on notions of meaningful silence and the ways in which words, once spoken, can be misunderstood; on images of voicelessness and ventriloquism. There is a sensuousness about all her work but also, in this novel, a profound engagement with ideas of myth and morality. And on top of that she has a wicked sense of humour.

The poetry award went to John Agard for his Bloodaxe collection *From the Devil's Pulpit*. Characteristically wry, earthy and rich in wit, the book also represents a profoundly serious analysis of the hypocrisies of contemporary life. Sometimes Agard's talent to amuse has too effectively disguised the real edge of social commentary that informs all his work, but in this collection the balance is beautifully poised. Sensuous, seductive and even salacious though many of the poems are, we are conscious of both the artfulness of their language and the seriousness of the poet's engagement with issues of myth, theology, politics and culture that inspire his barbed word play. Agard's poems engage all our senses as well as our conscience and intellect. In a wonderful short poem, 'Coffee in Heaven', he reveals all his – and his Devilish persona's – guile in just nine wicked lines. He writes

You'll be greeted
By a nice cup of coffee
When you get to heaven
And strains of angelic harmony

But wouldn't you be devastated
If they only serve decaffeinated
While from the percolators of hell

Your soul was assaulted
By Satan's fresh expresso smell?[3]

Can't we all smell that fresh brew wafting under our noses! It's more than poetic craft Agard has employed there, all done with such economy and such a light touch, but asking us the provocative, disquieting questions.

The Drama prize turned out to provide a nice resolution to that tension between the literary and the popular. Paloma Mohamed is a locally based playwright who sometimes works in that popular tradition but her play *Duenne* draws more on folklore and mythology than on topical issues, though it raises important questions about the dilemmas and responsibilities of women whenever they lived. In Caribbean folk legend a *Duenne* is the spirit of a dead child which first appears to humans as an abandoned sack that may draw attention to itself by wailing like a newborn baby. The play explores the symbolic and material responsibilities of a woman who accepts the burden of a child, for, as the folk-legend goes, if anyone so much as touches the sack then the spirit of the dead child fixes on that person like a parasite, gradually wearing them down. The play is not a simple re-enactment of the myth; rather it is a complex and dramatic engagement with the ideas that resonate from it in contemporary life.

The day before I was due to fly to Guyana for the meeting of the judges I had to sit in on – in my role as 'literature advisor' – a meeting between the Literature Officer of West Midlands Arts and the committee of the Birmingham Readers and Writers Festival. The festival is the major literary event in the Midlands, it has run successfully – at least in artistic and more broadly cultural terms – for many years now, though it has never had the fashionable *cache* of events like the Cheltenham or Hay-on-Wye literature festivals. So the festival has always been pretty much on the edge financially and depends on its grant from the regional arts council for its continued existence. The festival committee, themselves writers and unpaid volunteers, were having to ask for more money because the City Council's grant to the festival had been much reduced for reasons too mind-numbing to go into here. At the same time, the literature officer – just doing his job of course and fundamentally sympathetic to the festival – was having to quiz and criticise the festival about commercial this and sponsorship deal that, about 'growing the audience' and 'social exclusion'. It was painful, like watching a meeting between a world-weary DSS official and a bemused claimant. There was no vision of the fundamental importance of literature and writers, (who would dare to say such things these days!) no acknowledgement of the extent to which literature contributes, in ways the accountants and bureaucrats would never allow for in their forms and tick lists, to the quality of the life of the region, no appreciation of the real extent of the work the festival organisers have to put in. Of course, there are good reasons for these questions; we must expect to account for public money spent on minority interests, must do things in a professional way, must try and reach out to the widest audience... of course, all those things are important. But the amount of money they were asking for was, really, so small – half that devoted to the Guyana Prize – in Britain, in the English second city, with a population several times that of Guyana and, by comparison, massively wealthy. I couldn't help but make the comparison between that reluctant, carping, petty-minded version of state patronage and the vision, the essentially Caribbean generosity of spirit, that underpins the Guyana Prize.

BARBADOS @ THE CROSS-ROADS.COM: CALYPSOS IN BARBADOS

Speaking to a radio reporter at the height of this year's Crop-Over festival in Barbados, a Trinidadian visitor responded to being asked how this compared with the Trinidad Carnival by laughing derisively and remarking 'Well, is the sort of thing we have for a village, or maybe a small town *fete!*' This wasn't what his interviewer wanted to hear but he shouldn't really have been surprised; back in the early 1950s the legendary Trinidadian calypsonian Spoiler (immortalised three decades later in Derek Walcott's magnificent satirical poem 'The Spoiler's Return'), sang a condescending calypso about the Barbados Crop-Over festival titled 'Small Island Carnival'. In that song Spoiler ridiculed Bajan pretensions to host a festival that might even aspire to rival Carnival. The first prize for the best band, he observed, was 'a basket of breadfruit', while his account of a Bajan steelband is positively scathing,

> Ah laugh, ah roll, ah dirty meh clothes
> When I saw the steel band they have in Barbados
> Two old box and a butter pan – a bottle, a spoon
> and a old bell in dey hand[1]

Crop-Over is on a grander scale and is somewhat better organised these days – the calypsonian who won the Pic-o-de-Crop competition this year got a car and around $10,000 – but it still retains that sense of a genuine *festival*. In fact it dates back to slavery days, one of those hybrid holidays – intended to signal the end of the sugar-cane crop and allow the workers to, as the English would have it, 'let off steam' – that the displaced Africans turned into something more than the plantocracy intended or understood. And even though, these days, Crop-Over has become an excuse for a more general *fete,* still the festival begins with the crowning of the king and queen of the crop – the cane-cutters who have harvested the heaviest load through the season – and ends with the symbolic burning of a straw Englishman, 'Mr Harding', a hated overseer out of that colonial past. So while the government and the tourist industry may have moved in on Crop-over to try and capitalise on the Carnival image of a Caribbean bacchanal, in truth it resists such glossy packaging and retains both a frisson of that historic resistance and a kind of amateur spirit. But it's the amateur spirit that informed the way Gary Sobers used to play cricket – it may be fun but it's serious fun; the calypso competition inspires fiercely partisan engagement from the individual calypsonians and their followers!

Crop-Over culminates in The Grand Kadooment, a parade of floats, costumes and dancing bands that closes many of the streets of Bridgetown, the island's capital, for most of the public holiday on which it is held. But on the evening before Kadooment, the finals of the calypso competition is held in the National Stadium before a crowd of, I would guess, about twenty thousand people – a significant percentage of the total population of Barbados [about 8%]. This is the real heart of Crop-Over; the calypsonians have become by now figures of national importance; their photos adorn the pages – often the front pages – of the island's two newspapers while their calypsos have dominated the radio waves for the past month, displacing the reggae, soul and gospel imports that make up the bulk of the stations' normal fare. The calypsonians who have reached the final got there through a competition that began some months before, but comes to a head in the semifinals, held at the beginning of Crop-Over in a makeshift open-air arena on the island's east coast. This concert is even bigger than the final and virtually closes that whole side of the island. Of the fourteen singers – some long established as wry social commentators and polished in their performance, others young, raw but passionate in both their ambition and their sense of the social injustice that drives most of the calypsos – only half of them will make it through to meet the reigning Calypso Monarch in the finals and their fans are loud in both their support and their advice to the judges.

The competition this year was particularly controversial; there were great ructions over alleged bias and irregularity in the judging, particularly at the semifinals. Indeed two of the defeated calypsonians decided to contest the results in the High Court. The court declared for the calypsonians, which meant that the finals were contested by ten rather than the regulation eight contenders, and the competition judges resigned *en masse*!

So at the Pic-o-de-Crop Finals there was a new set of rather reluctant judges and the sense that the attention of the whole nation was focused on that stage for the evening. The competition is sponsored by Cockspur, one of the island's major rum companies and manufacturers of what I can confidently assert, on the basis of serious fieldwork and research, is the mellowest and most seductive rum in the whole Caribbean. Certainly the liberal quantities of the sponsor's product imbibed all around the stadium helped to create the atmosphere of affable tension that gradually built up as the final judging approached. The real competition this year came down to a fight between three figures; Li'l Rick, The Mighty Gabby and reigning champion Red Plastic Bag.

Li'l Rick was the favourite of a younger and perhaps less sophisticated crowd who cared more for his in-your-face critique of the government's economic and social policy in his 'We Survivin' than for the fact that he clearly can't sing and that his song wasn't, even by the most liberal definition of the genre, a calypso at all. Rick made his name as a dub ranter on the dancehall scene and his popularity in the calypso competition perhaps derives from that reputation. 'We Survivin' did seem to touch a nerve with a broader crowd, however, the whole audience joining in the litany of lamentation and celebration as the song's persona lists – and acts out – the difficulties of the day-to-day hustle and grind for many Bajans who don't have jobs in government or the tourist industry, nor relatives abroad to send them money. Rick may be the 'rude boy' of the current calypso crop and his lyrics generally rather simplistic, but there is at least one stanza of 'We Survivin' worthy of praise for its poetry. Are these not wonderful rhythms and rhymes?

> 'Cause we underprivilege always depriving
> take nuff bad treatment and nuff criticising

but know all about cutting and contriving...
and we surviving....

The singer knows where the blame lies, too:

All these things poor people got to expect
And how the boys up there aint give a heck...[2]

Everyone in the crowd knew who 'the boys up there' were and
sang those lines with particular relish and vehemence. Politicians
in the past have been foolish enough to take on the calypsonians,
either by banning them from state-owned radio or by taking them
to court. Such tactics almost inevitably fail, indeed just feed the
potency of the singer and his song. Li'l Rick's disgruntlement was
too generalised to offend anyone in particular, but the way the
crowds took up 'We Survivin' as a popular anthem may yet signal
some difficulty for a government perceived as not having kept its
promises to the poor.

Despite his popularity I don't think many people really expected
or even wanted Rick to win the competition. The real contest
was between the two figures who have dominated Bajan calypso
for the last decade: 'Gabby' and the 'Bag'.

If Li'l Rick is the *enfant terrible* of the Bajan calypso scene then
Gabby is its grandfather; in his late 40s now, he has been singing
folk song, spouge and calypso for more than thirty years; indeed
at the age of 19 he was the youngest ever winner of the Calypso
Monarch title in Barbados. He has won the title more often than
anyone else and, perhaps most remarkably, he has won it at least
once in each of the last four decades. Gabby is truly a legend in
Barbados, his most famous calypso, 'Boots', asked pointed questions
about the need to maintain a heavily armed Barbados 'Defence
Force' when there was so much poverty on the island and there
was hardly much likelihood of Barbados being invaded or – still
less – invading anywhere else, was there? Well just after he wrote
'Boots' the American invasion of Grenada – supported by 'local
forces' – began. Gabby's perceived protest was picked up by US
media and he was featured in an edition of Time Magazine.[3]

A concern with more covert US imperialism has been a consistent theme of Gabby's and was the subject of his major calypso this year, 'Massa Day Done'. Recycling the famous anti-colonial motto coined by the late Eric Williams – historian and first Prime-minister of Trinidad and Tobago – Gabby's calypso addresses the perception that paternalistic American attitudes to the Caribbean amount to a kind of re-colonisation of the region. In the calypso Gabby offers a history lesson of his own, cataloguing the victims of white American imperialism, beginning with the Indians and the buffalo, through Marcus Garvey, Martin Luther King and Mohammed Ali:

> every black man who stands straight and strong,
> America make sure she shoot him down.

He lists recent examples of direct US intervention in the Caribbean – putting 'them big foot on Cuba,' 'invad[ing] Nicaragua' and dropping 'their bombs like flies all over spicy Grenada' – before moving on to more immediate and topical incidents, focusing particularly on the Ship-Rider Treaty most Caribbean governments were 'persuaded' to sign last year. By that treaty the American government asserted its right to board and search any ship or plane in the region it regards as its own backyard, regardless of the origin of the ship or the territorial waters in which it is travelling. Ostensibly this is part of the US drugs control strategy, but Gabby suspects it has more sinister overtones as far as the sovereignty of individual Caribbean states is concerned: 'You tell America from me /She don't own the Caribbean sea.' The generally combative, challenging tone of the song, with tiny Barbados standing up to the over-mighty USA, – 'We aint frighten for she' – was a major aspect of its appeal, culminating in the roared chorus 'America mus' understand / Massa day done!'[4] 'Massa Day Done' is a fine calypso, if not perhaps among Gabby's very best. Some people felt the lyrics were a little predictable and, no matter how he played the historical resonances to his own purpose, there was a feeling that borrowing Eric Williams' phrase in that way was a little dubious. But Gabby is a marvellously polished performer and there is no doubt that on the night of the Pic-o-de-Crop finals he was the real showman, using all those years of stagecraft, his talent for developing a little 'picong' bad-mouthing of his opponents and his general rapport with his audience to deflect attention from any weakness there might have been in his lyrics.

Red Plastic Bag, on the other hand, had what was by popular acclaim the most original and witty calypso in the competition. RPB as he is known to the thousands of fans waving red plastic bags stamped with his initials all around the stadium, was the reigning Calypso Monarch and hot favourite to retain his crown until Gabby made a late entry into the competition at the semifinal stage. Even then RPB – real name Stedson Wiltshire – seemed sure to win with his song 'On Line' which contained the hauntingly sonorous chorus:

> We're trapped in the world wide web
> Caught up with the rest of the world
> We are doing all that is wrong:
> Barbados at the cross-roads dot com.[5]

Barbados presents itself as being the stable, clean, safe West Indian society where tourists may safely graze and rich tax exiles can live a comfortable, air-conditioned life with all the amenities of home and few of the hassles associated with other Caribbean islands – drugs, crime, violence, corruption, and an irregular electricity supply! If you believe the propaganda, RPB implies, then Barbados is both on line for a sound economic future and literally 'on line' through reliable connection to the Internet, which makes America and the rest of the cyber-world that much more accessible. The Bag suggests that things may not always be as rosy as the image makers pretend; indeed he paints another face of Barbados altogether, where prostitution – fuelled by high unemployment and tourism – is rife, where there is considerable poverty behind the glitzy tourist facade, where racism is still entrenched and 'racket and scam' are the order of the day.

> You say economically we are fit
> Morally and socially we are sick
> And all the talk about sovereignty
> We need social justice in this country

In a crafty dig at Gabby's boldface assertion of Bajan defiance RPB demands:

> Ask yourself a serious question
> Are Massa days really really done?
> On racism we put a mask
> We have some serious problems with class

And where Gabby stood up for Bajan Prime Minister Owen Arthur's reluctant signing of the Ship Rider treaty, demanding 'plenty alterations' to the agreement before he would sign it, Red Plastic Bag sees evidence of a neo-colonial cringe in the way President Clinton's visit to the island was handled, particularly at a time of severe water shortage

> Everybody around here knows
> All about our water woes
> But we took a hose
> And washed down the roads
> For all of Clinton's limos

It's true that RPB didn't give a particularly vibrant performance on the night of the finals and some people said he even got a couple of lines in the wrong order. (Of course, by the night of the Pic-o-de-Crop just about everyone on the island, including the judges, knew the words of most of the calypsos by heart.) But 'On Line' is such a good calypso; witty, pointed, punning, particular to Barbados but also resonating more widely, and Bag's performance wasn't by any means poor… But after a tedious two hour delay the judges decision was announced, with Gabby and 'Massa Day Done' taking the crown. Well, trouble come! Debate rage! Many people felt that RPB was robbed and Gabby's upbeat, us-and-them, pro-government sentiments might just have got the vote for dubious reasons. Another of the calypsonians in the finals, the imaginatively named Colin Spencer, sang a popular calypso satirising the way the whole competition was judged, suggesting incompetence, bias, and even a hint of political corruption. Needless to say his song, '10 Points' didn't feature

among the prize winners but with hindsight some of his lines
have a certain poignancy,

> I want to make a point
> but I wondering, what's the point?
>
> The judges givin you
> Ten Points
> for mediocrity
>   Ten Points
> if you over forty
>   Ten Points
> if you is a natty dread
>   Ten Points
> For not attacking the government
> ....
> and if you from the rulin party
> yu know yu gone through already...
>
> I LIE?[6]

POSTSCRIPT TO BARBADOS @ THE CROSSROADS.COM: A STING IN 'DE TAIL'

The one element of the competition that was uncontroversial in Barbados but would have been news elsewhere was the blatant and unapologetic homophobia evident in many of the calypsos. Just about all the Bajan calypsonians have written and performed such songs, some of them quite sinister, and the prevalence of such attitudes here adds a dimension to the ongoing debate about homophobia in West Indian popular culture. The reggae/dancehall lyrics of the Jamaican singer Buju Banton, for example, have drawn opprobrium from gay groups in Britain and America but have been defended by cultural critics like Carolyn Cooper as accurately reflecting the attitudes of the Jamaican 'folk' to those they call 'batty men' and their 'nastiness'. As I say, some of the Bajan calypsos on this theme had a sinister edge but there were also some witty treatments – best perhaps being Romeo's 'I don't believe/ God made Adam and Steve…!'

The paragraph above was included in the original published essay. In my innocence I had assumed the couplet had been coined by Romeo himself as part of his contribution to the topical debate in Barbados over the status of homosexuality – the nature/nurture, deviant/genetic debates that has been popular currency around the world for some years now. In fact it turns out that the 'Adam and Steve' line is well known in both gay and homophobic circles as a by-now somewhat trite put down. So Romeo was sampling or recycling the phrase by applying it to the particular Bajan context.

I don't remember the rest of Romeo's song, nor – accurately – the several others that I heard by various calypsonians that year which carried a similar homophobic message, only that the impact of the number of songs on that theme was surprising and rather disturbing. For someone who had begun to take for granted contemporary European and (parts of) North American frameworks for talking about homosexuality, the open contempt of the Barbadian calypsos was quite shocking. Many gay people might say that the UK is still a homophobic society, but here the blatant homophobia of those calypso lyrics would draw, if not legal sanction, then a furore from the gay community itself and from organisations and individuals concerned with notions of social justice and minority rights.

All the same I doubt I would have thought much more about it if I hadn't been so impressed by the work of Red Plastic Bag. 'On Line', in particular, seemed to me an outstanding calypso, indeed a song which transcends its genre (and I am in no way intending to sneer at calypso) to become a genuinely important expression of popular political consciousness which would bear scrutiny in terms of its language, craft, imagery and style with the best of West Indian poetry. 'On Line' is clearly the work of a sophisticated, intelligent, liberal-minded calypsonian who has a sharp sense of social, political and cultural realities and – apparently – a fundamental commitment to social justice.

It was only when I was able to buy the CD of *Barbados @thecrossroads.com*,[1] which included 'On Line', that I came across Bag's song 'In de Tail'. 'In de Tail' is a whining siren of a song, in turns paranoid and sinister, defensive and threatening. It is blatantly and crudely homophobic, seeming to accept without question the prevailing social stereotypes, negative stereotypes, about homosexuality. The song presents gay men as dangerous, diseased and predatory, child abusers and instigators of child prostitution. It accuses them not only of being personally corrupt and of corrupting the island's youth, but also, in an extended pun on 'billing' (a variant I guess of the Trinidadian term for homosexual acts, 'bulling'), with undue and unhealthy influence over business and government in the island. A gay conspiracy theory in other words. RPB or his persona is at great pains to distance himself from this homosexual activity and to insist that he couldn't be 'bought' even for 'a billion billion' dollars. 'In de Tail' ends with the moral assertion that 'If you bill bill everyday/ Then bill bill bill you will have to pay'. The threat of the bill that must be paid carries the weight of all the negative scenarios the song has rehearsed – AIDS, moral corruption, the inevitable disgrace of exposure as child molester or crook. Indeed it is possible – perhaps even intended – that the last line is understood as a more direct threat of retribution from the incorruptible, unbuyable RPB and the community he might claim to speak for. The sound of gunshots is suggested by an insistent cymbal strike throughout the piece.

'In de Tail' is quite witty in its way, it is self-consciously and artfully constructed – the argument is coherently structured and the main points reinforced by repetition and chorus, as well as by the pitch and cadence of the musical 'vehicle'. So this is a piece that has had as much artistic consideration as 'On Line' and yet presents us, apparently, with a very different facet of RPB's character – insofar as we can read across from the songs he writes and performs to his personal values. One explanation of the seeming contradiction between the stance of 'On Line' and the paranoia and crude stereotyping of in 'In de Tail' might be that in both songs he is doing what the best calypsonians do, tapping into and reflecting popular consciousness. Calypso is by definition a popular, even populist, art form, so the calypsonian *must* please as many of the crowd as he can both by what he says and the ways he says it. So *is* RPB just acting as a 'voice of the people' in his portrayal of – and hostility towards – homosexuality? Given the frequency with which the topic is addressed by other Bajan calypsonians – almost always with the same negative attitudes – it would seem to be so. Many of the island's leading calypsonians have either devoted an entire calypso to the subject or made passing reference to current angles on the debate during calypsos focusing on other topical issues.

But how can we really know what the views of the broad mass of Barbadian people are on these issues? A trawl through the archives of the island's newspapers of recent years reveals considerable discussion of homosexuality. There is much furore over any attempts to modify the law in Barbados or, for instance, to admit gay clergy to the island, and disquiet over the spread and threat of AIDS. The controversy that brought up all those issues and deep felt prejudices was a debate over the appropriateness of issuing condoms to the all male inhabitants of Glengary Prison after a huge rise in the number of HIV positive inmates was discovered. To be fair to the Bajan press, a genuine debate is reflected in the stories and features they present, but the balance of both the editorial comment and letters from readers is very much a traditional, conservative hostility to homosexuality as a 'condition' and particularly towards practising homosexuals themselves. In a recent survey undertaken by the *Barbados Advocate*, sixty percent of Bajan respondents declared homosexuality an unnatural practice and a significant percentage thought that gays should be excluded from 'important positions in the community.'

I realise that these sources hardly constitute hard academic data but in my –admittedly rather cursory – trawl of the available literature there is not much evidence of recent serious sociological exploration on this subject. In what seems to have been for many years the standard sociology textbook for students working on Barbados, Graham Dann's *The Quality of Life in Barbados*, first published in 1982, there is no mention of homosexuality except, implicitly, in the context of what is termed 'Moral Decay' and sexually transmitted diseases, which in 1982 – pre AIDS – was already perceived to be a significant problem. It would seem that homosexuality was too obvious a perversion and homophobia too 'natural' an attitude to justify comment in what is otherwise quite a detailed catalogue of social mores.

If, then, Red Plastic Bag and the other calypsonians could be justified in claiming that their negative portrayals of homosexuals *are* merely a reflection of the generally and commonly held attitudes of 'the folk', the ordinary people of Barbados, that they are fulfilling their role as 'the voice of the people', then several questions arise. First of all, is that really a good enough justification for the threatening tone, the incitement to hatred – if not worse – that 'In de Tail' seems to me to inspire? I suppose it comes down to a tension between the calypsonian's right and indeed duty to speak out forcefully about the issues of the day as he sees them and other groups or individual's right not to be harmed or persecuted over their sexual identity. The idea of the singer as 'the voice of the people' serves to extend this discussion because it was the justification given by the Jamaican dancehall star Buju Banton for what he called his 'straightforward' attack on homosexuality in his song 'Boom Bye Bye', which sparked an international controversy. The lines in 'Boom Bye Bye' that caused particular offence were certainly more direct that RPB's punning word play, 'Burn im up bad like a old tyre wheel / Boom Bye Bye Mr Battyman' and 'Shoot them now, come le we shoot them'[2].

When asked why he employed such lyrics in an interview he gave for the film 'The Darker Side of Black', made by Isaac Julian, Banton argued that those sentiments were a reflection of the attitudes of the great majority of Jamaicans and that he was simply 'the voice of Jamaica' – although he quickly modified that assertion to being '*a* voice of Jamaica'. Gay rights campaigners across the world, but particularly in North America, were outraged at the sentiments of the song, as indeed was a significant section of the Jamaican public.

The most articulate commentator on the affair was Dr. Carolyn Cooper of the University of the West Indies, herself an outspoken and controversial commentator on Jamaican popular culture, who argued that if – and she seemed to accept that it was – if the song was an accurate reflection of widespread Jamaican feeling, then whether or not it offended either gay rights groups or a more general liberal/humanitarian constituency internationally, the sentiment should be expressed, heard and taken seriously, *particularly within Jamaica*. It could not be just dismissed because it came from a class or constituency whose views are not generally heard in the kinds of forum where such debates about morality and natural law are traditionally discovered. However, she also insisted that Buju Banton and other DJs representing this position must 'mind their backs', and be aware of the likely consequences and repercussions of promoting those views beyond the relatively safe waters of the Caribbean.[3]

According to Ian Lumsden, author of *Machos, Maricones and Gays: Cuba and Homosexuality*,[4] which details the mistreatment of gays in Castro's Cuba, 'the oppression of homosexuals is a common phenomenon throughout the region'. So, insofar as these singers *are* voicing popular attitudes, why should this intense prejudice towards homosexuality persist so virulently across the Caribbean? The most obvious (and most often made) explanation for the taboo are the several Biblical injunctions against homosexuality (at least that's how they have been interpreted) and the continuing importance of a quite fundamental Christianity among the 'ordinary people' of much of the region. There might be other, more pragmatic reasons, such as the concern with AIDS – both as a disease and a drain on the resources of these still relatively fragile economies.

There may also be some deep hostility borne out of the region's grim past. Isaac Julian's film, mentioned earlier, seems to want to locate the machismo, which is such a seemingly important aspect of some versions of Caribbean male identity, as being the remnant of a necessary masculine assertion, a tactic of survival and resistance through the centuries of slavery. I'm not sure how far we can go with that conjecture as an explanation of a hostility that expresses itself in terms of violence – both verbal and actual – towards women and the effeminate qualities associated with homosexuality. Another, perhaps equally tendentious contributory explanation for the strength of homophobia in the Caribbean might be that through those same centuries of slavery, homosexuality was perceived – at least in Barbados – as a particularly *white* perversion and so was held in especial contempt and taboo by the people who were the slaves. Then, the argument goes, that view was 'naturalised' as a given by the slaves' descendants and reinforced by Christian prohibitions.

My only evidence, such as it is, for that last suggestion, comes from a surprisingly useful and provocative little book entitled *Sodomy and the Pirate Tradition: English sea rovers in the Seventeenth Century Caribbean* by B.R Burg[5] in which I found a survey drawn from the historian Ligon's account of his stay in Barbados around 1650, in which he remarks on the severe gender imbalance among the white population of the island at that time, with males outnumbering females by 10:1 in all classes of white society. While we all know how many of those white men may have satisfied their sexual appetites, it is also reasonable to assume, from those statistics and other evidence, as Bing does, that 'homosexuality has a long history in Barbados.' And it would seem that there is an almost equally long history of literary disapproval of the practice in the island. Burg cites the writing of one Thomas Waldwick, a Barbadian colonial, who commented on homosexuality in Barbados in a verse letter written in 1710 which might almost be the text of a contemporary Bajan calypso,

> All Sodom's sins are centred in thy heart
> Death in thy look and Death in every part
> O! Glorious Isle in Vilany Excell
> Sins to the Height – thy fate is HELL!

So perhaps little has really changed – except colour and attire – in 300 years!

'NOTHING ABOUT US AT ALL': OLIVE SENIOR AND WEST INDIAN POETRY

One way and another I am quite often asked to introduce Caribbean poetry to a new audience, whether to a fresh class of students, most of whom wouldn't actually be able to point to Haiti or Guyana on a world map, or, as in this case, writing something to set the scene for a selection of West Indian poems in a magazine or anthology. As I cast around for a way to frame such an introduction it invariably strikes me again how remarkable it is that this amazing body of work is out there at all. A hundred years ago it would have been inconceivable that the West Indies, for centuries the site of some of the worst atrocities of human history, would produce some of the most life-affirming and spiritually uplifting poetry of the twentieth century. Although verse in English had been written in and of the region almost from the beginning of the colonising enterprise – Sir Walter Raleigh was, after all, to borrow Derek Walcott's line, "ancestral murderer and poet"[1], the best that can really be said of most of that literary material is that it is 'interesting' in an historical or sociological sense. The voices that spoke out of those poems were the voices of strangers or exiles; the language they spoke had been forged elsewhere. Those literary texts were, of course, only one part of the poetic word culture generated in the islands through those centuries of slavery and colonisation, but inevitably very few of the oral poems, songs and stories of the majority of the people who made up the populations of the region survived to be recorded in the anthologies of West Indian poetry that have appeared in recent decades.

So, silence and the voices of strangers, it is from such unpromising ground that the contemporary flowering of West Indian poetry has grown. Through the course of the twentieth century, major figures such as Claude McKay, Louise Bennett, A. J. Seymour,

Derek Walcott, Kamau Brathwaite, Lorna Goodison and Martin Carter have chronicled the evolving West Indian cultural consciousness, claiming a multifaceted identity in the process of retelling the region's history, discovering its land and seascapes and giving voice to the dreams and nightmares of its peoples. Since the independence decades of the 60s and 70s, West Indian poetry has extended its range both formally and thematically. The chorus of voices modulates the variety of accents, registers and creoles which distinguish the islands and territories from each other and reflect the diverse heritage and cultural traditions of all those peoples who came to the archipelago over time. Formally, too, the diversity of styles is remarkable, from writers who adhere, more or less strictly, to the conventions of English or American verse, to those who experiment with dub, calypso, reggae or jazz models, reclaiming and reshaping the oral traditions of the region for contemporary circumstances. But in fact most West Indian poets resist easy classification, even in terms of style, the most apparently formal sometimes moving across shifting boundaries of the oral and the literary, the private and the public, as the poems they are writing demand. Contemporary West Indian poets are as diverse and idiosyncratic a fraternity as British or European poets, but insofar as they share a common aesthetic it might be found in terms of attitudes towards history and authority and – bound up with that – in ways of thinking about and using versions of the English language. Those elements come out in the wit, the rage, the verbal energy, the delight in linguistic play, the use of voices and characters and notions of storytelling that derive from the history of the region.

Another surprising aspect of the story of contemporary West Indian poetry is the way that women have come so much to the fore in the last decade or so. With very few exceptions (most notably the Jamaican Louise Bennett who has been actively crafting and – one way or another – publishing her poems since the 1940s) West Indian poetry was dominated by men through most of the twentieth century. That in itself isn't so surprising, given what we know from closer to home about attitudes towards gender roles, access to education, control of publishing opportunities etc. What is so striking is that in the last couple of decades so many powerful and accomplished women poets have emerged on the West Indian poetic stage: Lorna Goodison, Grace Nichols, Jean Binta Breeze, Merle Collins, Olive Senior, Mahadai Das, Velma Pollard, Marlene Nourbese Philip, to name just some who have established international reputations. Together – although what I've said earlier about the diversity of attitudes and approaches among West Indian poets probably applies even more to the women – they have certainly changed the focus and the tenor of West Indian poetry. That said, the themes and issues which have preoccupied West Indian poets over time – history, exile, identity, roots, landscape, childhood, race – remain as primary concerns but are now presented from different perspectives and augmented by other themes directly linked to women's experience and values – including questions around gender itself.

Among the most interesting of those writers is the Jamaican Olive Senior. Perhaps best known as a writer of short stories – one of her collections of stories won the Commonwealth Literature Prize – she is also a social historian, a journalist and a poet. As poet she distils qualities from those other roles – as storyteller and social historian – to inform a quirky and original poetic voice. Quite often she comes at 'big issues' from an unexpected angle, surprising us, as readers, into connections we had not foreseen. In her first collection of poems, *Talking of Trees,* a seemingly 'quiet' poem, 'Birdshooting Season' opens out – if we want to read it that way – from a commentary on the rural Jamaican world of her childhood to become a critique of male aggression and patriarchal values on a global scale. I'll quote the whole poem as it says much about her style and approach:

> Birdshooting season the men
> make marriages with their guns
> My father's house turns macho
> as from far the hunters gather
>
> All night long contentless women
> stir their brews: hot coffee
> chocolata, cerassie
> wrap pone and tie-leaf

for tomorrow's sport. Tonight
the men drink white rum neat.

In darkness shouldering
their packs, their guns, they leave

We stand quietly on the
doorstep shivering. Little boys
longing to grow up birdhunters too
Little girls whispering:
Fly Birds Fly [2]

It may be because I'm writing this on the day that some of the
biggest anti-war demonstrations ever staged in Britain have been
held – directed in part at a trigger happy U.S. President – that the
poem opens out and resonates so as a critique of 'macho' values.
Set so concisely in rural Jamaica through the names of food and
drink – 'cerassie', 'pone and tie-leaf' – and a couple of distinctive
usages – 'from far' and the wonderful 'contentless women' – a
very Jamaican mashing up of conventional English – the image
of the men setting off for 'sport' invokes more sinister images of
armed men setting off for combat. The real force of the poem,
though, comes in the final stanza, the ambiguous 'we', the division
of the response between the boys and the girls raising all sorts of
questions about gender stereotypes, innate and learnt values, loyalty
and treachery, about memories of childhood and the associations
of *home*.

In 'Birdshooting Season' the poet convinces us that this is a
world known intimately. That sense of a voice speaking with an
insider's knowledge of a rural Jamaican struggle is borne out in
many of the poems in the first part of *Talking of Trees*, as in the
brutal, brusque opening stanza of 'Epitaph':

Last year the child died
we didn't mourn long
and cedar's plentiful [3]

Although there can be little space for sentimentality in such a
hand-to-mouth existence, there is a certain dignity about the

characters who occupy that rural setting in Olive Senior's account. Elsewhere in *Talking of Trees* she engages with a very different – though equally brutal – Jamaica: the urban stress and violence of Kingston. Another woman's voice speaks in 'City Poem' describing the forced removal of squatters on the dungle – a notorious shanty-town slum area of Kingston. The trauma of this dispossession deprives everyone of 'all we have', including any vestige of human dignity:

> Wen de bulldoza come a back-a wall
> we jus pick up all we have and all
> we have is children an we leave
> Mavis doan wan leave Mavis aksin
> why why why A seh Mavis
> move fus aks question las
> de ting out dere biggern yu
> an it caan talk
> so Mavis move too but is like
> she leave all sense behin. Fram dat
> all Mavis good fah is aksin
> why. [4]

This is a voice not much heard before in West Indian literature, and hardly ever so credibly pitched and nuanced. Other poems in that section of the book touch on child-abuse, drug culture, class and race antagonism, gun and gang violence. In a poem written much later in her career, to be included in the forthcoming collection *Over the Roofs of the World*, Olive Senior has a poem entitled 'Rejected Text for a Tourist Brochure' in one part of which a character speaks in the – ironically pointed – voice of a hustler, a tourist rep selling out the island and its natural treasures one last time:

> ...Take for a song
> the Last Black Coral: the last Green Turtle;
> the last Blue Swallow-tail (preserved behind glass)
> Come walk the last mile to see the Last Manatee
> The last Coney, the last Alligator, the Last Iguana Smile. [5]

So there is a commitment in Olive Senior's work to confronting the unpalatable realities of Jamaican life and experience, notwithstanding that on the surface at least her poetry appears measured, restrained and in the context of much recent West Indian poetry, formally conservative.

If those poems from *Talking of Trees* address the Jamaican present in its various dimensions, in her second collection, the much praised *Gardening in the Tropics*, Olive Senior uses the metaphor of gardening – delving below the surface of things – to address hidden histories and forgotten stories:

> Gardening in the tropics, you never know
> what you'll turn up. Quite often, bones [6]

The bones she uncovers tell tales from the past that help to explain how this Jamaican present came to be. And that discovery of truth through her own effort contrasts with what she, as a pupil at a prestigious 'Colonial Girls School', was taught during her formal education, which:

> Told us nothing about ourselves
> There was nothing about us at all [7]

In the process of her gardening the persona discovers characters and stories from the Amerindian period of the Caribbean's pre-European-conquest history. Olive Senior has always had a particular affinity with the Arawaks – more properly the Taino – the Amerindian people who occupied the island at the time of the European 'discovery'. Little tangible remains of their culture but she has argued that 'some cultural transmission took place' which in some way informs the life of the island even into the present. The drama and dilemma of first encounters between the Amerindians and the Europeans is explored in 'Meditation on Yellow', which also considers the parallel experience of the Amerindians and the Africans imported to the region to work the plantations. In the final section of the book, 'Mystery: African Gods of the New World', Olive Senior looks in more detail at that African inheritance which she feels powerfully underlays Jamaican culture. She turns research on Yoruba myth and religion into praise-songs for the gods in their Caribbean manifestation, so her 'Shango: God of Thunder' is making style, Caribbean fashion:

He come here all the time
sharp-dresser
womaniser
sweet-mouth
smooth-talker
– but don't pull his tongue
is trouble
you asking
his tongue quick
like lightening
zigzagging
hear him nuh:

I SPEAK ONLY ONCE [8]

Even in this praise song there is an irreverence about Olive
Senior's poetry that goes back to that spirit of defiance – that
take on history and authority – I suggested might be said to
characterise recent West Indian poetry. But in fact the irreverence
is entirely appropriate in a poem modelling itself on West African
praise-song, which often involves satire and ridicule as well as
more uncomplicated forms of praise. By taking the fragments
of a long buried oral tradition and re-imagining them as a
contemporary literary artifact, Olive Senior is holding true to
the essential spirit of all Caribbean art, which – to a greater or
lesser extent – acknowledges, (to borrow a phrase from the current
critical/theoretical debate) 'a hybrid muse'[9]. Indeed if anything
can be said to define West Indian poetry it is that sense of an
engagement with the diverse and often hidden sources of Caribbean
history and culture and the determination to refashion those
materials into a poetry which speaks of and into the present in
voices that the peoples of the region would recognise as their
own.

MARTIN CARTER: 'THE POEMS MAN[1]

A poet cannot write for those who ask
Hardly himself even, except he lies:
Poems are written either for the dying
Or the unborn, no matter what we say. [2]

Across the Caribbean Martin Carter is regarded as one of the great poets of the region, one of those revered voices who have chronicled the journey from colonialism to independence, alongside such figures as Nicholas Guillen, Aimé Césaire, Derek Walcott, and Kamau Brathwaite. As I noted in an earlier essay, outside the region his reputation has been confined by the focus on his early 'political' verse. It was too easy for a lazy critic to settle for a version of Carter as the anti-colonial radical who swore to use his shirt 'as a banner for the revolution', putting his cause before the necessary craft of making poetry.[3] Such a view of Martin Carter's poetry could not have been sustained by anyone even halfway seriously examining his work, even if they were restricted to the early pieces collected in *Poems of Resistance*. The linguistic cunning and rhythmical measure underpinning a poem like 'University of Hunger', for example, contributes as much to its mesmeric power *as poem*, as do the ideas that drive it and the imagery that so haunts anyone who reads it:

is they who rose early in the morning
watching the moon die in the dawn.
is they who heard the shell blow and the iron clang.
is they who had no voice in the emptiness
in the unbelievable
in the shadowless.
O long is the march of men and long is the life
and wide is the span. [4]

One quality of that poetic language is its subtle use of a Guyanese creole construction – 'is they' – a device which opens the poem up to all sorts of echoes and resonances.[5] And while the written language of the poems never ventures far from standard English, that same cast and inflection of voice is evident in many of the later poems, helping to establish a verbal connection between the philosophical musings of "the poems man" – as one small girl dubs him – and the life of the society he speaks to and from. Indeed looking at his work overall it is hard to think of a contemporary poet who showed more concern for craft, who measured his utterance with greater care, who thought more about the intricacies of the relationship between art and society, than Martin Carter. As he put it in his poem 'Words', written in 1957: 'These poet words, nuggets out of corruption / or jewels dug from dung or speech from flesh'[6].

Like many poets across the world writing in the teeth of political oppression and cultural disintegration, Carter knew the real value of words, knew that they might be both weapon and the means of spiritual survival; 'the bread that lasts', as Derek Walcott put it. But Carter also had a profound belief in the power of poetry to work at all sorts of levels and in all sorts of circumstances. Those famous poems-of-resistance, smuggled out of prison to be read aloud at political rallies, at trade union strike meetings, recited by crowds at popular demonstrations of dissent against colonial oppression, those poems acknowledged that particular context in their language and their form. Carter wrote them with a simplicity and directness that is not at all typical of his poetry as a whole, and while they remain crafted literary artefacts they were liberated from the constraints of the library or the elite literary soirée, as he knew they would be, by their appropriation as orature, as a public poetry-of-resistance. Poems such as 'University of Hunger', 'I Come from the Nigger Yard', 'This Is The Dark Time My Love' not only bind Carter to his local audience, his comrades in struggle, transcending issues of class and race in that period of national crisis and outrage, but also established Carter as a figure of especial respect among Caribbean intellectuals, wherever they might have found themselves.

In 1991 Carter came to the UK to take part in an Arts Council sponsored reading tour with other Guyanese writers based in Britain. At a packed reading in central London he read to an audience which included many exiled Guyanese - few of them I'd guess regular attenders of literary events. As he read from those poems that audience began to recite them with him, not read them from a book but recite them from memory. They were there etched in the memory banks, a part of their being, fundamental to their identity as Guyanese people. And just as Martin Carter seems to have moved easily among the whole spectrum of the Guyanese people, from the most desperate to the most distinguished, so his poetry seems to speak across the race and class divisions that have so scarred Guyanese society. Few poets in our time – and fewer still writing in English – have made such an impact on the consciousness of a people.

And yet, in English his work is hardly acknowledged beyond the Caribbean. To be fair, access to Carter's poetry has always been a problem for would-be readers outside Guyana, for unlike so many colonial writers of his generation Carter didn't migrate to the metropolis to pursue a literary career; he stayed in the Caribbean, in Guyana. As time went by he came to understand the full implications of the choice that had to be made, between leaving the region in order to find publishers, an audience, the possibility of commercial success – but at the cost of that sense of exile and alienation so many Caribbean writers of that period expressed – or to stay and feel his ambitions frustrated by the narrowness of life in a post-colony, the parochialism, the lack of a developed literary culture, the sense of being, as he puts it in one of his essays, 'a displaced person' in the very society he has stayed to serve. So when he writes that 'The artist cannot change the nature of his fate: all he can do is endure it...'[7] we cannot but be conscious of the personal pain in that assertion. But to stay and write was to make a statement of commitment and integrity as a poet *of* – rather than simply from – Guyana.

Martin Carter was active in Guyanese politics one way and another throughout the forty years following his release from detention in 1954; disowned by and disowning in turns the two charismatic figures who dominated Guyanese politics in that period,

Cheddi Jagan and Forbes Burnham. He served for while as Minister of Information in a Burnham government in the late sixties, at a moment when it seemed possible that a new, multicultural politics might be forged out of the old divisions – but that prospect proved illusory and he soon resigned, publishing a snarling poem which announced both his departure and his reasons:

> And would shout it out differently
> if it could be sounded plain;
> But a mouth is always muzzled
> by the food it eats to live.[8]

Carter's natural position seemed to be on the margins of formal politics; an outspoken agitator, his poems spoke to – and for – the conscience of the nation. It was a dangerous position to fill: he was a friend of Walter Rodney, the Guyanese historian and radical activist murdered in 1980 and Carter was himself badly beaten when he joined a demonstration against the then government's attempts to manipulate the constitution to try and keep themselves in power. After those – and other, similar, events – Carter seemed to stand back somewhat from the public struggle. As Rupert Roopnaraine, the Guyanese scholar and political activist, put it, Carter:

> embraced the pure practice of poetry as the only available practice for a seeker of truth in an era of degradation. He turned inwards and so did the poems. In the end, the truth of craft was all. [9]

All his writing life Martin Carter published primarily in local journals and newspapers, and for many years his work was only available in very fugitive, limited circulation collections. As George Lamming has observed, Carter wasn't at all interested in self-promotion or fame, indeed he seemed 'philosophical' about the success or otherwise of his poetry to the point of complete indifference, trusting rather that time would sort the 'true poems' from the rest soon enough.[10] The 1989 edition of his *Selected Poems*, again published in Guyana, quickly sold out and a revised second edition was published just a few months – as it turned out – before

Carter's death, by the Red Thread Women's Press in Georgetown. It is a beautifully made book, illuminated by two leading Guyanese artists, but even that is a hard book to lay hands on outside of Guyana.

In many ways that early fame or notoriety set a misleading burden on Carter's reputation. His later work, while it never lost its political edge, was more oblique and cerebral than the overtly political poems of his youth, seeming to have more in common with the so-called magical realism of many of his fellow South American poets than with the naturalism of much socially committed African-American and Caribbean poetry of the second half of the century. Carter's work represents a sustained poetic and philosophical *process;* the individual poems are part of a much more ambitious intellectual undertaking that went on throughout the poet's life.

Consequently his later poetry didn't really 'fit' in terms of the prevailing orthodoxies and has not been read with the attention it deserves, has not found the kind of publishers and audience that might have followed it if it had been translated from the Spanish, say, with Vallejo, Neruda and Paz. They are his contemporaries in every sense, his work is of that originality, force and stature.

> This day
> is an old one. It is as old
> as a petal or a flower
> or the rain or the still air
> of a child's wild guitar
> shuddering in the silence
> of parents.[11]

At one level it is possible to read Martin Carter's poetry as a kind of testimony of despair, tracing a movement from the optimism and assertion of those early poems towards the world-weary meditations of his later years when that dream had been shattered by the intrigues and disappointments of Guyana's postcolonial and post-independence struggles for survival as a nation. Faced with such a situation, it is perhaps not surprising that a poet of Carter's sensitivity should resort to a kind of personal code in shaping his responses. Hence perhaps derives the perception that Carter's poems shift, over the course of his career, from the heart-on-sleeve accessibility of the early, optimistic poems to a more closed, cryptic kind of verse.[12] There is no doubting Carter's despair over the betrayal of the possibilities that the end of colonial rule offered, or of his bitterness at the way Guyanese politics has been reduced to the self mutilation of ethnic rivalry – the old colonial tactic of 'divide and rule' internalised and exaggerated for short term advantage.

Carter understood, perhaps more profoundly than any of his literary contemporaries, the real depths of desperation and despair that was the lot of so many Guyanese people through the twentieth century. And that bitterness is certainly apparent in many of the later poems:

> I
> keep working for a storm, some
> kind of fury to write new dates
> in our vile calendar and book [13]

But on reflection, and in the light of more attentive rereading, it is clear that such a view of Carter's achievement is too simple, leaves too much out of account. Rather Martin Carter's poetry offers its readers the chronicle of a life committed to *being*, in Guyana, and traces the evolution of his commitment to the notion of social justice, beyond the contagions of racial politics, through the tumultuous period his 70 or so years spanned. The poems witness to the fundamental integrity which characterised so much of his practise as both a man-in-society and as a writer. They provide a kind of record of that fiercely intelligent, sternly poetic sensibility responding not only to the political turmoil but also to the personal and domestic claims on his emotions and energy – he wrote several beautiful love poems through his career – as well as to the spiritual and the elemental dimensions of life in Guyana. Reading the poems across the span of this collection it is clear too that, beyond the despair and bitterness, there is an emphasis on the possibility of redemption through creativity. But that possibility of redemption depends, the poet insists, on the people taking responsibility for their own society, for their own futures. The later poems bear the evidence of that intense self-scrutiny in their pared-down compression, in the pithy density of their language, in their lack of unnecessary ornament or dramatic pause. His poem 'Rice', for example, is much more than simply a complaint about rural poverty and exploitation

> What is rain for, if not rice
> for an empty pot; and pot for
> in a hungry village? The son
> succeeds his father in a line
> to count as he did, waiting,
> adding the latest to the first
> of his losses; his harvests
> of quick wind padi... [14]

Rather the poem is a meditation on the cycle of life and death and the futility of that necessary struggle in the context of an elemental time scale. Guyana is a place of immense natural forces – the sea, the rainforest, the rivers, the distant mountains, even the power of the rain when it falls – and like most Guyanese writers Carter was ever conscious of that contrast between the cruel grandeur of those forces and the puny self-aggrandisement of mankind's ego. Martin Carter was a great poet, one who 'dreamed to change the world' but came to accept, as he put it in one of his last poems,

> Here is where
> I am, in a great geometry, between
> a raft of ants and the green sight
> of the freedom of a tree, made
> of that same bitter wood. [15]

'INCALCULABLE FLOTSAM': THE MINOR POETRY OF FRANK COLLYMORE

In the Foreword to his *Selected Poems* (1971) – and in what seems to have been a characteristically self-deprecating way – Frank Collymore described the contents of the volume as 'minor poetry'. Critics and anthologists of West Indian poetry have generally agreed that – in terms of his own output and achievement – Collymore, the great facilitator and champion of other people's writing, can only be considered a minor poet. Some have wondered whether Collymore's own talent for poetry was sacrificed in the cause of developing and promoting West Indian literature more generally through his work with *Bim*[1] and in his promotion of writers such as Derek Walcott and (Edward) Kamau Brathwaite in the early stages of their careers. Others have suggested that Colly simply spread his talent too thin as it were, trying to be painter, poet, actor, critic and prose writer as well as a full time school master and the editor of *Bim* – with all that entailed.

But what does it mean to be accounted a 'minor poet'? In the long history of poetry only a tiny fraction of the poems ever written survive more than a few years beyond the occasion of their composition or the death of their author. To have written poems that anyone thinks worthy of preservation or study more than half a century after their composition is quite an achievement – it is a salutary experience for any contemporary poet to read through the literary journals and anthologies of an earlier decade and to realise how few, if any, of the poets or poems are still read or referred to today. Fifty years after their deaths the entire work of the great majority of poets has effectively disappeared from view except to the serious and determined scholar. In the crude critical 'major-minor' scale, their work hardly registers at all. Frank Collymore wrote virtually all of his 'serious'[2] poetry in a relatively short period in the 1940s – very few British or American poets whose work appeared in the literary anthologies of the 40s and 50s are remembered today – yet Collymore's work is, if anything, taken more seriously by scholars and the general reader of Caribbean poetry than at any time before. This is partly due to his position in relation to the development of Caribbean literature, of course, and to the fact that there were relatively few West Indian poets writing in the decades before Independence, so the work of those who were active is investigated as a matter of course by scholars wanting some sense of the history of the region's literature. But beyond those circumstantial and instrumental readings, I want to argue that Frank Collymore's work survives into – and speaks into – the twenty-first century because of the intrinsic qualities of the poems themselves. Or at least *some* of the poems do. The term 'minor poet' tends to be applied to writers of past periods whose poetic output as a whole was relatively slight or who are remembered for only a few, or even a single poem that somehow captures a moment or a quality of the time in which it was written. The anthologies which survey historical periods are thick with such poets, whose work provides a necessary context and backcloth for the poetry of the major figures of the age. In all of these senses, Collymore was right to think of himself as a 'minor poet' but as I want to argue, that is not necessarily a title to be sneered at. Collymore wrote relatively few poems overall (and published only a proportion of those) and of those only a handful make it into the modern survey anthologies of West Indian/ Caribbean poetry, where – alongside the work of such 'minor' figures as A.J. Seymour, Philip Sherlock, Eric Roach, Una Marson and Phyllis Shand Allfrey – they make up the poetic *ground* of the pre-independence period which produced the great poets who dominate modern West Indian poetry, Walcott, Brathwaite and Martin Carter.

Of the hundred or so poems that Collymore chose to publish, only that anthologised handful – with maybe another handful that have perhaps been unjustly overlooked, so about a dozen in all – really bear close scrutiny now, or at least seem to a more-

164

or-less objective reader to stand and work, as poems, without relying on the apparatus of a cultural or social contextualisation that might explain the seeming weaknesses of the other poems in various ways.[3] And of that dozen only one, 'Hymn to the Sea' is without question, and in anyone's terms, a 'true' poem which transcends claims of time or place or even authorship and lives a kind of independent poetic life, available to – and acknowledged by – readers around the world and across time. 'Hymn to the Sea' is a beautifully made poem, and it is a profoundly moving and challenging poem, opening up and suggesting more and other connections each time one reads it.

In terms of the evolution of Caribbean poetry, though, Collymore's poetry is of particular interest and importance. It is interesting because he was writing at a time when there were relatively few West Indian poets and in that situation his work both reflects and represents the times in terms of our understanding of 'the story' of West Indian poetry – its themes, styles and voices. It is interesting because of everything else that Collymore did, particularly his long time editorship of *Bim*; to know the kind of poetry Collymore wrote tells us much about his literary and cultural values, his own sense of what a poem was. It is important because of the impact and influence it may have had on younger writers, casting around for regional models to follow – it is certainly possible to speculate that there are moments in Collymore's poetry which anticipate moments in early poems by both Walcott and Brathwaite, and to wonder if they were – consciously or unconsciously – influenced by Collymore's work.[4] But I want to argue that Collymore's best poetry is important in the sense that all good poetry is important, in that it enriches the spirit of those who encounter it in various ways, and certainly there are several Collymore poems that keep their place in the canon of Caribbean poetry for that reason.

A discussion of Collymore's poetry has to begin with questions of language and technique. Here we have to locate Frank Collymore as a man of his time, the beneficiary – as he and other Caribbean writers of that generation saw it – of what Derek Walcott called, almost without irony, 'a sound colonial education', which is to say, in matters that bear on his notions of what constituted fine writing, a solid grounding in the European Classics, including some knowledge of Latin and Greek literature and mythology, and a wide reading in English literature, especially Shakespeare and the 18th and 19th century poets. Born in 1893, Collymore is essentially, at least temperamentally, in the terms of twentieth century English poetry, a Georgian poet – that is to say his verse is 'well mannered', formally quite conservative and concerned 'to express the truth of feeling'.[5] In terms of his poetic contemporaries he owes much more to Hardy than to Eliot, indeed there is little to suggest the impact of modernist ideas in Collymore's poetry. In terms of what he wrote about, some of Collymore's more bucolic work sits comfortably with that idea of a Caribbean-Georgian sensibility, but much else doesn't. There is a toughness of thought about strands of Collymore's work that suggests he was more in tune with the style of thinking of the English poets associated with the 1930s – especially Auden and, in his satirical mode, John Betjeman. These English comparisons are not irrelevant to a discussion of this avowedly Caribbean man of letters, because at the time that his literary sensibility was being formed the colonial order was still securely in place and notions of independence hardly considered. The cultural values embedded in the kind of education he received and went on to promulgate were bound to be essentially those of the kind of English public school on which Combermere was modelled. But Collymore was no simple mimic man copying – as several would-be West Indian poets of his generation did – the approved metropolitan styles. For someone of Collymore's intelligence and sensibility the fact of his being in Barbados rather than Bayswater was bound to colour his interpretation and adaptation of those metropolitan influences, and indeed one clear strand in Collymore's verse is the endeavour to valorise the local, the particularly Barbadian, the landscapes and seascapes and – to borrow one of Brathwaite's terms – the manscapes of the island.

It is perhaps surprising then that there is little in the language and voices of the poems to suggest a nonstandard English enunciation. This may be largely because they are mostly 'personal' poems, to be spoken as it were in the voice of the poet, and we know, from the few recordings that survive, that Collymore's manner of speech was a West Indian standard English, hardly inflected by a Bajan accent even, far less a distinctive Bajan vocabulary. On the other hand we know, of course, that Collymore was very interested in the language people spoke. His work in collecting the *Notes for a Glossary of Words and Phrases of Barbadian Dialect* [6], however amateurishly he pretended to have taken the enterprise, was an important early foray into West Indian linguistics. But nowhere is that interest in – or ear for – the spoken language of the island evident in the published poetry.

If we concentrate on the fifty or so poems in Collymore's *Selected Poems*, which must represent his own sense of the best of his work, we can see that the poems fall into five broad thematic areas:

1. What we might call 'poems of spirit' – catching or responding to moments of revelation or epiphany – including 'Beneath the Casuarinas' and 'Words are the Poem'.

2. Poems of social satire, or at least poems that offer a more-or-less direct critique of the values of his society, best represented perhaps by 'Voici la Plume ...' and 'Ballad of an Old Woman'.

3. Poems concerned with place and 'the local', and particularly with an emphasis on the sea, like 'Schooner' and 'Return' and 'Hymn to the Sea'.

4. Love poems – or rather poems about love, usually love gone wrong, the disappointments of love, including poems like 'The Kiss' and 'The Culprit'

5. Memorial poems, written to commemorate the death and loss of important figures in his life – the best is probably 'In Memoriam: Michael Foster.

Simply as poems, the pieces that fall comfortably into the latter two categories are the least interesting of all Collymore's work. The memorial poems are heartfelt and worthy, honouring friends and family members and in one case – revealingly – his nurse 'Amanda – the negress'. The poem dedicated to the young Barbadian poet Michael Foster, tragically killed in a car crash, was one of two poems included in the *Selected Poems* written considerably later than the rest of the collection, which were otherwise taken from his 1959 *Collected Poems*. Most of the memorial poems are written for people who died in old age or in war, so that the extra element of the shock and futility of 'a young life plucked... too soon' while full of promise adds an edge to the story of Michael Foster's death.

The sequence of poems written about love are almost without exception wry, rather bitter responses to the disappointments of a young(ish) man's amatory career. Fashionably melancholy and sometimes – by today's standards – patronisingly coy, they seem perhaps the most dated of all Collymore's writings, stepping painfully among the conventions, prejudices and hypocrisies of high colonial society in a language that – in its formality as much as anything – seems alien to contemporary ears, as in 'So this is Love'

> Yes, the little fellow used us remarkably well
> Brought us together quite aptly,
> And a certain fortuity in the occurrence
> Achieved a remarkable completeness
> Which the romantic approach
> Might well have failed to accomplish.[7]

These poems are interesting to the social/literary historian in a gossipy, speculative way, establishing Frank as 'a bit of a lad' in his youth – at least if we accept them as tales from the life of the poet – and they suggest something about the nature of Bajan society at the time, at least in the social circles in which Frank Collymore moved. But simply 'as poems' there is not much to hold our attention in either the group of memorial poems or the poems about love. Indeed, if these poems represented Collymore's best work then it is unlikely his reputation as a poet would have survived, even as the most minor of literary figures.

However, the dozen or so poems that distinguish Frank Collymore's work fall in the other three broad categories I have suggested. The most nebulous grouping is those I have called 'poems of spirit' which includes 'Beneath the Casuarinas', 'Because I have turned my back', 'That Day', 'Words are the poem' and 'Blue Agave', although the latter might as easily belong in the group of poems that comment on the nature and style of Bajan society. There are other poems, too, in the *Selected Poems* that might seem to belong in this group, poems like 'That Day', 'Music at Night' or 'Minute's Magic' but they are all rather laboured in their working out.

Of this group 'Words are the Poem' is perhaps the most interesting piece, both for itself and in the way it serves – as the opening poem in the book – as a kind of 'proem', a self fulfilling definition of what Collymore thinks poetry is and how it works. It is significant, given the importance of the sea in Collymore's personal mythology that he describes words as 'the incalculable flotsam' and later says that 'words float upon the surface, a broken message.' The island poet's task, it would seem, is to discover the potentialities of those words he finds, as in more recent times some Caribbean sculptors regularly walk the tide lines of particular beaches and draw their inspiration from what they find washed up there, to become transformed as the substance as well as, sometimes, the subject of their work. So Collymore asks the finders of words – the poets and storytellers of the Caribbean, himself of course among them – 'what voyage shall he now essay?' The alternatives he offers take on a particular resonance when we read them with the hindsight that knows the position Frank Collymore was to fill in the evolution of West Indian literature. He poses the choice between the exotic but superficial exploration of an imaginative 'glide' along 'the trade routes' which may be, to borrow another phrase from Brathwaite 'what the world requires' or to attempt the more daunting task, to peer

> 'Below the restless surface, discovering,
> Tangled among the seaweed and obscured...
> ...A shape that might have been a man.[8]

Although 'Words are the Poem' is primarily a challenge by the poet to himself, the darkness of that vision and its challenge anticipates the struggle of several West Indian writers in the succeeding decades who struggled with words to disentangle and illuminate images, stories and themes that had been obscured in the process of – and the telling of – West Indian history. Not least, literally, the stories of those many shapes that 'might have been a man' that inhabited the sea bed on the routes of the middle passage. In a more general sense, however, the poem is a version of one that many poets have written down the ages, trying to understand or image their own practice, as a kind of counter-spell, or a rational explanation for what happens when a poem gets written.

Of the other poems I would put in this 'poems of spirit' grouping, only 'Beneath the Casuarinas' and – if we include it here – 'Blue Agave' is often reprinted or anthologised. The other two poems deserve more careful attention, however, and are interesting as a pair. The one 'That Day' suggests a moment of revelation and exceptional 'seeing', the other, 'Because I have Turned My Back' is a poem of closure, or turning away from a mysterious kind of 'vision'. 'That Day' opens mundanely enough with the image of the schoolmaster 'standing by the open window/while the boys wrote their exercise' – both pupils and master seemingly caged spirits dutifully intent on their work. However the teacher's eye is caught and inexplicably held by a sight that is both ordinary and – as the definite article suggests – familiar, 'the slim tree/In the round grass plot'. The language of the poem then becomes almost the heightened prose of religious revelation, the teacher's eyes 'were suddenly opened' and he engages not only the physical landscape 'but that which springs/ From the moment as it passes.' It may be that this is indeed a moment of Christian revelation, the tree perhaps standing for the cross, with the holy spirit 'clutching/The heart like love' as the persona's eyes are opened to 'delight' as if 'with balm anointing' and then the powerful final lines (cited below) a statement of Christian assurance. But in fact the source of this affirmative revelation is not spelt out, and a more convincing reading – given some of the issues that Collymore explores elsewhere in his work – is perhaps the implicit suggestion that the mysterious vision is more a kind of pagan/ animist connection with the spirit of the earth itself, an engagement with:

> ...the heart of the cold stone
> Whose slow long pulse echoes
> The peace within the bone [9]

It is interesting to recall that, around the time this poem was written and first published, the young Derek Walcott was encountering his first experience of literary and religious censorship when one of his early poems, celebrating a similarly 'animist' vision of God in nature, was condemned by the Catholic Bishop of the West Indies as a statement of blasphemy. Collymore's poem is perhaps more subtle and coded than the teenage Walcott's effort but, if read in this way, none the less controversial in staidly Anglican Barbados.

'Because I have turned my back' could also be read as a poem in awe of god-in-nature, though the force the persona has turned his back on – God or art or love – is never quite identified. The poem seems to lament the persona's failure to dedicate himself to:

> The frail immemorial flowers
> Sprung from the stillness
> Where the will is of no avail [10]

Rather the persona has – albeit reluctantly – settled for the mundane life of ordinary human commerce. The acknowledgment of some spiritual/elemental life-force is very strong in these poems, though its form or nature remains tantalizingly vague. 'Because I have turned my back' is an intriguing and mysterious poem, complicating our understanding of the spiritual dimension – and spiritual tension – to the poet's life. That mystical sense is most famously explored in 'Beneath the Casuarinas', a beautifully measured evocation of a silent walk through a wood of Casuarinas trees that inspires in the poet/persona a feeling of connection to an immemorial or ethereal other world. The dappled 'unreal' light, the eerie atmosphere of the wood, the stillness and silence of the place – a kind of sacred grove – contribute to the sense that this is a place apart, not of the 'real' world the poet/persona normally inhabits. Once noticed, the silence is disturbing; it suggests mystical and profound spiritual questions, asking whether this sound-less sound that fills the poet/persona's consciousness might be:

> The empty mouthing of the long forgotten dead...
> The winds' secret...the old lament
> Of all creation.......?

A beautiful and haunting poem, it is perhaps marred somewhat by a slightly stagey ending. The mystery of 'silence made/ manifest in sound' that the previous lines have so vividly established in that sequence of unanswerable questions is deflated by the trite and obvious assertion, 'we shall never know', and the rather unnecessary and melodramatic account of the return to the sunlit, 'ordinary' world:

> We pass from their shadows out into
> The sunlight
> And the silence echoes and re-echoes
> Within us as we go. [11]

While those lines are as measured and musically balanced as the opening lines of the poem and formally work very well – the pace and music of the poem contributing much to the overall effect of a mysterious, other-worldly encounter – they do suggest that the poet doesn't fully trust his words and images to do their work.

Indeed if one was to make a general criticism of Collymore's poetry – and it is the classic fault of the isolated poet – it might be that he does tend to 'explain' too much and in the process risk explaining away the very mysteries that inspire the writing of the poems in the first place. Several of the poems that fall outside this dozen or so that I argue represent his best work are over-written in that way. It is a tendency that reminds us of just how isolated Collymore was as a serious poet in Barbados at the time he was writing these poems. He may have been the convivial man-of-culture in the elite colonial high school, a member of the amateur dramatic society and quite possibly involved in groups interested in 'literary appreciation' but in terms of the actual writing, I suspect there were very few – if any – people he could have discussed such matters with. Across the Eastern Caribbean that generation of writers and artists who determined to stay in the region – Eric Roach in Tobago, A.J. Seymour and E. R. Burrows in Guyana, Harry Simmonds in St. Lucia, Phyllis Shand Allfrey in Dominica, all were struggling to find ways to write in the tradition of the education that had formed their sensibilities but also to be true to their personal feelings and the realities of their particular places. One can only speculate as to how much that sense of isolation underpinned Collymore's determination to make *Bim* – as a regional forum for exchange of ideas and literary efforts – a success, but it must have played some part.

The final piece in the 'poems of spirit' group I want to mention here is 'Blue Agave'[12], which straddles this grouping and those I have called the poems of social commentary and critique. On first reading, 'Blue Agave' seems a straightforward praise-song to the unconsidered 'weed' that is Blue Agave, a hardy, salt-tolerant creeping plant that survives and indeed thrives on the uncultivated and uncultivatable outcrops of the Bajan coast. Precisely but unobtrusively crafted, 'Blue Agave' is a 'poem of spirit' in that – like most of the other poems in this group – it begins in an expression of awe for the unquenchable life-force in the natural world, expressed particularly by the Blue Agave's against-the-odds persistence and its 'untamed beauty'. But 'Blue Agave' seems to invite another reading, as a metaphor for the tenacious qualities of other ubiquitous but unregarded locals in colonial Bajan society, particularly the rural peasantry or 'folk', as some literary shorthand styles them. In this way, it is possible to see the poem as one of social commentary or critique. I'm not sure how much of that reading Collymore himself would have acknowledged, but it is hard, with hindsight, not to read something of the sort into the poem.

Generally, however, Collymore's poems of social commentary are more direct. They rely more on satire and mockery than metaphor, the tone avuncular rather than reverential. And although he is in many ways a champion of 'the local', Collymore is not, by any means, an uncritical apologist for the mores and manners of the 'ordinary folk' of his island. The best known poem in this style is 'Voici la plume de mon oncle' in which the persona adopts the patrician tone of the worldly wise – but also world-weary – senior schoolmaster, surveying his past and present pupils' lives and values. The poem is a wry critique of the process of

173

secondary education at this time and on the values of the society that strove to put its boys through such a system. There is a sharply satirical edge to the poem – particularly apparent in the recording of Collymore reading the piece on the LP recording of poems from John Figueroa's *Caribbean Voices* anthology[13] – and while the satire is mostly directed at the recipients of the education, the poem also makes uncomfortable reading for those, like Collymore himself of course, who were the providers of that education. The poem is interesting in all sorts of ways, not least as a valuable resource for students of the history of education in the West Indies, revealing much about the content and style of delivery of elite education in the years Collymore was a schoolmaster:

> And for those who can't take it all in by the prescribed method
>   There's a road to the brain via the backside by blows....

> ...Then there's Prayers every morning and Double Entry
>   Bookkeeping
>   One foot in Heaven and one on the Things That Matter

Collymore is obviously unhappy with the materialism and the social hypocrisy of a society that sees education purely in terms of narrow notions of economic success:

> Physical geography, the Cadet Company and the Tables
>   Will have taught him all there really is to know.
> He won't need to seek other pleasures in dreams
>   Or visions, he can shut out from his mind that morbid
>   stuff
> The schools ignore: love, truth, and beauty;
>   He's got a damn good job and that's enough [14]

Collymore's life – beyond the necessity of making a living by teaching – was dedicated to the pursuit of 'love, truth, and beauty', so we understand the irony of his situation, inside a system that – as he presents it in the mood of the poem – is very much skewed against such a quest.

Like all of Collymore's best pieces, this is a very well made poem, carefully measured, an unobtrusive but consistent and effective use of rhyme, the language of the speaking voice a crisp, standard English with no suggestion of a West Indian inflection or linguistic construction.[15]

That this is clearly an educated voice narrating the critique, spoken by someone obviously very much part of the social world he describes, adds to the sense of irony that drives the poem and colours our understanding of the criticisms that are being made of both the school system and the society.

This satirical take on the society of which he is a part is evident in several more of Collymore's poems in the *Selected Poems*. The most interesting I think is 'Ballad of an Old Woman' which is presented as a cross between a nursery rhyme and a hymn:

> There was an old woman who never was wed;
> Of twenty-one children was she brought to bed,
> Singing Glory to God [16]

But there is clearly something sinister beneath the light-hearted façade; the old woman is abandoned by all her twenty-one 'illegitimate' offspring and dies an unremembered pauper in the workhouse, the poem touching on issues of migration, remittances, ungrateful or at least forgetful children, and the treatment of the poor and destitute in society. The contrast between the old woman's simple, uncomplaining Christian faith and an apparent lack of charity or compassion on the part of the institutions of the Church is underlined by the subversion of the hymn format – achieved in part by the way the repetition of the phrase 'Singing Glory to God' takes on an ironic charge. As a companion piece to 'Voici la plume...', 'Ballad of an old woman' extends the range of Collymore's social critique. Similarly 'Portrait of Mr X', which is quite a complex poem, examines the social realities disguised by an outwardly respectable Bajan life.[17] One has a sense in many of these poems that Collymore is to some extent taking himself to task. He was, after all, a respected and respectable member of the community, but he was also someone very interested in masks and, as others have argued, he was someone for whom the private self was an identity very much to be protected. The final stanza of 'Voici la plume...' opens out from the satirical focus on the spiritually mean domesticities of a suburban colonial life to ask, implicitly, more profound questions about the nature of existence and the meaning and purpose of any life.

That sort of opening up and contemplation of the mysteries not only links these poems back to Collymore's 'poems of spirit' but connect too with the essential thrust of the final group of poems I want to discuss, those that celebrate – and worry at the significance of – the sea. In many ways the refrain of 'Hymn to the Sea' sums up the poet's fundamental philosophy, that as 'small islanders' the people of Barbados 'must always be remembering the sea', that – particularly in the era before mass air travel – the sea shaped and framed and in many ways determined the lives of every Barbadian and – by extension – all West Indians. Indeed in the three poems I want to discuss, the sea is reverenced in ways that must have been quite controversial at the time the poems were written. 'Hymn to the Sea' may seem at first glance a simple mellifluous praise song, suitable for some of the purposes to which it has been put – for school children to learn by heart or the island's politicians to 'sample' and quote from in various more or less appropriate contexts – but just below the surface is a much more radical presentation of the fundamental relationship between the sea and the islanders. It presents a quasi-religious view of the origins of life derived partly from various myths about the sea and partly on a version of Darwinist evolutionary theory, which many might have found quite shocking. In different ways these radical ideas appear in each of the three poems I want to address here. 'Schooner' is the most conventional and least contentious of the three, a sensual and romantic celebration of a voyage through the night on a schooner plying – we assume – between the Caribbean islands. It is a beautifully evocative piece of writing:

> The ship's prow slips into the kiss of the wave, and
> The sail's saga is told in slow syllables as we plunge onward
> Towards the shore of the horizon where the clouds are wrapped
> About a shadow. [18]

But the heart of the poem is a human-humbling contemplation of the 'sea's endlessness' and the image of the voyage across it from which there is 'no end.' The sea is presented as an elemental force impervious to human reason or understanding, 'No meaning here but the song of the sails'.

On its own that kind of statement of awe in the face of the sea's scale and force and otherness would not be particularly remarkable but read in conjunction with 'Return' and 'Hymn to the Sea' it seems to prefigure elemental, mythic imagery that those poems develop. 'Return' is a strange, almost pagan poem, declaring the inevitability of all humanity returning to the sea from whence our ancestors once 'Crawled landward/To rear our gardens and palaces and temples'. It's not clear how much this idea might have been triggered by the – then still contentious[19] – scientific debates about the origins of human kind, the theory that all modern land-based species evolved from fish or other sea creatures.

There are also, of course, various creation myths around the world that posit a similar story, most significantly perhaps, given Collymore's Classical background, the Greek version of the Babylonian creation epic in which the sea monster Tiamet, whose name translates as 'the bitter ocean', was said to personify the 'Chaos from which all things came forth.'[20] Anyway, the reference in the poem to Leviathan – usually envisioned as a sea creature – refers the reader back to the Biblical story in which the Creator God battled and defeated the monster. The poem asserts that 'we too' will come down to the sea, passing the sands 'where the shattered bones of leviathan/Are strewn', implying that the return to the sea takes the representative human 'back' before history, before the Biblical stories, to that primordial place of origin. That evolutionary connection may be true for all mankind but is particularly significant – the poem implies – for islanders, who in some special sense are aware of 'the ancient memory/ within the bone' which calls them to the sea.

But more radical than the suggestion of human origins in the sea, is the poem's insistence that, 'We shall return' and the final stanza of the poem invokes a kind of underworld afterlife, using imagery associated with some Christian (and indeed Islamic) ideas of Paradise:

> See,
> On the bright sands her waves have spread
> Golden coronals to welcome us!
> Crowned as kings we shall return – [21]

However, the final image of the poem is confusing; the descriptions of the sea shift from a vocabulary of mothering and 'embrace' to the startling image of 'The crowding sea, vomiting her living and her dead.' That image might suggest the awesome power of the sea, its cruelty and indifference, but it seems at odds with the tone and argument of all that has preceded it in the poem. 'Return' is an intriguing and disturbing poem, developing the sense we have of Collymore's ambiguous attitude towards the sea, and where that places him in terms of conventional notions of history, of science and of religion.

'Hymn to the Sea' is a more complex poem than either 'Schooner' or 'Return', taking up and in various ways embroidering upon the central ideas explored in those poems but also developing other issues and dimensions of the promise of allegiance that the poem's refrain reiterates. It is formally a much more substantial and mannered poem than either 'Schooner' or 'Return'. Blank verse structured in five eight-lined stanzas, measured and musical, with spare and subtle use of half rhyme, assonance and alliteration to bind the poem and suggest the sensual and sensuous elements of what the poet sets out to explore. Although there is some slightly awkward diction here and there – words like 'cognizant' and 'apertures' in the first stanza for example – and the formality of the language emphasises the period in which the poem was written, there is no argument that 'Hymn to the Sea' is a finely crafted piece.

The poem opens with the seemingly simple assertion that

> Like all who live on small islands
> I must always be remembering the sea [22]

This gives us the central theme of the poem and establishes the voice in which the poem is spoken. 'Must' is an interesting word there, an imperative, both a bounden duty and a self- interested necessity, acknowledging the power of the sea in both the spiritual and the physical realms. If we don't automatically assume that the voice in the poem is that of the poet we wonder who is speaking and who he is speaking to.[23] Many of Collymore's larger scale poems are written as first person narrations, and couched in ways that make us think that the poet is talking to himself, so that we as readers are in a sense overhearing the poet literally 'musing'. This is very much the case with 'Hymn to the Sea' when we read this as the poet Collymore working through his own feelings about the sea and its significance for him personally. However, by that enfolding identification of the first line, 'Like all who live on small islands' the poet implies that these personal reflections have some wider resonance – for Barbadians in particular, for other West Indians and for anyone who thinks of themselves as living on a 'small island'.

The opening stanza presents a very sensual response to the sea, Collymore refers to it always as 'she' and through the poem there are images of the sea as both mother and lover, as well as Muse. There is something slightly voyeuristic about the line 'viewing/ Her through apertures in the foliage', suggesting not only that the sea is often times lost from sight but also that this observing is somehow sly, furtive, illicit. This sensual imagery is played up in the next few lines, 'hearing' her music and smelling 'The warm rankness of her; tasting/ And feeling her kisses on warm sunbathed days'. 'Rankness' seems a strange word to choose for a praise-song, meaning, according to the OED, a rancid or offensive smell. However according to Richard Allsopp's *Oxford Dictionary of Caribbean English Usage*, in the eastern Caribbean the word is particularly associated with a strong fishy smell and there is also the sensual association, in an alternative definition, of 'lustful or licentious'[24]. All of which suggests that the 'kisses' the narrator enjoys are perhaps more than the innocent blessings of a mother.

The second stanza is a more naturalistic description of the sea in its many moods and appearances; the language is heightened and with the reference to Titan the mythic associations of the sea are introduced. This is a more traditional praise song, the persona affirming his knowledge of – and the attention he has paid to – the sea. The third and forth stanzas explore the ideas about origins and destiny that 'Return' develops. The approach to those ideas in 'Hymn to the Sea' is less dramatic, less explicit, couched in terms of the many associations of the sea in human myth and history – the myth of Atlantis is invoked as is the story of the birth of Venus and the associations of Stella Maris – the title given to the Virgin Mary as 'the star of the sea' and which many sources also associate with Isis, the goddess of ancient Egyptian belief. The approach to the sea is prosaic enough, 'Go down to the sea upon this random day' but quickly the experience becomes more loaded as the beach underfoot includes 'saltfruit/ Torn from the underwater continents'. The entry into the sea is also couched in more religious terms. The image is of the sea as life-giver, mother, and in some sense a god-like force – our beginning and our end –

<blockquote>
cast
Your garments and despondencies, re-enter
Her embracing womb: a return, a completion
</blockquote>

Where the working out of that idea is the sum of 'Return', in 'Hymn to the Sea' it is part of this more complex evocation of the sea as a source of many visions and myths and theories and attempts to understand the nature of existence. The poem is rich in literary echoes and allusions, to John Masefield and Keats and perhaps most obviously to Wordsworth. The sea as Muse is invoked in this stanza in a phrase that inevitably calls the lakeland poet to mind: 'the patterning of her rhythm / Finds echoes within the musing mind.' The grand and rather sweeping final stanza of the poem has the quality of many more traditional seafarers hymns, acknowledging the destructive power of the sea as both 'Mother and destroyer, the calm and the storm'. But the poem then turns back to the image of the sea as an all powerful creator goddess who must 'always' be attended to, particularly if – as in the case of Barbados, as a coral island it was in a very literal sense 'born of the sea': 'This swarming land / Her creation, her signature set upon the salt ooze'.

'Hymn to the Sea' is Collymore's best poem but it is also a characteristic Collymore poem in terms of being the contemplative vision of a poet struggling to make sense of the world in which he lived. It embodies all of Collymore's qualities as a poet and reminds us of his weaknesses, but half a century after it was written it remains a beautiful and profound and relevant poem that all who live on small islands – or even those who only ever visit small islands – will respond to and honour. So while Frank Collymore may be accounted a 'minor poet' in the long sweep of literary history, his best work remains intriguing and rewarding in all the ways that poetry can.

'BETWEEN ME AND THEE IS A GREAT GULF FIXED: THE CRUSOE PRESENCE IN WALCOTT'S EARLY POETRY

In his essay 'The Muse of History', Derek Walcott asserts that the great poets of the New World perceive man as 'a being inhabited by presences, not a creature chained to his past'.[1] It seems to me that the notion of a poetry inhabited by presences is a useful way to approach Walcott's own poetry; indeed, by any definition, he is by now one of those 'great poets' himself. I have suggested elsewhere[2] that those presences – masks, personae, figuras, voices – which the poet has 'entered'[3] represent a strategy for dealing with the complexities of the history which has obsessed his imagination. The presences I would identify are overlapping and related categories which serve to focus aspects of that obsession. At one level they are wilfully adopted masks, in the traditional literary sense, devices to enable the poet to speak in other voices, but at another level they are the consequence of Walcott's perception of his cultural and historical situation as a West Indian poet: they occupy him. These presences serve to liberate his imagination from the chains of 'historical realism',[4] from the limitations of a voice compromised by the contradictions of his personal situation, and allow him to comprehend and confront those very contradictions. Robinson Crusoe, I want to argue, is one of the voices, along with Homer's Odysseus, through which Walcott explores the condition of being a castaway.

For a child of Walcott's disposition and education, growing up in the colonial Caribbean of the 1930s and 40s, it was perhaps inevitable that his imagination would be fired by those mythic figures of literature whose stories seemed particularly relevant to his own circumstances and situation. Certainly, from the evidence of his earliest surviving verses, the extent to which the authors and fictive characters of the classics had infiltrated his imagination is obvious. This is in some degree an expression of the colonial situation, in other ways it reflects Walcott's notion of a literary apprenticeship: 'as a young writer, he said, you just ravage and cannibalise everything'.[5] But beyond that urge to imitate, to find models of both style and substance, certain figures and stories seem to have spoken so immediately to his condition that they recur, modified, adapted, translated into very personal metaphors, over and over again. The most striking clusters of characters, which meld into the faces of a presence in the poetry, are to do with the personal, racial and historical condition of feeling and being cast away. The Odysseus figure deals particularly with the voyage, the quest for home, for a sense of roots, for a lost father/ land. The related Crusoe/ Friday figures focus on the idea and experience of the shipwreck on an island that must become home. The Odysseus story – worked and reworked – obviously continues to inspire him.

If the Crusoe figure in Walcott's work can be seen to grow out of the Odysseus figure, especially out of the turmoils of identity which beset the Odysseus of the early poems, the Crusoe persona, on the other hand, seems to have dominated his poetic imagination for a relatively short period. It focused his concerns at a time when he was trying to reconcile his seemingly contradictory ambitions to be true to his personal muse – writing private poems of inward exploration – and his sense of a kind of vocation to be the West Indian poet, the public voice of the society's culture, speaking out on topics of regional and international concern. Crusoe, although his story does serve to focus several of the poet's personal dilemmas at that time, is very much a consciously political, public construct, a voice for the situation of the Caribbean people making home from their shipwreck with the detritus of the good ship History scattered along the beach.

The Crusoe figure retains many of the universal resonances of the Odysseus metaphor – the concern with history, with exile, with memory – but he crucially grounds (beaches) the mythology in a distinctly Caribbean setting and introduces related concerns that are more parochial: the language debates, questions of race and isolation, the role of the writer in West Indian society, and so on. It is these areas I will consider here.

Walcott's appropriation of Crusoe begins in his assertion that, 'Crusoe is a figure from our schoolboy reading. He is a part of the mythology of every West Indian child.'[6] Indeed, Walcott was not the first West Indian poet to employ the Crusoe figure as a means of dramatising a personal response to a particularly Caribbean experience. Saint-John Perse, for example, whose work Walcott much admires, wrote a sequence entitled 'Images à Crusoe'[7] in the 1920s. Crusoe is not a simple mask for a West Indian poet to adopt, however. Is he castaway or coloniser? Can he be both? What is his relationship to Friday: master, friend, fellow castaway, all of those? Is he not always in awe of Friday, afraid of his prior claim on the island? Walcott drew the lineaments of his Crusoe in a lecture he gave at the University of the West Indies in Trinidad in 1965 entitled 'The Figure of Crusoe'. In that lecture Walcott argues that the poet's vision of the world should be like that of a 'true hermit', a character he defines by what he is not: neither 'naturalist', for whom, 'order is what is/change is its own law and nothing is shapeless,' nor 'cleric', for whom 'all that is shapeless must first be blest...' and who finds 'God's form' in the 'mosaic' of creation. For the hermit/poet on the other hand, 'All coheres/ both evidence and doubt, nature and faith' in a kind of perceptual frenzy. Walcott suggests that his own position as a poet in the West Indies in the 1950s and 60s felt like that of a hermit, a shunned outsider, at least in part because his activity as poet was conducted in that kind of frenzy, and yet there were so few in the society who understood or could imagine what he was about. In his lecture he tried to explain to his audience what that state of frenzy was like by likening it to the actions of a lonely man on a beach who has heaped a pile of dead bush twigs to make a bonfire.

> The bonfire may be purposeless or it may be a signal of his loneliness, his desperation, his isolation, his symbol of need for another. Or the bonfire may be lit from some atavistic need for contemplation. Fire mesmerises us. We dissolve in burning. The man sits before the fire, its glow warming his face, watching it leap, gesticulate and lessen and he keeps throwing twigs, dead thoughts, fragments

of memory, all the used parts of his life to keep his contemplation pure and bright. When he's tired and returns into himself, then he has performed some kind of sacrifice, some ritual.[8]

Walcott proceeded to read 'Crusoe's Journal' as an example of the poetry that is made in such a manner, in the contemplative frenzy of inspiration. The Crusoe/castaway figure that emerges in the poem is multifaceted, not simply Saint-John Perse's self-pitying exile but a protean mask with many voices. Walcott says: 'He is... Adam, Christopher Columbus, God, a beachcomber and his interpreter, Daniel Defoe.'[9] Walcott, then, is not simply taking a ready-made character and speaking through that voice, he is imaginatively entering the character and remaking him to his own ends. Later in 'The Figure of Crusoe' he says that although his Crusoe is not the Crusoe of Defoe and may seem 'for everyone else... an exaggeration and distortion' it was not until 'my imagination settled on that symbol that I understood what Yeats meant when he wrote: "Give a man a mask and he will talk the truth".'[10]

Perhaps the most significant truth Walcott's Crusoe voices – in terms of Walcott's overall concern with history – is his coming to terms with the psychic disruption of exile, a recognition of the trauma of those who feel, as he puts it in 'Laventille', that they 'left somewhere a life we never found'.[11] Throughout the castaway poems runs the idea of cultural amnesia, which is the nadir of human experience but also, even if it is hardly recognised, the point from which new growth must begin. Crusoe, washed ashore on a strange and seemingly hostile island, with nothing but desperation and a fundamentalist faith born out of that desperation to sustain him, makes a kind of Eden for himself. In that sense he is an 'emblem' for Caribbean endeavour.[12] Crusoe moves from the desolation of knowing himself lost on an island far from any shipping route, to loving the island as his first and only real home. As Walcott puts it in 'The Figure of Crusoe':

Crusoe's triumph lies in that despairing cry which he utters when a current takes his dugout canoe further and further away from the island that, like all of us up-rooted figures, he had made his home, and it is the cynical answer we must make to those critics who complain that there is nothing here, no art, no history, no architecture, by which they mean ruins; in short, idolisation, it is 'O happy desert!'[13]

However, in several of the Crusoe poems it is the desolation of that initial sense of isolation that is examined, the Adamic rebirth from amnesia can only begin once the desolation of arrival at that nadir has been endured. Although the Crusoe persona does not emerge until *The Castaway*, there are poems as early as the first self-published collection, *25 Poems*, that deal with that sense of being cast away, hence the conviction in the very early poem 'Travelogue' that 'these lands belong to no one but the luckless'.[14]

It is in 'Laventille' however that the force of the West Indian people's estrangement from their past is fully understood. The persona's feeling of being lost without Gods – having faith in neither the old gods of the African past nor the white man's, Christian, God – is a crucial element in the poem, but that sense of being abandoned derives from the notion of the castaway condition of the West Indian people. They are the 'luckless' people marooned on these islands between worlds, trapped in the mimic-man/Friday condition the poem describes:

> We left
> somewhere a life we never found,
>
> customs and gods that are not born again,
> some crib, some grille of light
> clanged shut on us in bondage, and withheld
>
> us from that world below us and beyond,
> and in its swaddling cerements we're still bound.[15]

Although the castaway experience is a particularly Caribbean theme, 'A Village Life' reads a wider resonance into the metaphor, suggesting that in a fundamental way all human beings carry this sense of themselves as castaways.[16] But to acknowledge the desperation of that 'natural loneliness' by losing the facade of normality, as the woman who is the focus of 'A Village Life' does, is to make oneself doubly castaway. And to be doubly castaway was, in another way, the state of the mulatto; in a world divided along colour lines, he is the ultimate outsider. This is a further aspect of the metaphor that Walcott has employed to confront a deep hurt in his own psyche; in more than a literary sense he felt himself the 'schizophrenic, wrenched by two styles'[17] who was only, ever, half-home.

The many-layered individual, regional and universal resonance of the Crusoe metaphor is clearly one of its attractions for Walcott, allowing him to consider large issues without ever 'losing/sight of the single human'[18] in the analysis. So the horrors of the Middle Passage and its castaway inheritance can be examined in terms of individual instances rather than in the easy slogans of so much protest and 'history' poetry. By considering the ordeal of one fictive castaway, we are implicitly directed to consider the wider implications of the castaway condition.

It is a logical development, then, when, in his third major collection, *The Gulf* he moves on from examining one man's personal alienation to a consideration of the fundamental stresses of human society. The image of the gulf begins in Walcott's quotation from *Robinson Crusoe* which is also the epigraph to 'Crusoe's Journal': 'Between me and thee is a great gulf fixed.' 'The Gulf' defines that distance in terms of both the separateness of even the closest lovers and the conflict between races and nations. But the obsession with man's fundamental isolation is perhaps most starkly drawn later in that volume, in the 'A Map of the Continent' section of 'Guyana' where Walcott contrasts the lives and world view of the blind but hyper-civilised Borges with that of the Amazonian Indian:

> The lexicographer in his cell records the life and death
> of books;
> the naked buck waits at the edge of the world.
> …
> Between the Rupununi and Borges,
> between the fallen pen-tip and the spearhead
> thunders, thickens and shimmers the one age of the world[19]

That isolation is a condition of man's being is a theme returned to again and again in the group of poems Walcott wrote about

America at this time. His own consciousness of being a stranger in a seemingly hostile environment – during his first visit to New York as a student he 'was a frightened cat in that grey city'[20] – is expressed again in terms of Crusoe's desperate longing for human contact, for home. In 'God Rest Ye Merry Gentlemen' the combination of loneliness and fear of racial attack recalls Crusoe's mixed feelings of joy and terror when, after many years alone on his island, he comes across a single human footstep in the sand. Reeling out of a New York bar into the dark December street the persona

> froze before the tracks
> of footprints bleeding on the virgin snow.
> I tracked them where they led across the street
> to the bright side [21]

With typical irony it is the barbarism of the white man that this black castaway Crusoe fears, just as Defoe's hero feared the stereotype of black savagery, the cannibal. Like Crusoe, Walcott's persona both desires human contact but fears the form it is likely to take.

Walcott's preoccupation with isolation, with man's 'natural loneliness' perhaps reflects his own experience of outsiderness, a condition which seemed to intensify as he became more and more committed to the role of the poet who remained in the West Indies, but was only emphasised, in fact, once he became a fortunate traveller, a self-appointed exile. It began, however, with a consciousness of being different in childhood; first by reason of his colour, then by his religion and again in terms of his class, he was set apart from the life of both the street and the country. He was almost compelled to explore and settle in the cave of the imagination that Crusoe has resort to. In 'What the Twilight Says: An Overture', the essay which forms a preface to his first collection of plays, *Dream on Monkey Mountain and Other Plays*, he describes that sensation of being excluded from the life of the 'black and poor' and the ambition it fired. He and his brother were watching a street parade:

Yet, like the long, applauded note, joy soared further from two pale children staring from their upstairs window, wanting to march with that ragged, barefooted crowd, but who could not because they were not black and poor, until for one of them, watching the shouting, limber congregation that difference became a sadness, that sadness rage, and that longing to share their lives' ambition.[22]

He felt himself isolated in another way too, isolated from the world of culture and art, feeling that real life went on elsewhere. In 'Crusoe's Journal', the relevance of the Crusoe story to that felt isolation is dramatised in the image of the 'one boy signalling at the sea's edge / though what he cried is lost.'[23] The boy waving out to sea, which is both his gaoler and his hope of escape, is trapped on an island which his colonised literary imagination views through the eyes of a stranger:

> Some noon-struck village, Choiseul, Canaries,
> with crocodile canoes,
> a savage settlement from Henty's novels,
> Marryat or R.L.S.[24]

and takes Crusoe's plight as a natural example. That in itself further embeds the metaphor, for in taking Crusoe as an example he adopts the pose of Friday who takes from the white master a 'style and voice, [that] make[s] his language ours'[25] and begins to see the world through the perspectives that the language carries. In 'Crusoe's Journal' Walcott is playing all those resonances and ironies against each other, the poet – a 'good Friday' in the linguistic sense if ever there was one – usurps and adapts the master's language and literary modes to satirise both the master and his own ambivalent position.

The poem 'The Castaway' provides a model of the process of poetic creation for such a poet, driven back into the cave of imagination and to his writing – 'publishing each day the newspaper of himself' – in order to keep a grasp on his 'sanity', albeit that the world he inhabits, because it is created in the kind of frenzy described in 'The Figure of Crusoe', is essentially a fiction, that 'loud world of his mind.' The sense of living in the mind, cast away from the ordinary discourses of the world, is a major element of the Crusoe metaphor in the poems in *The Castaway* collection.

At one level, it is the common creative experience of poets everywhere that their imaginative life conflicts with the norms and manners of the society in which they function. Arguing that the Crusoe experience was one common to all writers Walcott suggests that it is 'the despair of Crusoe... the despair of always being alone. That is our condition as writers'. Like the writer in 'Exile', their 'first indenture' is always to the Word. However, for West Indian writers of Walcott's generation, the despair has been intensified by the absolute alienation they have felt between their writing 'islands' and the kinds of lives, values, priorities that the societies they would nominate to be their audience had developed.

The Crusoe mask's function, Walcott argues in 'The Figure of Crusoe', is to get the poet past that double despair of isolation and alienation from his audience by going deeper into himself and finding the creative centre, the cave of the Muse as it were, Crusoe's cave. The isolation is in this sense creative in that it allows the poet access to that 'somewhere else' where 'the hermetic skill, that from earth's clay/shapes something without use,/and separate from itself'[26] – which is his poetry – can be exercised.

The Muse who claims his imagination puts him apart from 'all that I love'; it is Crusoe's condition, and the condition of being a poet; it is the condition of Van Gogh, Baudelaire, Dylan Thomas, Hart Crane, Harry Simmonds, Eric Roach – all figures whom Walcott admired – it is the Romantic artist's other life which comprehends the deepest isolation and failure but is also the means by which the poet might be saved from that despair.

'Mass Man' explores another angle on the alienation from his community that Walcott feels. Carnival, the supreme expression of a 'popular culture' unites the several races and classes of Trinidadian society in a shared celebration, a shared forgetting of their divisions and antagonisms, a cathartic frenzy of fantasy. The crowd are masked in costumes which reveal their fantasies of themselves – the timid clerk 'enters' a lion, Boysie – son of one of the most powerless nations on earth – plays Cleopatra. One of Carnival's arts is the art of escapism, a Bacchanal of forgetting. The poet, on the other hand, feels that he must not forget, must not engage in empty fantasies but must look behind and beyond the immediate sensation to the sources of a more lasting truth. So his response to the mocking invitation to join the masquerade: 'Oh God, child, you can't dance?' is to insist on his own kind of 'frenzy': 'my mania, my mania is a terrible calm' and to argue the role of the poet as neither the entertainer of the people who uncritically reinforces their prejudices, nor the simple patriot who celebrates their ways and beliefs without question, but as the conscience of the people, one who looks for the meaning behind the facade of the masking spectacle, hence:

> Upon your penitential morning
> some skull must rub its memory with ashes
> some mind must squat down howling in your dust
> some hand must crawl and recollect your rubbish
> someone must write your poems.[27]

That kind of poet is inevitably an outsider, one who observes the dance rather then loses himself in it. Though it constitutes his subject he is cast away from the common experience by the nature of his art. He is the pale child again, looking down on the black people's street parade. Yet though such isolation breeds despair he must cultivate it for it is only in such a condition that 'the intellect appraises/objects surely.'[28] That paradox only heightens the sense of being cast away; as Helen Vendler puts it, his destiny seems to be to inhabit 'an isolation that deepens with every word he writes – regardless of the multitudes by whom he is read.'[29]

A further aspect of the Crusoe metaphor, growing out of the castaway status of Walcott the poet, is the felt necessity to 'invent an appropriate language'[30] adequate to the natural and historical world in which he functions. The debates around the importance and significance of developing a language that can both accommodate the intellectual and technical demands of sophisticated poetry but which is at the same time clearly rooted in the experience and expression of the West Indian people has been a site of constant literary, educational and political battle. The Crusoe story, with Crusoe having to adapt his language first to accommodate the range of new experiences his island exile introduced and then in order to communicate with Friday, provides a clear metaphor for the poet's endeavour. The whole colonial relationship is imaged in the Crusoe-Friday story. Significantly it is not force of arms or recognition of superior technology, or even simple fear that cements the relative status within their relationship – master/slave, tutor/pupil, missionary/convert – but Crusoe's enforcing of his language on his slave.

Walcott has made much of the Crusoe/Friday relationship and the imposition of and accommodation to the colonial language. The psychology and cultural violence of the colonial experience for the 'saved' slaves is brilliantly revealed and the mentality of the civilising colonists satirised in his play *Pantomime*. The idea of a skit involving a role reversal, black Crusoe saving white Friday, seems hilarious to the white liberal hotel owner Trew until he actually begins to act it out.

> He comes across this naked white cannibal called Thursday, you know. And then look at what would happen. He would have to start to . . . well he'd have to, sorry,... This cannibal, who is a Christian, would have to start unlearning his Christianity. He would have to be taught... I mean... he'd have to be taught by this – African... that everything was wrong. That his civilisation, his culture, his whatever, was... *horrible*. Was all... wrong. Barbarous, I mean, you know. And Crusoe would then have to teach him things like you know about... Africa, his gods, patamba and so on...[31]

'Crusoe's Journal' is the poem which most intensely explores the interrelationship of the colonial/linguistic heritage and the West Indian's struggle for a language true to his inner history and experience. As we have already seen the poem establishes the relevance of the Crusoe story in terms of the poet's felt isolation, but it also develops the image of language as the agent of colonial domination:

> like Christofer he bears
> in speech mnemonic as a missionaries
> the Word to savages,
> its shape an earthen, water-bearing vessel's
> whose sprinkling alters us
> into good Fridays who recite His praise.

But, the poem goes on, the adaptation of that language is the means by which that domination can be broken:

> parroting our masters'
> Style and voice, we make his language ours.

When, having come to acknowledge the island as home – 'O happy desert' – 'Friday's progeny' take the detritus of Crusoe's occupation, his journals, and 'learn to shape from them, where nothing was/the language of a race',[32] they are putting the words into the New World Adam's mouth.

Although Walcott discards the Crusoe mask as such after *The Castaway* poems, a 'Crusoesque' perspective on events lingers, as we have seen, in *The Gulf*, and echoes from time to time throughout the later poetry. The image of the 'good man', the complete man, who is free and true and uncompromised by crude desire for things which are not natural to his world, emerges in the poetry with the figure of the New World Adam who represents the positive side of the Crusoe experience, the new man emerging from the ashes of desolation that the middle passage and shipwreck engendered. Crusoe is a bridge between the lost Odysseus and that 'found' New World Adam.

Before Adam emerges however there is one further face of Crusoe that can be said to know that Adamic experience before it occurs in the poems. It is the face of the old man, the old poet, looking out to sea, contemplating his life and his essential loneliness. As Walcott describes him in 'The Figure of Crusoe' he seems to have resigned himself not only to abandonment, but to discomfort. He seems bored with the idea of salvation, because he has resolved his own. He has reached, as he:

> sits there on his sand dune with parasol and dog, an anonymity so complete that it is past despair.[33]

That is the face of the young poet's ambition in 'To Return to the Trees'

> a gnarled poet
> bearded like the whirlwind

his metres like thunder ?

...

going under the sand
with this language, slowly[34]

In 'XXXIV' of *Midsummer,* that face is given a name that returns us to the origins of the exile/castaway metaphor in Walcott's imagination. The 'salt grizzled gaffer' perched on 'the stern of an empty pirogue' is Homer, the blind poet/myth-maker of the old world Mediterranean. Like any poet of an archipelago, he had 'the sea's silence for prologue and epilogue'[35] and is, by implication, both the father of Crusoe in his role as the creator of a new language that will define a nation and, in the person of Walcott – who rides 'the great hexameters' that 'finish up as Caribbean surf'[36] – the contemporary questing-poet blind to the distractions of the material world that makes him outcast, attending only to his inner ear: 'the loud world in his mind'. Homer, claimed as an ancestor by the New World/ Mediterranean analogy that Walcott explores, as a contemporary in the 'timeless yet habitable moment', is a synthesis of the roles of Odysseus and Crusoe in Walcott's imagination, a symbol of both public and personal honour, the voice of both conscience and duty. His fate anticipates both the contemporary condition of the Caribbean people and the situation of the poet who would understand and chronicle it.

'WRITIN IN LIGHT': ORALITY THRU TYPOGRAPHY, KAMAU BRATHWAITE'S SYCORAX VIDEO STYLE

This essay is developed from a presentation given at the round-table conference 'The Pressures of the Text: Orality, Texts and the Telling of Tales', held in the Centre of West African Studies, University of Birminghan in 1993.

This essay has evolved from what seemed to me, at least initially, a paradox: that Kamau Brathwaite should assert that his discovery of the word processor's hi-tech typographical possibilities was an agent for the development and presentation as text of the essentially oral 'nation language' of the Caribbean. I raised this issue with Brathwaite when I interviewed him in Jamaica in 1988, in a discussion about *X/Self*, the volume in which his poem 'X/Self's Xth Letters from the Thirteen Provinces' appears, which included the lines

(I'm)
learnin prosperos linguage &

ting

not fe dem/ not fe dem
de way caliban

done

but fe we
fe-a-we

for not one a we should responsible if prospero get curse
wid im own

curser'

……………

yet a sittin down here in front a dis stone
face/eeee

lectrical mallet into me
fist

chipp/in dis poem outa dis tablet
chiss/ellin darkness writin in light [1]

I had interpreted these passages, playing with the language of
the word processor and punning between the codes of his poetic
nation language and that hi-tech jargon as drawing attention to
a kind of conflict between technology and the history from which
nation language emerged. But no, Brathwaite said,

> Quite the opposite. What I was saying there was that technology
> makes nation-language *easier* ... the 'global village' concept, 'the
> message is the medium' and all that ... The poem was saying that
> the computer has made it much easier for the illiterate, the Caliban,
> actually to get himself visible ... Because the computer does it all
> for you. You don't have to be able to type, you can make mistakes
> and correct them or leave them, *you can see what you hear*. When I
> said 'writin in light', that is the main thing about it – the miracle
> of that electronic screen means that the spoken word can become
> visible in a way that it cannot become visible in the typewriter
> where you have to erase physically...The computer has moved
> us away from scripture into some other dimension which is 'writin
> in light'. It is really nearer to the oral tradition than the typewriter
> is. The typewriter is an extension of the pen. The computer is
> getting as close as you can to the spoken word.[2]

I want to explore, briefly, the evidence for that assertion and
to look at the ways Brathwaite's early work, both as cultural historian,
critic and poet, anticipated that concern with the representation
of an oral language as text and with the ways text could be arranged
to suggest the enunciation of the language. I would hope, then,

to trace the logic of the ways his subsequent work has developed towards such a visually distinctive presentation of – and experimentation with – language, particularly in terms of the 'Sycorax video style' he has evolved through his collections *Middle Passages, Dreamstories* and *Barabajan Poems*.[3]

The date of *Middle Passages* publication was significant – 1992 being the 500th anniversary of Columbus's entry into the/his New World. Kamau Brathwaite is an academic historian whose work has focused on the ramifications and distortions engendered by that 'discovery'. His historical research has always informed his poetry, indeed the two great trilogies for which he is best known in the literary world – *The Arrivants* and *Ancestors*[4]– represent his engagement with the human effects and issues of that brutal history. His historical imagination, as mediated through his poetry, is informed by his experience of living for many years in Ghana, and, on his return to the Caribbean, by his recognition of the submerged presence of Africa in the cultures of the region. Much of his work has been a kind of reclamation of that African inheritance, a reclamation that has inevitably involved a process of challenge and confrontation with the elements of the mercantilist/colonial culture which overlaid and often literally oppressed the African survivals.

Just as he insisted in his scrupulous, but also controversial, study, *The Development of Creole Society in Jamaica 1770 –1820,* that the slaves' most important act of resistance to the slavers' attempts at domination was through their refusal, adaptation and appropriation of the slavers' language,

> It was in language that the slave was perhaps most successfully imprisoned by his masters; and it was in his (mis-) use of it that he perhaps most effectively rebelled. Within the folk tradition, language was (and is) a creative act in itself; the word was held to contain a secret power...[5]

So Brathwaite's most fundamental challenge to the cultural status quo has been to the language of cultural domination itself, and to its most privileged form, as book-bound, grammar-bound script. He has consistently championed the use of non-standard vocabularies, resisting the implicit pejoratives of 'dialect' and even 'creole' as terms to describe the languages that Caribbean people speak, instead coining and asserting the appropriateness of the term 'nation language' to reflect both the status of that spoken tongue and the fact of the differences between the languages of the various nations of the West Indies.[6]

Brathwaite has argued, in his *History of the Voice*, for the cultural and psychological importance of nation language at many levels. Evolving from the very history of the places where it is spoken, it enables speech, he argues, where the dominant language cannot cope with the local referents:

> ...the models are all there for the falling of snow ...(but we haven't got the syllables, the syllabic intelligence, to describe the hurricane, which is our own experience... the hurricane does not roar in pentameters.[7]

In his lecture 'Caribbean Culture: Two Paradigms' published in 1983 but originating somewhat earlier, Brathwaite described his increasing frustrations with the resources of English in his quest to make an authentically Caribbean poetry, true to his experience and feeling,

> In addition to the natural poet's desire to transplode words, I find increasingly, as the struggle to express our particular experience in the general vocabulary of an admittedly generous language, that one has to create words to fit our particular and peculiar experience. It is the crisis of conscious Caliban faced with Prospero's thesaurus.[8]

Finding a argot for that which cannot be said in the 'official' language is clearly potentially subversive of that language's dominance and it is that subversive quality that Brathwaite fundamentally values. Nation language represents, he argues in *History of the Voice*, the enunciation of 'the African aspect of our New World/Caribbean heritage'[9] which must inevitably be at odds with the linguistic and grammatical as well as the cultural and ideological status quo. He argues too that nation language is an essentially oral/aural medium, its orality another aspect of its challenge to the dominance of a text-inflected English:

> [Nation language] exists not in the dictionary but in the tradition
> of the spoken word. It is based as much on sound as it is on song.
> *That is to say, the noise that it makes is part of its meaning,* and if you
> ignore the noise (or what you would think of as noise shall I say)
> then you lose part of the meaning. When it is written, you lose
> the sound of the noise and therefore you lose part of the meaning.
> [my emphasis][10]

But this does not mean that Brathwaite would limit a contemporary
Caribbean word-culture to its oral dimension alone; as poet,
publisher, historian, editor, essayist, critic, bibliographer and archivist
he has always been very much engaged with texts, with the printed
forms of language, and indeed argues the important place of texts
alongside the oral word-culture.[11] What his work more and more
reflects is his quest to find ways in which texts can be made to
accommodate the 'noise' of nation language, to represent the 'new
shapes and consciousness of ourselves'[12] which the use of that
language allows. It is interesting to note that even in the early
nineteen-eighties, when *History of the Voice* was being constructed,
he was beginning to think in terms of the computer in the way
he described that quest, speaking of trying to catch

> 'the actual rhythms and syllables, *the very software,* in a way,
> of the language.'[my emphasis][13]

There is evidence of this concern right through his work. His
use of a range of voices across the continuum of creole registers
in *The Arrivants*, privileging the peasant voice in crucial poems
like 'The Dust' – which has become now a classic expression of
West Indian consciousness – is in part an aspect of Brathwaite's
attempt to break, and break away from, the cultural constraints
of English. Brathwaite refers back to 'The Dust' in 'X/Self's Xth
Letters from the Thirteen Provinces'. Here the ending of the
later poem connects with the persona's somewhat frightened,
suspicious query about the sense of power this new technology
allows him: why is/ dat?//what it/ mean? This echoes the god-
fearing, awestruck questioning of the peasant woman's voice at
the end of 'The Dust', struggling to find a language to confront
the unknown. It is an intriguing echo, the poet perhaps inviting

his readers to see the connection between the quest for a language and the 'solution' the computer offers..? Interestingly, he omits that ending echo in 'Letter Sycorax', the revised version of 'X/ Self's Xth Letters from the Thirteen Provinces', which appears in *Middle Passages*.

Alongside that concern to allow more voices to be heard there has been an ever-present concern with orthography, as if the very technology of printing was loaded against the enunciation of the new/old/evolving oral-now-literary languages he wants to use. From his earliest collections Brathwaite has experimented with layouts and with syntactical 'calibanisms' as he calls them – spelling, breaking, spacing, shaping words in ways that dislocate them from their familiar associations and meanings but more importantly allowing nuances, echoes, puns, rhymes and particular kinds of music 'out' of the language that history has imposed on him to express his experience and vision.

That cultural imperative underpins both modernist and formalist dimensions to this linguistic experimentation. Brathwaite has acknowledged the influence of T.S. Eliot and Ezra Pound on his early attitudes to poetry. There was a cultural connection in the sense that both Eliot and Pound were 'colonials' who took on the poetic establishment, rebellious figures who wanted to make a poetry appropriate to their times and circumstances. As Donald Hall has observed, for them, breaking away from a colonial model, 'eccentricity – formal and spiritual – was an escape from Englishness.'[14] Pound's famous determination to, 'make it new', in a language which bore 'the taste of men's mouths' has obvious resonance for Brathwaite's project. Eliot's influence is particularly apparent in terms of his experiments with voices. Brathwaite has said that Eliot's major contribution to the development of Caribbean literature was via his validation of 'the speaking voice, the conversational tone.'[15] Eliot's interest in jazz and his adaptation of some jazz-like techniques also seems to have been a significant influence on Brathwaite's approach to the structure of his work and in terms of the freeing up of Brathwaite's poetic language. And it seems clear that Eliot's example in 'The Wasteland' serves as an important referent for Brathwaite, as he explored strategies for dislocating the reader from his/her expectations by mixing languages and scripts within the texts of his poems, by laying the poem out in unusual ways and using devices like the list or the repetition of phonetic/rhythmic sounds.

Eliot's experimentation was validated by Pound, who had himself learnt from William Morris and what Jerome McGann calls 'the late nineteenth century Renaissance of Printing' that 'the physical presentation of texts was a fundamental feature of their expressiveness.'[16] The resonances of the rediscovery spread wide, including, interestingly, some of the most important work of the Harlem Renaissance in the 1920s. McGann remarks that the radical/racial ideas and attitudes embodied in early works by Langston Hughes, Countee Cullen and in Alain Locke's anthology *The New Negro* are reinforced or reflected in the typographical and spacial manipulations of the text, which are recognised as significant 'resources for poetic effects.'[17] Brathwaite's experiments with the formatting of words on the page as a means of indicating the particular nuances of spoken voices perhaps owes as much to the work of another American poet of that period, Louis Zukofsky, who argued that "if print and the arrangement of it will help tell how the voice should sound,'[18] then typography was clearly a legitimate area of concern for the poet.

Although it may seem radical, such typographic foregrounding has a long history.[19] In a recent study, the linguist Willie Van Peer traces such devices back to Greek Bucolic poetry in the fourth century BC and cites examples through time, right up to the concrete poets of the 1970s and 80s. The reasons why individual poets in this tradition have chosen to draw attention to visual aspects of their texts obviously varies, but Van Peer's general assertion is that the conventional distinguishing characteristics of poetry as text (i.e. its layout on the page, its use of white space around lines and stanzas, its use of capital letters at the beginning of lines whether or not that word was the beginning of a sentence, etc.) in fact derive from poetry's roots in an oral tradition which was 'gradually reconstituted ... with a more predominantly visual character'.[20] One thing that poets who have deviated from that 'standard' layout and usage of typography have done is to draw attention back to the implicit signalling of orality by the textual 'surface' of the poem-on-the-page and then to have emphasised aspects of that oral presence by their particular breaking of the conventions in terms of the positioning of the text on the page, line endings, word spacing, type size, italicisation, etc.

Certainly that reorienting/re-oraling of the text has been a crucial aspect of Brathwaite's practice, but his motivations have been historical and cultural rather than primarily formalist or linguistic. His typographical experimentation has always been linked to his sense of the English language's complicity – perhaps especially the language-as-text's complicity – in the making of that history which so dominates his imagination and his poetry. Indeed, one of the things that distinguishes Brathwaite's experiments from the work of the contemporary concrete/sound poets[21] is that for those artists, as Berjouhi Bowler remarks in her book *The Word as Image*, the visual effect is, if not all, it is certainly their paramount concern. What they are interested in is the idea that:

> by disassociating the word from its usual setting, breaking it down to syllables, or even by giving us the merest reminiscence of a word, (they) make us perceive language spoken or written in a way we had not done before...

This is certainly part, but only part, of what Brathwaite's experiments are about; for the concrete poets the new word-images they construct '... want nothing to do with personality, psychology or biography. It is even removed from history.'[22]

That is very different from Brathwaite's purpose, in his experiments with the arrangement of words on the page, which has been rather to construct a language that *enables* the expression of personality, psychology and biography, and while he may wish to make a language able to shuck off the cultural baggage of its received history, he also very much wants that new language to express his alternative view of history.

Although the calibanisms, the mutations and amputations of the standard language, the unusual line breaks and layouts, etc. were evident in his work from *Rights of Passage*[23] and had been becoming more pronounced as his work progressed, in *Middle*

Passages (1992) that typographic foregrounding seems to have reached a new level in terms of the challenge to grammatical and orthographic orthodoxy. A note among the publication and copyright details announces that 'the text is based on the Sycorax video style being developed by Kamau Brathwaite' and the book employs a variety of fonts, calligraphies and symbols, varying in scale from the miniscule to the massive, both within and between poems. The collection re-works and re-contextualises several of Brathwaite's earlier poems – as in a kind of jazz suite – and it is particularly interesting, in terms of the focus of this paper, to compare the version of 'X/Self's Xth Letters from the Thirteen Provinces' that appears in the volume *X/Self* with the one that appears in *Middle Passages* as 'Letter Sycorax' and the further version that appears in Ancestors as 'X/Self's Letters from the thirteen provinces'.

Apart from a few changes in spelling – which I suspect may be corrections of the OUP editors' earlier 'corrections', i.e. 'reminton' in 'Letter Sycorax' for 'remmington' in the earlier version, in terms of the literary/linguistic content – the actual words of the poem – there is very little change between the first and second versions of the poem until near the very end of the piece. Then the image of the displaced Africans' journey as one 'perpetual / plantation' treadmill experience, as it is simply stated in the earlier version, is expanded and opened out. By the third version in Ancestors there is a visual/aural enactment-in-sound of that experience:

& how. evva yu
runnin up runnin up runnin up
it still

dung
dung
dung
dung

like de
sea

and with a catalogue of the names and titles of those implicated
in that seemingly endless decline, like:

> grannmaster sorrygent doe
> & de brann new imperial corporals
> smilin of cordite & leather strap-

> nel [24]

Finally, as I remarked above, the ending of the later version
of the poem is changed by the omission of that echo back to
'The Dust' that is woven into the conclusion of 'X/Self's Xth
Letters from the Thirteen Provinces' to become a more affirmative
– if equally problematic statement in terms of affixing meaning
– '& / mamma!'. Leaving the textual changes and the effect of
the ending aside, the main difference between the two versions
of the poem is in their layout and their use of typographic emphasis
like the italicizing of many of the words at the beginning of the
poem, the use of bold rather than standard typefaces in certain
places and the replacing of the conventional lower case 'x' in
'X/Self's Xth Letters from the Thirteen Provinces' with the large
and visually intrusive 'X' symbol from another font altogether
in 'Letter Sycorax'. The effects of those changes are interesting.
The major layout change, which does change the whole appearance
of the poem on the page, is the shift from a conventional left
justification of the text in the OUP *X/Self* version, to the centring
of each line in 'Letter Sycorax'. That change somehow makes
the poem much easier to actually *read*, perhaps because the layout
no longer asks us to read the text as conventional English poem,
with all the unconscious but powerful associations/expectations
of line endings, rhythmic patterns and patterns of narrative that
the recognition of that basic shape-on-the-page imposes on our
reading. Laid out as it is in the latter version, the poem visually
rejects those conventions; it no longer signals as the broken couplets
of an English poem but signals that this text will ask something
else of its reader. In effect, the Sycorax video style frees both
the text and the reader from those 'interference' effects that carry
over from those cultural expectations triggered by the essentially

traditional format of the original version and allow the rhythmic patterns and linguistic effects to make their own music. We do not unconsciously read this text against our expectations of the ways poems conventionally work. In his provocative book, *Poetry as Discourse*, the critic Anthony Easthope is at pains to establish the significance of such expectations, arguing that poetic forms are never ideologically neutral but signify particular, historic associations and allegiances on the part of the user which the reader will almost invariably pick up.[25] By arranging his text in the way he does in 'Letter Sycorax' Brathwaite is retaining the distinction between poetry and prose that the conventional poetic layout claims but distancing his text from the cultural associations of that layout.

Laid out under the Sycorax video style, the poem is visually much more distinctive than in the earlier version and recalls Brathwaite's remark that what he is trying to do with these new layouts is create 'word sculpture on the page, word sculpture in the ear',[26] creations which inevitably require a different set of aesthetic criteria for their appreciation than would be applied to traditional poems. But more significantly, as that remark makes clear, the layouts also serve to direct would-be reader/speakers of the poems into an understanding of the ways he intends the music of the poems to move, to be heard. As he said in the interview referred to earlier, the layout of the poems is 'part of my own concept of how they should sound and a hopeful aid to another reader'. Brathwaite's poems – while they repay careful scrutiny as texts – do *live* in their enunciation. To know a Brathwaite poem only from its text on the page, and then to see/hear him read it, is to understand how much of his work relies on the power of the spoken word. Brathwaite himself regards this as a very important aspect of his work. Asked about the importance of performance in that same interview, he remarked:

> I think there is always a little confusion about my work in that I *don't* perform at all, its my poetry that does it, I hardly move my body. And I think that the critics ought to begin to look at that because it's something that I think is my major contribution, if any, to the whole development of our poetry – that the words

on the page have a metaphorical life of their own. I do not depend upon walking up and down on the stage and doing things. People have the impression that I'm performing when in fact they are actually dealing with poetry as they ought to, that is, the poetry is singing in their ears.[27]

Understanding then that performance, in relation to Brathwaite's work, means enunciation, there is a sense in which the texts of his poems are 'scripts for performance'. That is a phrase which has some resonance in the discussion of West Indian poetry – a phrase which Louise Bennett, or at least her critical champions, objected to when it was applied to her work by some well-meaning TLS reviewer, because it seemed to limit her to an oral arena and deny her poetry the status accorded to 'real' literature. In Brathwaite's case, however, given his statements above, it is perhaps possible to read such a judgement as a *liberation* of the poem from the limitations of the conventions of text-bound 'literature'. So the world turns! Brathwaite has used versions of the Sycorax video format in the three other books that have appeared since *Middle Passages: The Zea-Mexican Diary, Barabajan Poems,* and *DreamStories.*[28] Although the *Zea-Mexican Diary* employs a larger than conventional typeface and makes use of some of the strategies for emphasis that the other texts employ in order to stress particular emotional changes in the lamentation/celebration that is the substance of the diary, it is essentially a conventional prose narrative and the typographical effects are minimized.[29] By contrast, the *DreamStories* couldn't be more unconventional either intrinsically, as narratives, or in the ways that they are laid out on the page in the Longman edition. As Gordon Rohlehr observes in his introduction to the collection, the devices of the Sycorax video style:

> create an arbitrariness in the appearance of the text, corresponding to the arbitrariness of the different dream worlds of these stories.[30]

The text is full of calibanisms and perverse punctuation marks which jar and disrupt the conventional flow of the narrative and Brathwaite employs all the devices of emphasis mentioned above, particularly in terms of varying the scale of the letter forms within and between words and being aware of the white space of the page to create the DreamStory effect. Part of that effect is to blur the divide between the visual-verbal language of dream as it is experienced and the capture/re-creation of that experience *as text* that might assist the re-enactment of the experience by the 'reader' as sound and (in)sight. The analogy seems to me to be with a musical score, particularly the scores of some contemporary composers who are trying to break new musical ground, in that the score is made of symbols that can be read and coded instructions that can be followed, so that practised readers can 'play' the music in their heads from the printed score, but the music only really fulfils its potential/ becomes itself in its performance. Similarly, the Sycorax video texts demand enunciation or at least a kind of active engagement on the part of the reader beyond the 'naturalised' process of silent reading or study. In a note to the story 'Dream Chad', Brathwaite refers to the story as it is written in light, in the word processor, as 'oratory'. The music analogy is perhaps better expressed, knowing Brathwaite's own taste in music and the experiments he has done throughout his career with jazz, if we think of the Sycorax video style as the *enjazzment* of the literary process, so that these stories become jazz texts.

The *DreamStories* text, as it appears in the Longman edition, while it may give the illusion of 'arbitrariness' is in fact far from arbitrary and – although it did not end up quite as Brathwaite originally envisaged it – much wrangling and hand-wringing was involved in the production of the book, even to get it as close as it is in this edition to his original idea. Indeed the author spent an entire summer re-formatting the text, as the best version the publisher could make – by reducing the scale of Brathwaite's original typescript to match the format of the series in which the book appears – did not meet Brathwaite's requirements in terms of the text's appearance and the aesthetic effects it generated.[31]

Given that Brathwaite could effectively act as publisher as well as author of the text, *Barabajan Poems*, published by Savacou North in 1994, represents the first opportunity to fully utilise the Sycorax video style format. The book is a mammoth tome, over 400 A4 pages, and utilises all the graphic potential of the word-processor's manipulation of printed language. The book is an expanded version of the 12th Sir Winston Scott Memorial lecture given in Barbados in 1987. It is, in effect, a kind of autobiography, a reprise of the ways in which Brathwaite's poetry has engaged with Barbados, its landscape, history and people over the course of his career. *Barabajan Poems* explores Brathwaite's relationship to earlier writers and his view of the potential for a flowering of Bajan consciousness in literature. The text is laid out and shaped according to the particular effects Brathwaite is trying to achieve, from a more or less conventional prose layout for the passages that stay close to the text of the lecture, through the by now characteristic calibanisms and use of different typefaces, interspersed with graphic devices like arrows, boxes and clip-art histograms within the texture of the piece, through to whole pages of poems in which the text is centred and very large pitch letter forms are used, so that on several pages there are only a dozen or so words. One purpose of the large type texts, centred in a field of white paper, is to lend a particular importance to the words thus emphasised, and one whole section of the book in which that technique is used is devoted to Bajan proverbs and 'small-ilann saying(s)' like

And then there is the great small-ilann

saying

sea

doan have no

BACKDOOR

Common speech, everyday language, ordinary usage is here made extraordinary by the manner of its presentation as text. The Sycorax layouts also develop on the effect observed in 'Letter Sycorax', above, of easing, directing and enabling the transition from text to speech. More generally, the Sycorax layouts challenge the readerly presumptions inscribed into traditional/conventional texts, but as the *Barabajan Poems* project is essentially an academic intervention, the overall shape of that academic discourse places some limits on the appropriate application of the Sycorax video style.

So we must wait for the appearance of a new book of new poems/stories, composed and conceived in the new format rather than translated up into it as most of the poems in *Middle Passages* and *Barabajan Poems* were, and which is also designed/published according to Brathwaite's specifications rather than reduced by the conventions/demands of a publishing house as *DreamStories* was, before we can fully measure the impact of the Sycorax video style. However, if we accept that the Caribbean isles are indeed 'full of noises' which formal, traditional English-as-text cannot adequately represent, it is clear that in the process of resisting the conventional pressures of the text in order to give voice to the noise of nation language on the page, Brathwaite's writin-in-light Sycorax video style is a logical development of his own creative practice. It also represents an important step on the road Caribbean poets have been treading – certainly since Claude McKay – towards finding a means of accommodating the language of life as it is sounded in the Caribbean and the life of letters as they are printed on the page.

POSTSCRIPT TO 'WRITIN' IN LIGHT':
'TIDALECTICS OF THE WORD'

Notes for a contribution to the panel discussion 'Tidalectics of the Word' at 'The Second Conference on Caribbean Culture to honour Kamau Brathwaite: Griot, Poet, Historian'. University of the West Indies, Jamaica, January 2002.

1. Thinking about the title of this panel – 'Tidalectics of the Word'[1] and the 'tidalectics' metaphor I was remembering the low tide – as it probably seemed to Kamau – of the kinds of carping and negative critical response that much of his early work received in some quarters and which persisted – he certainly felt – for many years, even on this campus. By comparison, listening now to the flood of praise-song and celebration which has been – appropriately enough – the tone of just about everything said about his work in this conference, this might seem like the high watermark, as it were, of critical appreciation of his creative project.

2. But who are *we*, who find and take the time to read, and listen and reread, to explore nuance and context, to annotate with the care and attention of the 'professional' enthusiast. We are in a sense the 'converted', who accept and embrace Brathwaite's ideas and literary strategies pretty much without hesitation, ascribing 'difficulties' in the texts or our engagement with them as our problems, that we need to solve by yet more careful reading and contextualisation. But perhaps we needed a bit more of a critical edge, perhaps we needed to hear some more sceptical voices, asking less reverential questions?

3. Don't get me wrong, I am here as part of that mood of honouring and celebration too, but I do think that as the tide of our enthusiasm

210

in this gathering ebbs we will see that some of our certainties seem more problematic than they have here. For while it is clear that Brathwaite's work speaks to a broad and diverse public, there are still many – in the Caribbean and elsewhere – who are not so convinced of – and by – some of the literary and linguistic strategies that he has developed and employed in his more recent work, and particularly in the Sycorax video style publications of the last decade or so. It has seemed to me, listening to the papers, that there were several occasions when 'the other side of the story' might have been told to colour and at least nuance our understanding of issues, but I want to focus on just one cluster around the question of accessibility and audience, and the philosophy of a poetry that is not only about – but also for – a pan-Caribbean/pan-African community.

4. Brathwaite's early texts have proved to be very accessible to a broad popular audience – certainly a non-literary and even a non-literate audience when they are performed. The language and concerns of the poems in the books that make up *The Arrivants* spoke to – and indeed helped form – the mood of the times in which they were published. The impact of poems like 'The Dust', 'Rites', 'Ogun', 'The Emigrants', 'South', 'Tizzic' etc. reached out far from the classroom and the literary journals, especially when the poet read them aloud at public events. The power and authority of those poems derived, to some considerable extent, from the sense we had that these were genuinely popular works which connected with West Indian society in ways that hardly any other literary works had achieved.

5. Kamau's recent work, particularly since the development of the Sycorax video style, seems – as text – to be much less accessible to that popular, non-scholarly audience, even though the logic of the evolution of Sycorax is unarguable, developing from the ideas first laid out in *The History of the Voice*.[2] The effect of the Sycorax layouts and devices, however, has been to produce texts which many former and would-be readers have found difficult and obscure, even turning them away from the poet and the poetry in disappointment. (I have only anecdotal evidence for this assertion,

211

but it derives from my experience teaching across three continents, and in the general discussion one has over time with interested 'general readers') So one question to explore which hasn't really been examined in this conference is 'who now reads – who *can* read – Brathwaite?'

6. We have an irony here. Here was a poet who came to prominence partly in response to a wide spread feeling that the 'traditional' literature that had been on offer to West Indian readers was inaccessible and irrelevant in many ways, who produced, in *The Arrivants,* a foundation text for a counter-literature that would be from and of their world, speaking to them in a language they both recognised and understood. Now that same poet is producing poems which – while still and indeed perhaps more intensely of and for that audience in an intellectual sense – are yet generally perceived to be inaccessible in terms of their style or their presentation *as text.*

7. But while that situation, in as far as anyone else recognises it as being essentially true, raises many questions for the poet, it also raises questions around the role of the critic and 'friends' of these texts. How do *we* help to make them more accessible – other than by offering our own diverse readings – how *do* we read a page of text in *Barabajan Poems*?[3] What do the graphic symbols *mean*, what is the significance of the white space or the shifts of font or point size? I don't know that anyone has really tackled this yet, or that Kamau has offered us a key.

8. I think that situation also feeds into some of the questions around publishing and the dissemination of Brathwaite's later work that were discussed in one of the panels at the conference yesterday. Should the author compromise his vision to accommodate either the laziness of possible readers or the dictates of crass commercial publishers? No, of course not, but while it's easy to condemn publishers, the practical realities of publishing do need to be understood in terms of costs, sales, distribution systems etc.

9. Wearing my *Series Editor* hat, perhaps I should tell the 'other side of the story' of the Longman edition of *Dream Stories,*[4] at

212

least to say that in publishing terms it was extremely problematic.

10. And who, other than the dedicated and/or subsidised academic could afford to buy *Barabajan Poems*, especially in the Caribbean or African context?

11. For myself I don't really understand why the Sycorax video poems need to be 'reduced to text' as the linguists say about (other) oral languages. If it is a video style then its natural medium, it seems to me, is 'video' or at least the internet/computer screen, where its full impact and possibilities can be explored, and some of the frustrations of the printed texts avoided.

12. I go back to my interview with Kamau in 1988, 'Writin' in Light' (published in *Kyk-over-al*, 1989) when he spoke passionately about the potential of the word processor/computer to undermine the cultural imperialism of 'the book' (See quotation 2 of main essay.)

13. It seems to me that if these poems are writings 'in light' then they are best read 'in light' too. That media seems to offer all sorts of other possibilities of a different sort of accessibility.[5]

14. But then we come back again to the question 'accessible to whom?' To delve back into the forests of structuralism – which Kamau calls up in his analysis of the burden of cultural imperialism implicit in the shape of a sonnet on the printed page – we have to ask, whom, by its formal characteristics, does the *Barabajan Poems* text – or even screen-shot – nominate as its primary or intended audience? And whom does it exclude? And how much, if at all, should the poet – or the critic – care?

15. That's my carping done.

16. As I say I raise these issues not in the spirit of one who wants to spoil the party, but as an aspect of the 'tidalectics of the word' and in the belief that *honouring* means more than simply praising but involves being engaged in constructive criticism and dialogue – which lesson, in fact, is what I take most from Kamau's example, over thirty years of engagement with him and with his work.

CELEBRATION SONGS: THE POETRY OF JAMES BERRY

This essay developed out of an address given at the 'Celebration Song' Symposium – held in honour of James Berry's work and to celebrate the award of his OBE at the Horticultural Halls, London, in 1994.

It is possible to represent or understand the experience forever evoked by that now famous image of the S.S. Empire Windrush docking at Tilbury in 1948 in various ways, positive or negative, creative or destructive. One could read it as representing a voyage of discovery offering real opportunities for personal and material enrichment to those West Indians who opted, in Louise Bennett's words, to 'go a foreign/ seek yu fortune', or one could see it as just an extension of the 'Middle Passage' with the migrants still merely economic cogs in the Imperial machine. In truth, of course, the actual experience of just about everyone who came, literally or metaphorically, on that Windrush voyage from the Caribbean to Britain has been a mixture of the positive and the negative. There has certainly been much disappointment, reflected in the pervading sense of having been betrayed by the supposed Mother country. The racism, the exploitation, the appalling ignorance of the realities of Imperial history on the part of British people, the sense of loss and isolation and rootlessness – all these are well chronicled and must be a part of any account of what it has meant to be a West Indian in Britain through the second half of the 20th century. But the other side of that story; the excitement of 'leaving', of escaping the constraints of small island society into a space of possibilities, and the challenge of making a life, intellectual as well as material, in a new place despite those social and racial barriers... that side of the story features much less prominently in the literature of exile and accommodation that is the migrant theme in West Indian writing. It is an important element in Sam Selvon's *The Lonely Londoners* ; the sense of light as well as darkness in his tall tales is in part what convinces contemporary readers of the 'truth' of those novels of 'making life' in the early 50s. But the chroniclers of that experience have, on the whole, concentrated on giving voice to the hassle, the injustice and the pain of the process of claiming that multicultural space in Britain.

One of the things that distinguishes James Berry's work from that of other writers who began to write about the experience of 'settling in' – to use a pretty euphemism – and from most of the Caribbean-heritage poets who have come to prominence in Britain through the last two decades, is its essential quality of celebration. It is a celebration tempered by a consciousness of all in West Indian history and the migrant experience that would defy celebration, but his urge to find value and sometimes joy in both the remembered life of his rural Jamaican childhood and in his sojourn as a 'bluefoot traveller' in Britain through the last fifty years, is the real motive force of his work. It is important to qualify what I mean by this 'quality of celebration'. I do not mean to suggest that he goes in for simplistic praise songs, nor that he romanticises either the rural struggle to survive in colonial Jamaica or the bleakness of those early encounters with an unwelcoming Britain, but rather that his instinct is to recognise the possibility in situations rather than to settle for the complaint or the self-righteous, self-pitying expression of anger or protest. Berry celebrates in the same way that Chinua Achebe argues that he celebrates in his novels of Nigeria. Challenged to justify his use of the term 'celebration' when his novels are full of individuals who are corrupt or weak or seen to fail, Achebe argued that it was in his very portrayal of them as people, flawed perhaps, never quite fulfilling their potential but nevertheless striving, 'making life' – to use that phrase again – that he celebrated their being.[1] Similarly Berry celebrates the migrant experience through his sustained exploration of the many dimensions of what it has meant to be a West Indian in Britain, both the good times and the bad. So while he is often justly critical of the attitudes he finds in

Britain,[2] he is also both self-critical (there are many poems of doubt and self-scrutiny throughout Berry's work) and willing to take unfashionable stances with regard to issues of race and identity in Britain.[3] While he has been very conscious of what it has meant to be black in Britain in the last half century, he has never been willing to settle for isolation or the brand of black solidarity that amounts to a kind of willed segregation. In all his work – poetic, editorial and as a public spokesman/ statesman for black people in Britain – Berry has been engaged in another process of creolisation, of bridge-building, of changing the culture of Britain in such a way that he could write, in his introduction to his collection of poems *When I Dance* (1988):

> When one's previously excluded cultural experience becomes naturally and properly included in mainstream learning material, one is bound to feel that something validly human has happened to both oneself and the old excluding culture.[4]

Cause for celebration indeed. That rounded view of 'the people who came' and the society they came into and helped to change is the essence of his celebration of their experience, neither merely victims nor always innocent of blame themselves, but, to say it again, 'making life'.

Some of those early poems – collected in his first book *Fractured Circles* (1979) – chronicling the 'welcome' those West Indian immigrants to the London of the 1950s received – seem bleak enough; the doors slammed in black faces by affronted white landladies, the hustle for work and warmth, the petty and not so petty racism, a real sense of a betrayal by the colonial 'mother country', they are all there. But what his poems of that period also catch, uniquely, is the spirit of adventure and elation that the 'country bwoy' making out in the big city retained, despite all the aggravation. So the 'Migrant in London' declares:

> I stan' in the roar, man,
> in a dream of wheels
> a-vibrate shadows.
> I feel how wheels hurry in wheels.

> I whisper, man you mek it.
> You arrive.

That elation is quickly deflated by his realisation of the harsher side of what it means to be a migrant in London

> Then sudden like, quite loud I say,
> "Then whey you goin' sleep tonight?"[5]

The celebration of that man's experience is in the portrayal of both the elation and the despair, the sense of achievement and the sense of isolation. The one without the other would negate the truth of the whole.

In many other of the other poems of that period – while they vividly catch the struggle of that time – they also understand that there were two sides to the story and even the outraged, hypocritical landlady responding to the rap on her door by the 'field man of old empire' turned 'Roomseeker in London' has real fears, has her own illusions... As the poet says, 'His knocks hurt both ways.'[6] So while the poet's sympathies are clearly with the roomseeker, his compassion can encompass, too, the flustered, hidebound landlady, imprisoned by the conventional prejudices of her class and time. When she bolts him out she also bolts herself in and it is the field man who retains his hope as well as his hurt, his dignity as well as the desperation of wondering 'how many more doors' he would have to endure closing in his face. In his highly acclaimed stage and radio play, *Song of a Bluefoot Man* and in his poem 'Bluefoot Traveller' Berry explores the origin of the term 'bluefoot man' in the Jamaican context of village people's suspicion of, and hostility towards, strangers, even if they only came from over the hill:

> Man
> 		who the hell is you?
> What hole you drag from...
> 	...
> to come and put body
> and bundle down in we village
> 	...
> 			Why yu stop here?[7]

So, without excusing the racism and hypocrisy, he has some understanding of the hostility to 'strangers' he encounters in Britain, and by resisting the temptation simply to demonise the landlady the poet ensures our engagement as readers with the entire scenario and thus with the nuances of the roomseeker's experience. The effect is to celebrate the migrant's resilience rather than merely to complain of injustice.

Those are poems of personal encounter, vignettes of the migrant experience, essentially private occasions but celebrated in poetry. Other poems are more self-consciously public, sometimes angry, sometimes assertive but often also celebratory in the sense of validating struggle or ambition or achievement. In 'Black Study Students', for example, (also in the *Fractured Circles* collection), the poet observes a group of evening class students – he doesn't say it's night-school or that the students are grown-up men and women rather than children or adolescents, but that is the impression one takes from the poem, perhaps because these students have almost as much to unlearn as to learn – and he marvels at their determination and perseverance. For them this is another voyage of discovery, another migration of the spirit, and much that is discovered is painful: but they are also discovering 'strange familiar/footways'. The final stanzas of the poem culminate in this awed celebration of their determination to know themselves:

> All know they arrive
> from abysses to fill
> shapelessness with dreams.
>
> They go in pure and religious rage
> renewed in a feeling of freedom
> to grow.[8]

Another public poem is his bitterly ironic, spirit-wounded satire 'I am Racism', from the *Chain of Days* (1985) collection, which at first sight offers little to sustain my claims for Berry's instinct to celebrate. In the poem, 'Racism' becomes a character who speaks his own credo, congratulates himself on his insidious but ubiquitous presence, his privilege, his authority. Perhaps most disturbingly he boasts of his power to convince even his victims of the rightness of his views:

> After all
> I carry the supreme essence.
> I have a position to uphold.
> And I well know I am extolled
> in secret by nonspecials.
> You see I do deserve special rights.
> After all I am Racism [9]

But even in that bleak poem, plainly fuelled by Berry's rage and an immigrant's sense of civic impotence, is an occasion for celebration; the point of the poem is, of course, to draw the reader's scorn on Racism's blustering, grandiose arrogance. As a 'nonspecial' himself the poet's capacity to mock, to ridicule, to make of that most culpable of materials – the English language – something which damns itself and its putative speaker, is a powerful riposte to the apparent argument of the poem.

The significance of that achievement is the greater when we consider the poet's sense of the colonial language as an agent of subjection, as we shall see when we look at his poems about his relationship with his father.

If he demonstrates the ways that the English language can be made to damn itself, Berry has also been very much involved in the process by which Jamaican creole (one of his own 'natural' voices which, historically, enunciates its cultural resistance to that 'standardising' English) has been validated as a suitable vehicle for a Jamaican/ Westindian-British poetry (his term). Already in those early migrant poems the speaking persona's language established a distinctive way of saying that was both true to the poet's experience and invoked a whole culture's cadence. His affection for the life of his Jamaican childhood is largely expressed through dialogues between characters rooted in or displaced from that world. For them there is no other language for the landscapes and experiences of that life than the 'dialect'/'patois'/'creole'/'nation language' (whatever the currently acceptable terminology happens to have been!) through which they learned to know the world. One thing that Berry, the migrant, has wanted to do is to demonstrate that language's capacity to adapt to and accommodate new experiences. So, in the poems of the wonderfully evocative 'Lucy's Letters' sequence (in which Lucy, a long time exile from Jamaica, writes regular letters home to her friend Leela, who has never left the village, about her life in London and her nostalgia for 'home') the creolised voice of the more-or-less accommodated migrant in London becomes both the medium and the message:

> City speaky-speaky is mixed up
> here with bush talk-talk, darlin
> an' with Eastern mystery words[10]

The Lucy poems – which made up a large part of his second collection *Lucy's Letters and Loving* (1982) – often move towards conclusions that take the form of Jamaican proverbs, celebrating, again, the culture and its more than 'folk' wisdom. It is in the Lucy poems and others that catch the tone of affection, nostalgia and folkways humour, that Berry is most obviously a praise-singer. His evocations of the lighter side of Jamaican rural life are more vivid, more truthful to that will-to-laughter that *is* – not just romancing it, but *is* – characteristic of those communities, than anything else in poetry. They are matched only, perhaps, by Olive Senior's wonderful stories of country life. Of course, both Berry and Senior are able to portray that bittersweet humour so well because they understand its sources, know well enough the struggle and the pain and the injustices that are facts of that life, but also know that laughter has many functions.

Those qualities are perhaps best represented in the wonderful evocation of flattered outrage that is his 'Dialogue Between Two Large Village Women' in the *Lucy's Letters and Loving* collection. The complex voice-picture of those two rural matriarchs meeting at a standpipe is picked out in the nuances of their language. Bet-Bet is seemingly outraged but seems very keen to tell her story, to let her friend know both of the cheek of the boy who has propositioned her, but also to let it be known that he found her attractive enough to 'try it on'!

> Vergie mi gal, yu know
> wha overtek mi?

Wha, Bet-Bet darlin?

Yu know de downgrow bwoy
dey call Runt?

Everbody know de lickle
forceripe wretch

Well mi dear, de bwoy put
question to mi[11]

Berry evokes that whole drama and its 'local' context by his precise and confident use of the creole. Vergie's bemused response, "Wha? Wha yu say?" conveys disbelief, mock outrage and some amazement at the boy's force-ripe mannishness. But there is also, throughout the whole dialogue, some hint of a communal pride in the boy's boldface audacity and the virility of his ambition! The thrust of the poem reminds us that there is strong strand of sensuality running through Berry's work.

'Dialogue....' is a kind of honouring of those women and the life they represent in Berry's memory. There are many other such portraits of individual men and women throughout Berry's work: recognising, acknowledging, honouring their lives. Some are heroes – Paul Bogle, Edna Manley, Martin Luther King, Nelson Mandela – but most are 'ordinary folk' like Lucy and Leela, like Nana Krishie the midwife and Ol' Tata Nago the healer, the people Berry calls his "village cousins" and to whom he dedicated *Lucy's Letters And Loving*. He also writes of his family – there are several moving poems about his feelings for his mother – but the most intriguing are the several poems, spanning his whole writing career, that interrogate his difficult relationship with his father.

That hard-won, long-awaited first collection, *Fractured Circles* is dedicated to 'my father' and one has a sense that the poet is saying to his father, among other things, 'Look, I did it, I achieved something, I made something special of myself.' The poem, 'Thoughts on my Father', in that collection establishes that this was a complicated relationship. The poem ends with the assertion, spoken, it seems, son to father,

221

You scar me man
but I must go over you again and again.
....
I must assemble material
of my own
for a new history[12]

It is clear that his father and Jamaica are inextricably bound in the poet's memory and imagination; he is 'made' by both and remains in awe of both, but equally both represent a destiny he is determined to escape, as he says in a later poem:

I refuse to be Estate 'chop-bush' man
and a poverty path scarecrow[13]

His father is portrayed as a strong, stern man who demands a certain traditional respect within his family, 'And I wash my father's feet at sunset / in a wooden bowl'[14] but who still 'knows his place' in the colonial order and is passive in the face of insult and injustice:

My father stutters before authority
His speeches have no important listener[15]

That suggestion of a kind of shame at his father's failure to make a mark on the world beyond the village begins in the child-who-will-be-the-poet's shock at seeing his father ('my first lord/ my inviolable king') going 'cap-in-hand' to the local white landowner and standing:

Helpless, without honour
without respect, he stood indistinct,
called 'boy' by the white child[16]

Suddenly 'a black history I didn't know' swamps the consciousness of the black child looking on and his determination to escape the island is set because, 'I can't endure like my father.' That determination is restated in several poems, often alongside images of his father that recall his broken spirit, but also begin to understand the force of the ideology responsible for his apparent passivity. Two generations on from slavery, his father's seeming to be ruled by 'old scars (that)

222

warn you to yield and hide' becomes the spur that drives the younger man to dare to leave, to try and make more of his talents than life in the Jamaican village offered: 'I refuse / to walk my father's deadness'.[17] It is interesting that for the boy-who-will-be-the-poet it is his father's lack of words, the lack of a language that will empower him to change the family's lot, that most enrages. That line about stuttering before authority is reinforced in 'New World Colonial Childhood' by the image of him reduced to

> our language master dumb
> with forgetfulness, our
> captain without compass[18]

It is that dumbness, that lack of a voice, that humiliation by the language of the master that most terrifies and inspires the young Berry to break away. Elsewhere he writes of the necessity but also the magnitude of that journey:

> I must cross our moat of sea,
> and I have no way. I must list
> lost tracks, must write
> my scanning of time, must plant
> hot words in minsters like cool
> communion bread. Yet I should drown
> in language of our lanes.[19]

There is an implication that the son was not exactly encouraged in his determination to leave, that the father feels his son's attitudes as a kind of betrayal.

Significantly perhaps it is in a 'Letter to My Father from London', in which the poet-son begins by describing the great difference between what life is like in the metropolitan centre and anything his father could imagine, that we find the harshest judgement on his father's apparent passivity:

> You still don't understand
> how a victim is guilty as accomplice[20]

Such a notion carries over into Berry's general attitude to life as it is presented in his poetry; that refusal to be cowed into the role of the perpetual victim is the steel in his response to the frustrations of making a life as a black man in Britain.

Although these poems considering his father's life and its legacy are found right through Berry's work, they become more explicit and profound as he gets older, culminating in the exploration of that theme as a major element in his most recent collection *Hot Earth Cold Earth*, published in 1995, and mostly written, we can infer, when the poet was himself in his sixties and seventies. The collection is dedicated 'to the memory of my mother and father' and both are certainly strong *presences* in the book, focusing the theme of a reconciliation, albeit painful, with the poet's past. The final reference to his father in the book is in 'Meeting Mr Cargill on my Village Road'. Mr Cargill, a contemporary of his father, meets the poet on the road and praises him for his appearance of good health and worldly success. He goes on to commiserate on the death of the poet's father and recounts how, despite the son not being there for either the funeral or the Nine Night wake, all the formalities were observed to pay the father due honour:

> everything, everything, happen
> like yu was here, here on spot[21]

So the poet is left both reassured and chastened; but while there is a sense that even in his death his father has reinforced the image of his son as a wayward child who failed to conform to the community's expectations, there is also a sense in this poem of a kind of completion. The father finally laid to rest in the same patch of earth he had toiled over all his life ('we bury him... under yu mango tree') is visited by his successful, much travelled, internationally honoured, son – OBE – a man of words who has been driven, in many ways, by his father's struggle with words. This is a complex celebration of both struggle and achievement, which recognises the cost to both father and son of a history which eventually silenced the one but in a certain way gave the other his subject, his necessary anger, his voice. As Berry confesses in 'Faces Around My Father':

> I disowned you to come to know
> thanks to connections that someone may feel.[22]

This sense of the power of the colonial ideology which so distorted his relationship with his father led Berry to investigate a connection to Africa still 'submerged' in Caribbean consciousness. So, as we have seen, early poems like 'Black Study Students' responded to the energy that the communal rediscovery of African history released, while others like the cathartic 'Reclamation', from *Chain of Days*, chart a more personal rite of passage. 'Reclamation' is a remarkable poem both in its ambition and its achievement. Berry has written elsewhere of his sense, from early childhood, that something important was missing in his understanding of who he was, some part of the story was not being told. As he puts it in the poem:

> Yet there was a knowing I was
> marooned from. And I didn't
> know what or how or why.[23]

Recognising, perhaps after his encounter with those Black Studies students, that he needed to discover and face up to the African dimension in his cultural inheritance, he begins that psychologically daunting journey back through plantation slavery, Middle Passage and further, 'through change of name/ through loss of tongue / through loss of face', until he reaches a place where:

> unreachable time has turned
> familiar voices strange,
> but kept every face my own[24]

Two long poems frame his exploration of that concern: 'In our Year 1941 My Letter to you Mother Africa' addresses the spirit of the continent and asks fundamental questions about the relationship between Africa and the Caribbean and how it has evolved –

> you sold my ancestors
> labelled, *not got human rights*
>
> Will I have to store,
> or bag-up and walk with, inherited hurt
> and outrage of enslavement[26]

At the other end of the collection is 'Reply from Mother Africa', a poem which Berry tells us in his preface was a long time coming and 'when [it] came, its contents were a surprise.'[27] The poem seems to distinguish between Africa as entity – as a place of origin and spiritual sanctuary – and the people of Africa who were as corruptible and mendacious as human beings anywhere. The Africans and Europeans involved in the slave trade, either as warriors or raiders, merchants or sailors, planters or the slaves themselves were involved in something evil designed by men for men which 'Mother Africa' was powerless to prevent, the poem seems to argue.

Eventually emerging from that psychic encounter with origins back to this old/new world, the poet can assert 'I'm new spirit out of skin', who can celebrate a capacity to 'sing an old song like a first song.'[25]

It was a poem expressing his concern with that history – and for Africa in a more political sense – that really brought James Berry to national prominence, when it won the National Poetry Competition in 1981. 'Fantasy of an African Boy' is not so much concerned with the African past as with considering the innocent African child's musing on money as a metaphor for the contemporary relationship between the materially impoverished continent and the affluent West:

> We can't use money to bandage
> sores, can't pound it
> to powder for sick eyes
> and sick bellies. Yet without
> it, flesh melts from our bones.[28]

The concern with Africa and that subtle edge of earned political awareness informs all Berry's later work and underpins his pivotal role as cultural activist. As perhaps the first black-British poet (though the terminology and the concept is fraught) he has always felt a duty to be to some extent an educator, both in terms of raising consciousness within the black community and mediating that community's experience of the wider society. That commitment has led to his involvement in producing materials for schools and colleges, his teaching and reading (he has a reputation as an inspirational leader of workshops and writing classes) and his efforts in promoting, and celebrating, the work of other black writers in Britain.

His anthologies of poetry by Westindian-British writers, *Bluefoot Traveller* (1976) and *News for Babylon* (1984), provided crucial platforms for the work of writers who might otherwise have remained 'invisible' and unheard. His coinage WestIndian-British is interesting, carrying as it does a sense of both belonging and difference, and suggesting a genuine engagement between the migrants and the 'host' community which has led to the creation of a new forms of cultural expression. By their success, Berry's anthologies fundamentally changed both the complexion and the voice of contemporary British poetry.

Given the evidence of a real psychological struggle with the facts of Caribbean history and the poison of colonial ideology that this essay has explored, it is the more remarkable that James Berry should have been able to cultivate that quality of celebration in just about everything he has written. But that is what the poems do; without romanticising, without leaving out the hurt and the insult and the injustice that is, still, part of the everyday experience of black people in Britain, they celebrate the hard-won authority to assert, confidently, as the black child's voice does in Berry's poem 'One' :

> I am just this one.
> Nobody else makes the words
> I shape with sound, when I talk[29]

IAN MCDONALD: A CARIBBEAN LITERARY LIFE

In some ways Ian McDonald makes an unlikely Caribbean cultural
hero: a white, Cambridge educated, sugar industry executive,
steeped in English literature and European culture, a champion
of what some would regard as old fashioned or conservative values
as regards issues like language, family, education or regional identity.
In fact it would be hard to find a more self-consciously West
Indian man than Ian McDonald, born and educated in Trinidad,
with family connections in Antigua over generations, who, whilst
he could easily have lived comfortably elsewhere, has opted to
live virtually all his adult life in Guyana, a country that for the
last three decades at least has been losing most of its skilled people
and intellectuals to more sympathetic locations around the world.
McDonald has stayed and dedicated his life both to the business
of sugar, ('the emerald ancestral cane', which for all its negative
and economically distorting associations has been the major
employer, the major earner of revenues for Guyana) and to his
art, which as well as requiring a personal commitment to poetry
and writing generally has involved him in the practical business
of improving the cultural infrastructure of Guyana – for a long
time now one of the poorest countries in the world.

In a typically Caribbean way McDonald is a man of many parts;
the range of his interests is reflected in the subjects he discusses
in his regular opinion column in the *Stabroek News* – the country's
leading newspaper: from literature and art (he is on the management
board of the recently established National Gallery of Guyana)
through ecology (on which he has somewhat radical ideas) and
history (his subject at Cambridge) to the West Indian Commission
(of which he was a member) and sport. As a young man he was
a champion tennis player, captain of the West Indies Davies Cup
team, and sport, particularly cricket, remains a passionate interest

of his. He has written movingly of the power of West Indian cricket – in the glory years of the 80s – to unite and uplift people across the region in a way that virtually nothing else has been able to.

Those newspaper columns serve as an indicator of his range as a writer. Primarily known as a poet, though he has also published short stories and plays, he made his first real mark with his only novel, *The Hummingbird Tree* (1969)[1], which won the Royal Society of Literature Prize. One of the more interesting of the several Caribbean novels of childhood, *The Hummingbird Tree* explores the relationship between Alan, an eleven-year-old white Trinidadian boy, Jaillin, his family's Indian kitchen girl, and her elder brother, Kaiser. Set in the final decades of the colonial period, the novel is a subtle, poignant story of innocence and discovery, of power and poverty; the children's growing awareness of the checks and limitations on their respective lives and the sometimes brutal playing out of their doomed friendship enacts the pain of Caribbean history in a particularly lyrical and moving way.

Although *The Hummingbird Tree* was widely acclaimed at the time of its publication and was adapted into a successful TV film as recently as the mid 1990s, with the exception of a few short stories McDonald has not written any other extended fiction. His instinct for storytelling is apparent, however, in many of the early character poems that established his reputation as a poet and indeed his books of poems have each been written as collections of interconnected poems around a central theme. Many of those early poems such as 'Jaffo the Calypsonian', 'Yusman Ali, Charcoal Seller' and 'The Stick Fighters' have become minor classics of Caribbean poetry and staples of many a school anthology, catching in a unique way something important and otherwise untold about the time and cultural world in which they were written. 'Yusman Ali, Charcoal Seller' is typical of this strand in McDonald's work, observing and understanding – and essentially celebrating – the life and tragedy and spirit of an apparently very different kind of West Indian man than the poet would seem to be. The tragedy that scars Yusman Ali's subsequent life is briefly told in the second stanza of the poem:

He made an ordinary living by the long mud shore,
Laughed and drank like any other man and planned his four
    son's glory
His young eyes watched the white herons rise like flags
And the sun brightening on the morning water in his fields.
His life fell and broke like a brown jug on a stone.
In middle age his four sons drowned in one boat up a pleasant
    river.
The wife's heart cracked and Yusman Ali was alone...

and living through his grief and rage, the final stanza reads:

He is useful still. I shake with pain to see him pass
He has not lost his hating yet, there's that sweet thing to say,
He farts at the beauty of the iron-dipped moon.
The smooth men in their livery of success
He curses in his killing heart
And yearns for thorns to tear their ease.[2]

In other hands such a poem could be mawkish and patronising, but McDonald's fundamental respect for the character's human dignity and the sense we have that this is a known world, with all its cruelties and inequalities and uncertainties understood, guards against any such charge. The poem veers towards the melodramatic – it is a young man's work – but any weaknesses in the poem are redeemed for me in the opening lines of that final stanza, the calculated abruptness and pointed invoking of Caribbean history in the sentence 'He is useful still'. The whole plantation value system is in that statement, but also the pride-in-work of a people who know no other source of dignity; to be 'useful' as the ultimate measure of worth. And the measured lilt of the line, 'He has not lost his hating yet, there's that sweet thing to say' has a very West Indian logic to it – again the implicit invocation of a history of slavery or indenture where, for most people, identity depended on ancestral memory tied to a sense of injustice – the 'slave's defiance' as he puts it elsewhere. So the capacity to hate becomes a 'sweet thing', though the phrase, of course, is double-edged. As, often, in these poems, the poet brings himself into the account, observing, judging, but also judging himself for judging. So the final stanza begins, 'All pity taints the pitier' and ends, 'and no one knows the human heart.'

Another group of much anthologised early poems takes the form of compassionate musings on death, history and the social injustices of Caribbean life; poems such as 'On an Evening Turned to Rain', 'A White Man considers the Situation', 'The Weather in Shanty Town', and 'On an Old Woman, Half Gone Mad' ground those concerns in situations and characters that are both identifiably local and yet speak across regional and racial boundaries.

Eleven of those early poems were included in the Faber anthology *Poetry Introduction 3* (1975) but they were not widely available in book form until Peepal Tree Press brought out the volume *Jaffo the Calypsonian* in 1994. Most of those poems were written in the 50s and 60s and McDonald published little poetry for almost two decades, but in a remarkable burst of creativity in the mid-1980s, he wrote the poems that appeared in his first full collection, *Mercy Ward* (Peterloo Poets, 1988). The book (which won the 1992 Guyana Prize for poetry) chronicles daily experience in a hospital ward for the 'poorest of the poor', very like the ward in Georgetown's public hospital where McDonald served as a volunteer visitor, comforting those who had no relatives or friends to see them though their last illness. The book is full of characters and incidents from the life of the ward, and there is a surprising amount of humour considering the pervading presence of death. McDonald does not romanticise his subject – this is a hospital that has few painkilling drugs to offer its pauper patients and most die in agony – but rather the poet observes the strategies the patients and the staff employ in coming to terms with their situations. Several poem explore tensions between inner lives and 'exterior' experience, noticing both ruse and ritual as tactics employed to deceive that 'dark angel' which hovers over virtually every poem. Among the most poignant is 'God's Work' which stands out perhaps because it is one of the few poems where the poet's reserve, his trained – or more likely hard-learned – reasonableness in the face of so much grief and despair, so much suffering and injustice, cracks. Like so many other characters who become the subjects of these poems, Mister Edwards, sometime gardener and handyman for the poet, is in the Mercy Ward to die. In life he had been both physically strong and temperamentally stoical. His dignity is based, again, on his work, and on a faith that would not countenance any complaint at his lot in life, whether it was his place in the social order, or the storms that destroyed his work on house or garden or, now, the 'months of agony..../ripping his guts away slowly'. All were 'God's work' and so, all through his illness, the old man has refused to cry. But, the poem ends:

> ....his last day in my arms he cried.
> "God's work!"
> God should play more.[3]

Implicitly, throughout the collection, the poet's own rationale for dealing with so much suffering and death has been that it was all – in more complex ways than Mr Edwards perhaps meant – 'God's work' and as such could not usefully be resisted but rather had to be 'managed'. The distress informing the irony of that last line, 'God should play more', is the more powerful for being so understated, but still reveals the extent of the poet's own pain at the manner of his 'good friend's' dying.

When interviewed, McDonald has resisted the idea of the Mercy Ward serving as a metaphor for the social and political state in which it operates – he has always tried to avoid any overtly political agenda – but it is hard to resist the parallels. At the very least the collection provides a disturbing insight into the social conditions in Guyana at the end of the Burnham era, the period in which the poems were written.

If the poems in *Jaffo the Calypsonian* and *Mercy Ward* are essentially urban, describing the lives of people drawn or born to live and die in Georgetown (or, in some of the early poems, Port of Spain), in 1992 Ian McDonald published another collection, *Essequibo*, which explores and celebrates aspects of the Guyanese landscape beyond the reclaimed and cultivated coastal fringe of the country, the so called 'interior' of rainforest, gigantic rivers and spectacular waterfalls. In 'The Fix', a very revealing poem in *Mercy Ward*, in which the poet confronts his own motives in continuing his volunteer work on the ward:

> There's intensity in living through
> a dying that's not your own.
> There's always power in the air

he also describes the need to escape from that grim "ward-tension"
sometimes, and his escape is to spend time on the:

> Beloved Essequibo where my soul will go
> If hereafter good things happen.[4]

The Essequibo is one of the great rivers of the country, and
an entry into that other world of the interior. And just as he engages
so wholeheartedly with the Mercy ward, so these poems speak
of a profound engagement with the places and creatures and people
of the Essequibo. Although he is at pains to remind his readers
that he is a stranger in this place – just as he is in the Mercy
Ward – yet he is also a trusted guide and translator. There are
character poems in the style he has developed through his career
which recount and embroider the stories of figures met in various
situations along the river, but there are also many poems of place,
recalling histories and legends, writing that 'other world' into
the literature of the region. Perhaps the most powerful of those
poems is 'The Sun Parrots are Late This Year', which is dedicated
to the murdered Brazilian environmentalist Chico Mendez, and
is both a praise-song to the rainforest and a lament for Mendez
and the causes he championed:

> The great forests of the world are burning down,
> Far away in Amazon they burn,
> Far beyond our eyes the trees are cut
> And cleared and heaped and fired:
> Ashes fill the rivers for miles and miles,
> The rivers are stained with the blood of mighty trees.
> Great rivers are brothers of great forests
> And immense clouds shadowing the rose-lit waters
> Are cousins of this tribe of the earth-gods
> Under the ancient watch of the stars[5]

As emerges from the poems – but also from his newspaper columns
– McDonald is passionate about the survival of the rain forests
and the importance of a finding a balance between the needs of

poor peoples in places like Guyana for development and economic growth, and the absolute necessity to cherish and sustain the wilderness of the interior.

One quality shared by many poets writing in English in corners of the world as distant from each other as they are from the metropolitan centres of literary fashion is their indifference to the linguistic and stylistic conventions which mark – over time – the cast and cadence of a particular period of British or American verse. Indeed it's one of the ways we recognise the cultural difference of those writers, so its maybe not surprising that, read from the perspective of the conventions of contemporary British poetry, there is something 'out of time' about the tone and temper of McDonald's most recent collection, *Between Silence and Silence* (Peepal Tree 2003). It may simply be that living as he does in a relatively 'raw' society, where emotions are more openly expressed and where the cruelties and injustices of life and death are immediate and real, then the niceties of literary fashion just don't signify. It may also just be a function of age – a theme that runs through the collection – that by now McDonald's voice and style are established and the perceived urgency of 'telling it true' is the only consideration. He'll let time be the final arbiter of what's good.

In that attitude and indeed in other ways, the poet he most calls to mind in this collection – and whom he has acknowledged in interviews as an influence – is Thomas Hardy. That willingness to address the 'ordinary' flux of life in his time and place, and to see both beauty and portent in the apparently unremarkable, is very like some of Hardy. The collection is divided into four broadly thematic sections. In the first, 'It Passes' he writes of his love for his wife and children in simple and direct ways, risking sentimentality in beautiful measured poems like 'Behind the Rib-Cage Lies the Heart', which opens with the lines

> My six year old son is at my side
> Light-brown, glowing, olive-eyed,
> He's precious beyond compare.[6]

But the trick, of course, is to walk that line between sentiment and sentimentality. As the poem unfolds the innocence of the child, groping toward understanding and finding the words to be able to express his feelings, is pitched against the father's playful, well-intentioned, tale-telling in a way that turns the poem completely, so that its real subject is – very unsentimentally – the mystery and power of the 'new-born word'. In the second section of the collection, 'Middle Age', McDonald explores the ramifications of that process of aging, both its frustrations and disappointments – the losing of interest in the teasing games of young women in their 'tight designer jeans' – and its unexpected benefits, the solitary pleasures of:

> Opening a new book I have wanted,
> Alone in a chair that fits my back,
> Anticipating delight, fingers cracking the pages.[7]

But there are other aspects to this stage of life too, the loss of much-loved, aged parents – recalled in several moving poems – and also a sense of moral coarsening – or at least a wariness born of experience that overrides finer instincts. That idea is developed in what seems to me a very Hardyesque poem, 'We Do Not Stop for Strangers'[8] which – in a section of the book full of death and portents of man's grander inhumanities, ('smokestacks of the Central European plain,/the killing fields of Pol Pot's paradise') is based on a seemingly insignificant and disturbingly familiar incident. En-route for a party with friends, the worldly-wise middle-aged poet/persona drives past a man and a small child seemingly signalling for a help on the dark roadside. Perhaps they were in serious need, or perhaps, as some of the good fellows in the car suggest, the man was intent on robbery or worse, using the child as 'a lure' – a scenario not unfamiliar in the contemporary Guyanese context. But although the truth of the situation will never be known – it is a story passed over in the second it takes the driver to 'accelerate past the waving man' – that comfortable dismissal of the implicit claim on their shared humanity comes back to haunt the poet as he mingles 'in the chattering crowd/stuffing barbecued lamb, swilling rum'.

Perhaps because he spends some of his precious time helping out at the local public hospital for the terminally ill – a part of his life, as noted above, explored in his earlier collection *Mercy Ward* – McDonald is better able to empathise with the circumstances of Guyana's poor than most of his middle class, middle aged contemporaries. The third section of the book, 'Archive', extends the concerns of that earlier collection and explores the lives – and deaths – of some of the characters encountered on that ward, people for whom there would not normally be any kind of memorialising. Perhaps the most poignant – and characteristic of McDonald's sense of irony – is 'Mr Perfection', which begins, 'His name was actually that, Manuel Perfection', and plays on the nature of striving and success in a life 'full of meanings we can never know.'[9]

As a group of poems, the final section of the book 'The Birth of Poetry' demonstrates Ian McDonald's real strengths as a poet. The dozen or so poems represent the range of his concern throughout his career – the celebration of people and place, a profound sense of the mysterious, an eye for comedy, the importance of love and friendship, history and the power of story – especially as distilled through poetry. I would like to quote from all of them – from the wonderful and unlikely muse of the boil-encrusted and bespectacled 'Spinster Ganteaume and the Birth of Poetry'[10], through the glory of Viv Richards in full pomp letting his bat lash vengeance on West Indian history in 'Massa Day Done'[11], and the dread empathy of 'The Weather in Shanty Town.'[12] The poem from which the collection takes its title is a haunting exploration of the frailty of human endeavour, its vulnerability to the whims and fancies of a cruel god – however he/she/it might be styled. The poem turns around a wonderfully vivid and disturbing image of an Amerindian fisherman setting a nest of ants afloat on a river, to act as a lure for the fish he pursues. The final lines seem an appropriate commentary on the collection as a whole,

Friend, it is past the time when tears matter:
between silence and silence there should be only praise.[13]

However, if all that Ian McDonald had done was to hone his own writing skills and produce several volumes of fine poetry over the almost half a century he has lived and worked in Guyana he would hardly merit the title of 'cultural hero'. But as well as playing his important role in the sugar industry and producing such a distinctive body of creative work, he has also been hugely influential in many areas of Guyana's cultural life. Perhaps most crucial was his decision to rejuvenate the literary magazine *Kyk-over-al* in the mid-1980s. Founded initially in the 1940s by the poet A.J. Seymour, *Kyk*, was one of the most important catalysts for the development of West Indian literature, providing precious local outlets for the region's aspiring writers until Seymour finally ran out of energy and money as Guyana imploded in the 1960s. Initially co-editing the revived journal with its founding editor in the few years before Seymour's death in 1989, McDonald has produced the magazine to a more or less regular schedule ever since. Beyond any literary aggravations that the production of a journal like *Kyk* inevitably entails, the difficulties of funding, printing, distributing and most crucially sustaining a literary magazine in one of the world's poorest countries are immense. But at the same time McDonald was also instrumental in the establishment of the Guyana Prize for literature, which is the most valuable and prestigious literary award in the Anglophone Caribbean. Awarded in alternate years to acknowledge the achievement of Guyanese writers working in fiction, poetry and drama, the list of prize winners – from Wilson Harris and Roy Heath to Grace Nichols, Jan Shinebourne, Pauline Melville, and Fred D'Aguiar – reminds us of the outstanding contribution Guyanese writers have made to Caribbean literature.

In addition to that publishing and administrative work, McDonald has also done important work as a literary scholar. He co-edited *The Heinemann Book of Caribbean Poetry* and has been working for many years on the compilation of a comprehensive historical anthology of Guyanese poetry. He also spent many hundreds of hours on selecting, editing and bringing to publication major collections of poems by Guyana's two leading poets of the twentieth century, Martin Carter and A.J. Seymour. Both were prolific writers but in different ways left their life's work in something of a mess. It is unlikely that the achievement of either of those writers would be fully available to future generations of Guyanese readers if McDonald hadn't worked so hard – for no real personal reward – to rescue and then help organise the publication of substantial editions of their work.

So, 'cultural hero' is not an inappropriate accolade, though it's one that he would scoff at. Of course he has his detractors and literary enemies – which editor, critic, judge of literary prizes doesn't? There are a few writers with bruised egos who rattle the race cage, inevitably in a country like Guyana, and some, more considered, who complain about the 'power to exclude' of the limited number of cultural 'gatekeepers' in a small place like Guyana. But those quibbling voices are few and far between. To acknowledge his contribution to Caribbean literature Ian McDonald was awarded an Honorary Doctorate by the University of the West Indies a couple of years back, an honour of which he is immensely proud. We know that because he has written about it in his weekly column in the *Starbroek News*, among the hundreds of other topics he has touched on. He has the knack of writing in such a way that his readers feel they are being individually addressed, and because he is writing on things he feels strongly about, those readers are engaged and held. The columns – which are syndicated to papers around the Caribbean – have proved immensely popular and the *Stabroek News* is planning to bring out a selection of the essays in book form. There is a certain irony in the fact that of all the writing he has done, in fiction, poetry and scholarly contributions, the body of work that has had the widest impact on the general Guyanese and Caribbean public is the most ephemeral, these 'Ian on Sunday' pieces. There might be a poem, or a column, in that.

'STRAIGHT IS NOT THE WAY':
AN INTRODUCTION TO THE POETRY OF MERVYN MORRIS

> Every poem is an unmasking; someone may understand. And every poem, however 'confessional', is a mask, a face the poet has fixed.[1]

The lines above are from 'Behind the Poems', an autobiographical piece included in a prizewinning collection of essays *Is English We Speaking*, by the distinguished Jamaican poet Mervyn Morris, published in 1999. Although the observation is about poetry generally, the enigmatic cast of those lines – that every poem is both a masking and an unmasking – is particularly true of Morris's own poetry which is characterised by its formal brevity (many of his poems consist of less than fifty words) and by a delight in ambiguity and paradox, as in 'Data', which I quote in full,

> facts lie
> behind the poems
> which are true
> fictions [2]

The wicked, witty, play on 'lie' and 'true' and 'facts' and 'fictions' resonates for much longer than the poem takes to read and still teases long after the initial smile the poem evokes has faded. This is wryly serious stuff, especially when you consider the associations of the title, which – beyond mocking the poetry anthologiser's quest for 'bio data' to locate and contextualise the writer's work in some spurious way – calls up the whole realm of cyber-records, credit ratings and the military / intelligence data on which real life-and-death decisions are made. Morris's work invites such readerly embroidering of a one word title because his practice as poet, paring each poem down to its essentials, interrogating every word to justify its presence in the finished artefact, demands that his readers pay similarly careful attention to the words that remain. In another seeming paradox, Morris lists, among the writers who have helped form him as poet, both John Donne and Philip Larkin – the Metaphysicals and the Movement – but we can perhaps surmise something of their respective influences even in this apparently slight piece.

As the Professor of Creative Writing and West Indian Literature at the University of the West Indies, with many literary and academic publications to his name and a reputation as a fine teacher of creative writing, it is perhaps not surprising that Morris, as poet, should be so interested in the issues around the craft and process of making poetry. That concern is one of several themes that emerge from a reading of his four published collections of poetry. 'Data' is included in his most recent book *Examination Centre* (1992)[3] but a similarly wry reflection on the poet's art is evident in 'Stripper', from his first collection, *The Pond* published in 1973 (revised edition 1997)[4] where the routine of the nightclub stripper, ('She put on clothes to take them off' while 'riddling hard to music') reminds the poet of his own practice. And in *Shadow Boxing* (1979)[5] the poem 'Muse' is a reflection on the frustrations of the poet's courtship of that coy mistress:

> Extraordinary
> trade
> When you woo her
> she will fade
>
> This is how
> the game is played [6]

Other themes running through Morris's work include an interest in religion and questions of faith – his sequence of poems for radio 'On Holy Week' is widely admired – love and sex, ageing and death, friendship, the nature of art, fatherhood, time, questions of identity and self definition – and, in the broadest sense, cultural politics. Although the understated style and seemingly ambivalent cast of his poems has sometimes been contrasted with that of brasher and more outspoken Jamaican poets who foreground radical political concerns in their work, Morris's poetry is in fact profoundly engaged in and with the debates around the cultural values that would come to characterise post-independence Jamaican society. Apart from relatively short periods spent abroad as a student (he was a Rhodes Scholar at Oxford) or to teach, Morris has lived all his life in Jamaica and his poems reflect on events, social developments and changing attitudes that have shaped the island through the four decades or so of his writing life. Read in that light, his books present a sceptical, ironic but also affectionate and amused commentary on what it has been to live a particular kind of Jamaican life in that period. There are poems in *The Pond* that suggest the range of Morris's social and political sympathies – although he is always quick to insist that *all* the poems are, in the sense that 'Data' reveals, fictions. Some of the poems strike what was characterised as a conservative pose in relation to the black consciousness movement in Jamaica during the 60s and 70s, although reading the poems now it is apparent that they are an aspect of Morris's wide-ranging critique of what he sees as hypocrisy – or at least woolly thinking – in public (and private) life. Several of his poems take the form of mini-dramas, highlighting the inconsistencies and contradictions of social policies and fashionable attitudes in the lived experience of people who are directly affected by them. As, for example, in 'To an Expatriate Friend' in which a white British teacher comes to feel that the rhetoric of black power is creating a society in which he is so stereotyped by his whiteness that it is both dangerous and counterproductive for him to remain:

> And then the revolution. Black
> and loud the horns of anger blew
> against the long oppression; sufferers
> cast off the precious values of the few.
>
> New powers re-enslaved us all:
> each person manacled in skin, in race.
> You could not wear your paid-up dues;
> the keen discriminators typed your face.[7]

In his own commentary on this poem Morris is careful to draw attention to the word 'all' in the first line of the second stanza above (the third stanza of four in the complete poem), insisting that the poem is a musing on the effects of that radical shake-up of consciousness right across Jamaican society, so that when the poem ends with the line 'it hurt to see you slowly going white' the reader is as aware of the narrating, 'seeing' persona as s/he is of the character who is 'seen'.

Another of the poets Morris acknowledges as an influence on the ways he thinks about his own function as a West Indian poet is Derek Walcott. Rereading Morris's work, Walcott's critique – in his poem 'Forest of Europe' – that too often the politicians and social reformers 'lose / sight of the single human through the cause', often comes to mind. Walcott implies and Morris enacts the concern to reinstate those individuals – whatever their status – into the public story. Across the page from 'To An Expatriate Friend' is what seems a very different poem in style and focus, 'I Am The Man'. This speaks the despairing, threatening philosophy of the 'sufferer', the dispossessed and downtrodden inheritor of all the evils and iniquities of Jamaican history. It begins:

> I am the man that build his house on shit
> I am the man that watch you bulldoze it
> I am the man of no fixed address
> Follow me now

and ends, four stanzas on:

> I am the man that file the knife
> I am the man that make the bomb
> I am the man that grab the gun
> Study me now [8]

Although I say this poem speaks the concerns of the 'sufferer' (itself a Jamaican usage) there does not immediately seem to be much in this poem to locate it in a particularly Jamaican context; these could be the sentiments of the wretched of the earth wherever they are found. (Indeed I thought of this poem in the wake of the discussions around the 'causes' behind the September 11th atrocities.) But there are some features of the poem that do imply, for the a reader familiar with Jamaica anyway, a Jamaican locale. An infamous public waste tip in Kingston, the island's capital city, is known as The Dungle (dungle being the Jamaican creole term for a midden) and for years desperate people scavenged the tip and even built shanty town settlements on it which were periodically bulldozed by the city authorities – a reference in the opening lines of the poem that would be picked up by most Jamaican readers. Similarly, the final line of the poem, 'Study me now' is a particularly Jamaican usage, invoking the Biblical/slavery days injunction against 'studying revenge' in the face of a perceived injustice. However the other – and more potent – indicators of a Jamaican persona reside in the small but significant grammatical deviations from standard English usage in the statements that make up the poem; 'build' and 'watch' in the first stanza where standard would have 'builds' or 'built' and 'watched' or 'watches'. 'Correct' the voice of the poem along those lines and it takes on a very different cast.

That subtle use of language conventions to imply a particular voice and inflect poems which in standard English might not ring so true is another feature of Morris's work throughout his writing career. He has written versions across the linguistic continuum of Jamaican voices and registers, from a middle class Jamaican 'standard' which predominates (and which we might assume to be the 'natural' voice of the poet), through to a much broader creole in poems like 'Walk Good', which closes *Examination Centre* and might need 'translation' for a non Jamaican reader:

> Teck time
> walk good
>
> Yu buck yu foot
> an memory ketch yu
>
> like a springe [9]

Perhaps his most famous voice poem, however, is 'Valley Prince', which opened his first collection. It was written for – and we assume in the voice of – the great Jamaican jazz trombonist Don Drummond, who died in a mental institution in Jamaica in 1969 after having murdered his wife. But while the poem is clearly responding to aspects of that tragic life, it is also a commentary on the process of 'making art' and the isolation of the artist who would be true to his vision, no matter how it conflicts with prevailing orthodoxies:

> ...me one
> in the crowd again,
> and plenty people
> want me blow it straight.
> But straight is not the way; my world
> don' go so; that is lie.[10]

So we are back to truth and lies again. Morris seems ever concerned to explore the no-man's land between the two, or rather to understand how the same ground can seem to belong to both parties, often at the same time. Perhaps it is no surprise then that Morris also lists R.S. Thomas among the poets he admires and who have had some influence on his style.

All in all, Mervyn Morris is one of the most distinctive and original of the West Indian poets who have made such a striking contribution to poetry in English in the second half of the twentieth century. His voice may not have been among those shouting loudest for our notice but in its scrupulous attention to the subtleties and nuances of language, craft and the issues of his time and place, Mervyn Morris's poetry may prove to have qualities that will commend themselves to readers when the tricks and poses of some of his noisier contemporaries are long forgotten.

TAP NATCH POET: READING AND LISTENING TO LINTON KWESI JOHNSON

In his introduction to Linton Kwesi Johnson's first full collection of poems, *Dread Beat and Blood* (1975), Andrew Salkey, the distinguished Jamaican man of letters, praised the young poet's directness and 'gritty, truthful' plainspeaking that 'cut into abstraction and verbal shadow-boxing with the ease of a hot knife through lard.' Salkey recalls Johnson's observation that,

> My poems may look sort of flat on the page. Well that is because they're actually oral poems, as such. They were definitely written to be read aloud, in the community.[1]

Even at that early point in his career then, LKJ was alert to the tension between the demands of the poem on the page and the poem 'in the air', in recitation or musical performance. Perhaps because – as a migrant to Britain in his teens – he was denied any comfortable or simple sense of his cultural identity, he feels more intensely than some other more obviously literary West Indian poets, the real strain between the several poetic traditions that bear on his sense of what it means to be a poet in his time and place. Given the media hype about LKJ as the revolutionary voice of radical black youth in the UK it is perhaps surprising, that, even in the early, angry, 'messages from the front' poems of that first collection like 'Five Nights of Bleeding' and 'All Wi Doin is Defendin', he was clearly concerned with issues of literary craft and technique.

> brothers an sisters rocking
> a dread beat pulsing fire   burning
>
> chocolate hour in darkness creeping night

> black veiled night is weeping
> electric lights consoling   nights[2]

Speaking to Kwame Dawes in a more recent interview, LKJ recalls, in a passage that could have been lifted from Derek Walcott's memoirs of his youth, that as a young man he was 'reading lots of poems… I was struggling with my voice. I would imitate every poet I was reading at a given time.'[3] This only seems surprising because of the ways in which LKJ has been presented or packaged to appeal to a wider audience than that traditionally associated with, say, the readership of literary magazines. He is a 'dub poet' or a 'reggae poet' or a 'performance poet', each of those descriptors putting the poet – and so the poetry – *behind* some other characteristic which is more sexy, louder, more impressive than simply 'a poet' who cares about the ways the words work on the page or even as spoken 'dry', as LKJ describes his *a capella* recitals.

As Andrew Salkey's essay suggests, the abrasive and apparently direct manner of LKJ's early poems, especially when set against a reggae backing, spoke to a new situation – the race and class realities of urban Britain in the 1970s. They also spoke to a new audience, one not particularly interested in or impressed by the ornamental artifice of metaphor or the other devices of more traditional English lyric poetry. As Christian Habekost describes in his useful, if rather perverse, book on dub poetry, *Verbal Riddim*,[4] the crowds who swelled the halls where LKJ's band played – those who listened behind the musical occasion – were interested in a poetry of statement and assertion, an account of a world they recognised, vivid enough in its lived experience that it needed no embellishment by what Habekost calls 'useless metaphors'. However, while his work was plainly addressing that popular audience, Johnson was also striving to develop new forms that could accommodate both plain speaking *and* metaphor, both the driving bass rhythms *and* other other – subtler – speech rhythms. When, much later in his career, in the collection *Tings an Times*[5] LKJ is experimenting with more conventional poetic devices and ways of saying, Habekost notes, rather disapprovingly, that the 'political discourse is frequently clothed in allegorical constructions and mystical imagery.'[6]

In the interview with Kwame Dawes, LKJ speaks of his frustration at not being able to explore a more private, lyrical impulse in his verse. Rather he felt duty-bound to use his writing as if, as he put it, he was 'a journalist for the Black world in Britain'. That pressure even extended to his own band, who, he suggests, resisted the idea that there was a difference between a reggae lyric and a dub poem in terms of the relationship between the words and the music. He insists that

> I always, in each show with a band, do a number of pieces 'dry', to make the point that this is a poetry thing, really.[7]

One major reason why he stopped touring with a band in the mid 80s was that he felt his poetry was suffering from the pressure to conform to a reggae format.

Johnson's earliest publication, *Voices of the Living and the Dead*,[8] is a verse play, and in fact much of his work has employed the traditional devices of English literary poetry. As Fred D'Aguiar notes in his essay 'Chanting Down Babylon', which serves as the introduction to *Mi Revalueshanary Fren*, much of LKJ's poetry 'maintains… a regular iambic, mostly tetrameter line'.[9] Johnson has spoken of his early experiments with language, playing with the effects of onomatopoeia, assonance and alliteration, and there is a consistent exploration of rhyme in his work – not just end/chime rhymes but playing with internal rhyme and echo, half rhyme and phrase rhyme. My favourite passage of LKJ rhymes is in 'Inglan is a Bitch':

> dem hav a likkle facktri up inna Brackly
> inna disya facktri all dem dhu is pack crackry[10]

And beyond the reggae pulse – which is usually implicit rather than explicit – there is great rhythmical variation within poems that are generally quite tightly constructed. Johnson's early poems don't actually look 'flat on the page' although by the time you get to the *Inglan is a Bitch* collection the majority of the poems are simpler in both form and manner.

However, in more recent work LKJ seems to move towards a

more complex, densely textured poetry which demands to be read *as well as* heard. Johnson has spoken of being drawn – as poet – towards metaphor but also acknowledges some dissatisfaction with his own talent in terms of that mainstream *Eng-lit* tradition. This comes to a head in his poem of the early 90s, 'If I Waz a Tap Natch Poet' which is an occasion for LKJ's personal acknowledgment of a counter-canonical poetic tradition to which he aligns himself and his work. It is not simply that he lists several great African, Caribbean and African-American poets (plus T.S. Eliot, strangely[11]) but he also asserts the spiritual roots of that tradition in the forbidden Africanist religions of the New World and the 'songs of freedom' they inspired:

> Like a candhumble/voodoo/kumina chant
> A ole time calypso or a slave song
> Dat get ban[12]

The immediate inspiration for this poem seems to have been the poet's anger at the apparent disrespect paid to his work – and the work of other poets in that tradition– by the mainstream British literary establishment, which failed to acknowledge the different notions of crafting (to adapt Gordon Rohlehr's formulation), that might be appropriate to an informed appreciation of the qualities of such work. This disrespect was voiced most offensively, as far as LKJ was concerned, in the careless words of a senior black British/Caribbean poet who was reported in the *Oxford Companion to Twentieth Century Poetry* as defining Dub Poetry as 'over-compensation for deprivation'.[13] Although not directly named, he is scornfully referred to through the poem as the 'Goon poet'.

So that public, cultural politics agenda is being engaged by the poem, but there is also a confession, couched in the repetition of the phrase that serves as the poem's title, with emphasis on the 'If'. The tone is of disappointment, an acknowledgement that by his own lights the poet has not achieved the kind of effects with his poetry that he aspired – and aspires – to. But in this very literary poem ambiguity swiftly comes into play as the reader/ hearer is not quite sure to what extent the modest self assessment

– that he is *not* a 'top notch poet' – is ironic or is a genuine expression
of humility in the context of that list of great poets:

> if I woz a tap-natch poet
> like Chris Okigbo
> Derek Walcott
> ar T.S. Eliot
>
> I woodah write a poem
> soh dyam deep
> dat it bittah-sweet
> like a precious
> memari
> wha mek yu weep
> whe mek yu feel incomplete[14]

'If I Waz a Tap Natch Poet' is a measured, multilayered, intertextual
piece, (even – as text – footnoted) dealing with issues of cultural
and political history as well as venting – in a coded, artfully English
way – his sense of frustration and betrayal. The central metaphor,
invoking the power relations between – and relative moral authority
of – two black south African political figures of the apartheid
struggle, Chief Buthalezi of the Zulus and Nelson Mandela of
the ANC, can be read in various ways. The analogy seems to be
with Buthalezi's narrow, self-serving, essentially conservative vision,
which effectively aligned itself with and sustained the apartheid
status quo and Nelson Mandela's ANC radicalism and progressive
vision of a new social order.

One reading would be that the Oxford-validated 'Goon Poet'
whose description of dub poetry serves only to maintain the cultural
status quo is aligned with Buthalezi while LKJ, as spokesman
for the maligned dub poetry movement, which would subvert
and radicalise the literary establishment, is in the position of
Mandela. If that reading is sustained, then 'If I Woz a Tap-Natch
Poet' serves as a kind of manifesto for the progressive poets, among
whom LKJ is acknowledged a kind of leader. However, all of
this rather undermines the credibility of the poet's apparent humility
because if he is Mandela to the Goon poet's Buthalezi, then we
know who the tap natch poet is in that encounter.

As text, the poem is unchanged between the two versions in the Penguin collections *Mi Revalueshanary Fren* (2002) and the *Selected Poems* (2006)[15] Two audio versions of the poem are available – the 'dry' recital of the LKJ *A Capella*[16] collection and the musical version on the CD, *More Time*, where it is set to a calypso style beat.[17] The calypso format is significant, invoking the Eastern Caribbean tradition of a musical poetry of social commentary, wit, irony and multiple voices, and in that form it certainly reaches out to a wider audience than in either of its more literary versions, as text or as 'reading'. But it is the 'dry' reading of the poem that it is most powerful and compelling, allowing notice of sound rhymes, subtle rhythmic changes, occasions of pace and pause, and inflections of voice that are not necessarily understood from the text on the page.

I have tried, in this brief essay, to establish the literary qualities of Johnson's verse, which are too often overlooked in the focus on his more radical and outspoken oral performances. This takes us full circle to Andrew Salkey's observations on Johnson's first collection and the young LKJ's insistence that his poetry needed to be heard as well as read off the page. 'If I waz a Tap Natch Poet', like much of LKJ's work is only fully available to understanding and criticism when the reader/hearer has access to the poem in both audio and textual versions. This is not a weakness in the poems or something that has to be explained away, it simply acknowledges the tension Johnson's poetry works between voice in the air and verse on the page.

REGGAE AND REQUIEM: A BRIEF INTRODUCTION TO THE WORK OF KWAME DAWES

In what seems a very short time (his first book of poems was published only in 1994), Kwame Dawes' has established a reputation as a poet and critic of an unusually wide-ranging and sympathetic intelligence. His biography demonstrates what a broad definition 'Caribbean poet' can be: born in Ghana of West Indian parents, Dawes grew up mostly in Jamaica, was a postgraduate in Canada, lives and works in the USA, and is mostly published in Britain. As a critic of contemporary Caribbean writing, his analysis has been both generous and original, particularly in his work on the notion of a 'reggae aesthetic', as developed in his study *Natural Mysticism*[1] and illustrated both in his anthology *Wheel and Come Again*[2] and his collection of poems *Shook Foil*.[3] One has a sense, reading over Kwame Dawes' work, that his is an active intelligence, in the best tradition of the practitioner-critic, the different facets of his work – poetry, drama, public reading, reviewing, the interviews with other Caribbean writers and the academic criticism – each serving to inform his overall artistic project.

It is clear from his account of the evolution of a 'reggae aesthetic' that Dawes has a strong sense of the importance of tradition in understanding contemporary cultural expression, albeit that the tradition he identifies in *Natural Mysticism* and *Wheel and Come Again* is not that Walcottian 'mighty line of Milton and Marlowe' which ratified the Caribbean canon! *Natural Mysticism: Towards a Reggae Aesthetic* is a brilliant and original rereading of Caribbean literature and orature in relation to one of the most powerful cultural phenomena of the second half of the twentieth century; the emergence of reggae music and the philosophies that underpinned it. He explores the ways a complex reggae aesthetic, informed by a 'history of rebellion and defiance', but characterised, too, by a Rastafarian redefinition of 'love', permeates and liberates the writing of a whole generation of Caribbean writers. (Not to mention a significant group of African, American and European writers). His analysis fundamentally challenges prevailing orthodoxies but is argued with both authority and great subtlety. This is a period of redefinition for Caribbean culture and Dawes' work in *Natural Mysticism* and *Wheel and Come Again* sits alongside Carolyn Cooper's *Noises in the Blood*,[4] Kamau Brathwaite's *LX, The Love Axe/l*[5] and Antonio Benitez Rojo's *The Repeating Island*,[6] as seminal texts in that process of reassessment and reclamation.

The notion of a reggae aesthetic – of the language moving to a different rhythm, under different kinds of pressure – also underpins all Dawes' work as poet. It is, in part, what has established the distinctive voice in his poetry, which is in other ways both formally and thematically diverse – ranging from the exploration of intensely private emotion to a consideration of huge public historical issues, particularly around slavery, the Middle Passage and its consequences. But of course that history is one source of his private emotions, so again we have this sense of interpenetration in Dawes' work, of the wholeness of his intellectual/ artistic enterprise. The distinctiveness of the voice and the range of his concern is perhaps best illustrated in relation to three of his collections, the 1996 collection *Requiem, Shook Foil* (1998) and *Midland* (2001).[7]

Requiem is a linked sequence of poems responding to the historical facts of the Middle Passage, powerfully imaging and evoking the horror of the slaves' experience but also managing to transcend the conventional responses of outrage and horror to convince his readers that the voices s/he hears, the emotions s/he encounters, are genuine, are felt, and so enable the cathartic, healing energy of the sequence to come into play. It is in this sequence that we understand how much Dawes has learnt from both Brathwaite's historical vision and Walcott's facility with metaphor. *Requiem* represents an emotional counter-discourse to the ethnocentrism of the accounts of slavery that are fixed in the early histories of the Caribbean. In rewriting that history the poems are, to some extent, re-centring the colonial relationship, putting the experience of the slave at the centre of the story, the slave-owners very much at the margins. But the sequence is not just a re-imaging of the Atlantic crossing, it includes several poems that focus on the life-after-the-crossing, from those set in plantation times to others very much of the present. Inevitably then the legacies of slavery are addressed, particularly with regard to issues of race. 'Family Tree', which is written, pointedly, in a female voice, explores the complexity of ethnic identity – colour and shade – in post slavery societies

> Now her daddy, he was white,
> but my daddy didn't know him,
> saw him sometimes, but didn't know him.
> And her mother, his grandmother,
>
> she was black, she was a slave,
> and the daddy, the white man,
> he would go on and get his pleasures
> from her till she would swell.[8]

And in exploring the notion of shame – the subject of one of the most powerful poems in the sequence – *Requiem* confronts another taboo: the hurt bound up in the nagging idea that the people who were the slaves (and, more pointedly, their descendants) had in some neo-colonial sense 'connived' with plantation lore in order to survive. Again it is a woman's voice:

> while we lick our wounds,
> wipe the wet from our thighs,
> avert our gaze from the shame
> of men, still alive, now boys
> witnesses to our abuse [9]

As those quotations demonstrate, although there is a healing and cathartic element to the sequence – for the reader as well as for the writer – no-one emerges from a reading of *Requiem* shouting 'all a we is one'! Despite the intensity of the passions these poems draw upon, Dawes is a sophisticated enough poet to understand that such energies must be channelled, shaped and mediated through voices that will – in the terms of that most fundamental of axioms for the aspiring poet, – 'shows us, not tells us' of those feelings. The economy of the writing, the sense of 'measured' utterance, the gravitas and respect with which the poet addresses his subject, all this informs the complex truthfulness of the poetry. Not that these are in any sense 'decorous' poems; the emotion that most characterises them is anger which – in the character of particular personas – is both raw and violent. Take, for example, the poem 'Crime of Passion' which so powerfully evokes the rage of the man-who-would-become-the slave and the frustration of alienation in his descendant who might-be-a-poet:

> .....Oh to stay in the simple
> dialectic of hatred and brutality
> there at the edge of my flaming hut,
>
> to remain in that fire-bright place
> of purest hate, the stranger, a beast
> my fist clear-eyed, pounding life
>
> from his faceless howls. All this long before
> the gospel of crosses, blood; the strong
> of promised lands I have embraced,
>
> long before I copulated
> with his books and gave birth to words,
> long before he found my tongue,
> could sing my tongue, owned my tongue
> while I toyed with his. Now my fist
> is a cataracted beast, unable to shake
>
> the monkey of affinity from my back.[10]

The *Shook Foil* collection taps into deep feeling too. Clearly related to his scholarly work on the reggae aesthetic, the collection complements Dawes' recent biography of Bob Marley.[11] The style of poems like 'Some Tentative Definitions I' illustrates Dawes' formal awareness of the bass line that characterises the reggae aesthetic:

...the bass, a looping lanky
dread, sloping like a lean-to
defying gravity and still limping
to a natural half-beat riddim,
on the rain-slick avenue[12]

Shook Foil also suggests the sensibility, the sensuality, the one-love weight of spirituality and metaphor – 'light like a feather, heavy as lead' – that the reggae aesthetic encompasses

I stir from my trance hungry and thirsty,
And as sudden as a prayer formed, the sky is ashen –
Heavy and spluttering pellets of rain.
I stand before the language of this storm
Again an alien, a sojourner, waiting for a clue
To lead me homeward – a place of quiet rest.[13]

This is a poetry dancing to a different drummer: the range of reference, the cultural assumptions bound into the poems, the cast and turn of the language, the lyrical drive... all of these announce another way of thinking about poetry in English where both 'poetry' and 'English' are problematic terms to be challenged and redefined.

'Challenge and redefine' is essentially what Dawes is doing throughout his work, from the poems of alienation and lament in the Forward Prize winning first collection *Progeny of Air,*[14] through the extended verse narratives of *Prophets*[15] and *Jacko Jacobus,*[16] to the exploration of what it means to claim a New World African identity in *Midland,* which won the prestigious Hollis Summers prize in the USA in 2001. Like *Requiem* and *Shook Foil, Midland* is also concerned with the gifts – both welcome and burdensome – of cultural inheritance. Indeed the collection opens with a long poem titled 'Inheritance' which explores the idea of a poetic inheritance. In it the prolific and prodigious young poet, so often compared to Derek Walcott, and described as one who might take on Walcott's mantle as *the* poet of the West Indies, goes to sit (in fact or imagination) at the older poet's feet. The poem is an extended praise-song to Walcott's commitment and achievement and above all, his example of a life devoted to '..the chronic genius of crafting poems':

how he makes a parrot flame a line
or a cicada scream in wind; the names
he gives the bright berries of an island
in the vernacular of Adam and the tribe[17]

Striking the pose of the apprentice, the younger poet seeks the old master's benediction, but it is not forthcoming. 'He will not be drawn out/ he is too weary now.' The young poet has to acknowledge that his is a different inheritance anyhow, for one thing his sensibility is shaped by a more direct relationship to Africa and its cultural traditions. In another poem, 'Ska Memory', dedicated to his father Neville Dawes, himself a distinguished poet and novelist, Kwame Dawes recalls other – distinctively Jamaican – aspects of his cultural inheritance 'the way/ a melody could collect memories, could flesh and swell/ and bleed'. Through the rest of the collection, which is as stylish and original as Dawes' earlier work – that so invited the comparison with the young Walcott – Kwame Dawes explores other aspects of that New World African inheritance. A sense of displacement, a questing for home and identity and belonging runs through this book in the many voices and locations of the diaspora – Alabama and Guyana, Ewerton in Jamaica and Ewe country in Ghana, South Carolina and London's South Bank. One has a sense that as his career unfolds, Dawes sees himself cast in the role – to borrow a term from another tradition – of a 'peoples' remembrancer', or as he puts it in 'Liminal':

I am gathering the relics of a broken threnody,
Lisping psalms – all I have – and crying salt and wet.[18]

FELLOW TRAVELLER: 'A WITNESS IN MY TIME AND PLACE': THE POEMS OF DON BURNESS

An Introduction to Don Burness's Selected Poems, *The Bardie Clan*[1]

I first read Don Burness's poems while I was living in Kano in northern Nigeria in the early 1980s. I was teaching in the university there and one of my neighbours in the old city was an American teacher, Priscilla Starrat, whose family home was in New Hampshire. Priscilla knew I was writing poems about the experience of living in Nigeria and remembered that a neighbour of her parents', back near Rindge, had also written about his travels in West Africa, so she arranged for me to see a copy of his collection *Safari*.[2] So, a literary – and later a personal – friendship began by the unlikely coincidence of our sharing a neighbour, despite living on separate continents!

It was clear from my reading of the poems in *Safari* that Don Burness and I shared many interests, and in particular a concern with finding ways to represent and understand experiences encountered as a Western traveller in Africa at the end of the twentieth century. In some ways though, reflecting, perhaps, our different backgrounds, our approach to that challenge has been very different. As an expatriate Englishman working in parts of the former British Empire I have been obsessed with history, with my sense of walking – whether I would or not – in the footsteps of other such displaced Englishmen. Burness, however, will not recognise the notion of the expatriate – at least not in relation to himself. He writes in much the same spirit as he travels; initially as a wide-eyed and open-hearted stranger, enthusiastic to discover the life and culture of the many places he has seen. Then, after a little while, he writes as a friend to the places and particularly of the people he encounters. He has not, on the whole, got so hung up on history.

I do not mean to suggest that Don Burness's poems have no sense of the way history has shaped those places and those people he encounters, rather that his concern is with present possibility rather than past perversions. Indeed, Burness's poetry reveals a very sharp awareness of current issues and their historical roots in the places where he has spent any time, particularly Nigeria. Borrowing both techniques and sentiments from some of the Nigerian poets he was quick to befriend, Burness writes with chilling insight of the corruption of military dictatorship in Nigeria in 'The War Never Left Port Harcourt':

> While General Naira drinks his beer
> And whispers sweet nothings in his mistress' ear [3]

The naira, of course, is the main unit of currency in Nigeria.

A concern with Nigeria and Nigerian writers runs through this entire collection. Burness's Nigerian poems are essentially in two moods: his first instinct is always to praise – particularly to celebrate poets such as Christopher Okigbo, Chinua Achebe and Niyi Osundare – but that celebration is counterbalanced by the need to lament – as those same writers have – the demise of civil society there. Burness speaks as he finds, but he is always aware that his is a view from the perspective of a temporary visitor, a traveller; he is always going to be 'watching/ the masquerade from different angles', as he puts it in one of his pithy epithets from the *Watching the Masquerade*[4] collection.

Notwithstanding his determination to be positive, travelling in Africa can be an uncomfortable experience – morally and spiritually – for someone with Don Burness's sensitivities. He draws vivid pictures of those moments when the impoverished reality of one world impinges on the rich illusions of the other, in poems such as 'Along the Elegant Streets of Dakar':

> The countless armless, legless creatures
> who flock at the feet
> of the strong and the healthy

They are everywhere, these beggars
Fighting, cajoling, crawling, stalking
Their way to survival [5]

And in 'Safari', set in East Africa, Burness plays even more
pointedly on the ironies of such meetings in his beautifully measured
account of the encounter between the tourist who has come to
'see the sights' of Africa and the blind beggar with his ubiquitous
boy-guide,

Quietly – hand in hand –
the boy led the blind old man
on a safari to a land
we tourists could not see [6]

As that last quotation might suggest, the poetic persona that emerges
from this collection – while he can be angry and passionate, witty
and caustic – is essentially a contemplative. Don Burness not
only observes the world as he travels through it but he is also –
and this is a much rarer talent – someone willing to sit in silence
and wait and listen and watch. That is a talent he brings to his
poetry from another of his passions – for ornithology. As poet
Don Burness takes – to use a British term – a *twitcher's* pride in
spotting and naming the birds of all the regions of the world he
has visited, but what comes across in his many poems written
about birds is his undiminished delight in the sheer beauty and
'otherness' of those birds, whether they are the familiar black
ducks and chickadees of the countryside around Rindge or the
more exotic weaverbirds and grey-headed kingfishers he encounters
on his tropical forays. But, if there is one thing a bird watcher
must be able to do it is to 'be still and know' and it is that capacity
for *meditation* that characterises so many of the poems in *The Bardie
Clan*. I must confess to having been surprised at this discovery
as I reread the poems for this brief introduction. Surprised, I
suppose, because when I think of Don Burness's work I immediately
recall those ebullient 'African' poems, evoking the sights and sounds
and *engagements* of his visits to the continent, but surprised also
because the Don Burness I have come to know as a man is a

larger than life character: outspoken and unselfconsciously – and delightfully – 'up front'. But so many of the poems reveal this other, contemplative, side of his nature. The words I used most often in my notes to the poems were 'understated', 'restrained', 'simplicity', 'unornamented' and particularly 'meditative'. This comes across in poems such as 'Yad Vashem', recording his visit to the Museum of the Holocaust in Jerusalem. This is a man for whom his Jewish heritage becomes increasingly important as he grows older, so a visit to Yad Vashem was bound to be an emotionally searing experience. The poem he writes does contain that pain, but the horror of what that experience *means* is conveyed most powerfully by the whisper rather than the scream; he trusts his words to do their work:

> It is the normality of it all
> That appals at Yad Vashem
>
> A normality that makes us grieve
> As we take the bus back to Tel Aviv [7]

'Normality': ordinariness, the commonplace, unexceptional, the expected… that such terms might apply to such horror, both for the victims and the perpetrators. The resonance of that observation is more powerful than any number of outraged assertions of Nazi wickedness.

That sense of perspective, which allows him to understand that his own deeply felt pain must be a secondary focus in poems responding to places where evil is commemorated, is also evident in 'At Elmina Castle', in the selection from *The Cry of the Crow*.[8] In this brief poem he distils into eight lines both the complex history of one of the most notorious centres of the African slave trade and a sense of the immense distress that affects any thinking visitor to Elmina – African, American or European, black or white. Again Burness doesn't go for the easy target, rather he sees what happened at and to Elmina as a metaphor for contemporary circumstances:

> for the waves of lament are still heard on this shore
> and the cry of the crow warns that now as before
> the drumbeat of betrayal is heard throughout the hills [9]

Another thing that strikes the reader of these contemplative poems is their apparent simplicity. As anyone who has tried will know, to write simply, directly, without apparent artifice or adornment, and yet also to write memorably, is not at all a simple task. In the several elegies for dead friends (human and canine) and in more general meditations on what friendship means (such as the poem, 'I think of people I have not seen for years'), Don Burness manages to do just that:

> I think of people that
> I have not seen for years
> Amaranths that blossom
> In all seasons
> Offering beauty
> When cold winds blow [10]

There are many such moving remembrances in the collection, several dedicated to other poets or to distinguished friends. I was particularly moved by his 'Praise Song for Hilda Leach', an African American woman who knew, he says, 'Elminas of despair'. But there are also several elegies to dogs, pets who have really been, one feels, this particular man's 'best friend'. (Note the uncharacteristic viciousness of his response to a Nigerian newspaper headline reporting a man's death after eating dog-meat soup!) That he can write so unselfconsciously of his feelings for his dogs is another token of the emotional honesty that underpins all the poems in this collection.

Most of what I have said so far, Don Burness has anticipated in his poem 'Letter to the Future', which might well serve as his own introduction to this 'Selected Poems':

> I a witness in my time and place
> have often been ashamed
> of the human race
> but for reasons I know not
> I love the world
> The open laughter of markets in Africa
> ...

261

But mostly I love the world
birds, chipmunks, flowers, mountains
birch trees, elephants, ducks, thunder
the great sky in the West of my country
and dogs
all dogs but dachshunds above all [11]

It is all there, but I take this opportunity to draw attention to
a couple of other elements in his work. One of them is not listed
but enacted in that quotation: his wry sense of humour. Don
Burness knows that the last two lines of that quotation will raise
a smile in most of his readers, and he shares it with us, but he
has also used wit – in both senses – in more pointed ways,
throughout his writing career. The grim wit and humour of many
of his poems set in Nigeria is a response to corruption and injustice
that he learnt from his many friends among Nigeria's contemporary
poets. He can also mock the absurdity of obsessions closer to
home, as in 'Modern Love' which remarks 'These solemn suitors
/ have wed their computers' or in his beautifully spare deflating
of pomposities in his poem sequence, 'Couplets'. I particularly
empathise with his response to too many of the speakers at academic
conferences:

They are profound, sincere, earnest and deep
But when they speak I fall asleep! [12]

Burness can also use his wit to pay back an unsympathetic reviewer,
as in the tart 'Epistle to the Critic Russell Hamilton':

Russell, Russell is it scotch or vermouth
That causes you to stray from the truth?
Or do you have the critic's disease
to fart wherever whenever you please [13]

This critic is suitably forewarned!
But that sharp edge to Burness' poetic tongue is more often
an expression of his dismay at the larger injustices that pollute
the world through which he travels. It is the other side of his
compassion and his capacity for empathy that he should be so

affronted by corruption and cruelty. Whereas his earlier poems remarked on the wrongs of other people's societies as he encountered them, there is a strand in his more recent work that is much more critical of the state of his own country. That disquiet emerges in poems such as 'The Rosenbergs: Forty Years Later' which laments not only the injustice done to that particular couple wrongly executed for spying in the early 1950s, but expresses outrage that, even when their innocence was confirmed through recent access to KGB files, there was general indifference to the implications of that revelation:

> not even a shrug of the shoulder now
> …
> from government or the press
>
> twin actors in the nation's
> daily drama of self-congratulations [14]

And in 'Longfellow in Menton' the poet can't disguise the bitterness of the assertion that:

> in my country
> painter and poet are exiles
> in a land where money is the highest art [15]

This theme is most powerfully explored in 'I Hear America Crying' which formally, as well as in terms of its spirit, acknowledges Whitman's great epic and also recalls elements of Alan Ginsberg's 'Howl'. Burness – whose instinct is to celebrate – finds himself drawn towards despair by the seeming decline of moral values he perceives in contemporary America:

> I hear America crying
> the lamentations and ululations of mothers burying their
> children gunned down as they sit at doorstep or chat on
> the corner [16]

And just as he is drawn to contemplate the nature of his own society in the later poems, so there is a more personal and self-reflexive strand to his meditations, a concern with finding meaning in terms of his own life and work. Having looked out for so long, he now turns his gaze – informed by his knowledge of the world and its ways – back on himself. We notice a concern with ageing and with a sense of his own mortality, brought on, in part, by the passing of his own parents. That process of self-inquiry draws him to an investigation of what his Jewish inheritance might mean in poems such as 'The House on Griswold Drive', 'Now these are the generations' and, more bitterly, 'The Illustrious Anti-Semites'. If his Jewishness is an important part of his identity, then so is his poet-ness – for want of a better term. There is a strong sense here that Burness feels himself part of an extended family – extended in time as well as by geography – of the world's poets. In 'The Bardie Clan' and 'On Being a Jew' he links those two strands of familial identity, for as he says in the former:

> A People must have a poetry
> to map in song the soul of a race [17]

And that is what he does in 'On being a Jew', a marvellous poem that seems to me to represent the fruit of the various lessons learnt on his many journeys – as a man and as a poet – to enunciate a credo that is both humane and inspirational. The poem is by turns stern and compassionate, justly angry but also generous spirited, grandiose but also self-deprecating. It is a poem that asserts a particular heritage but claims, too, the right to other connections. There is a tension in the language, a sense of something having been carefully wrought about the poem, but it also has the quality of proverb, of something that has been handed on, the product of a collective rather than just an individual wisdom. 'On Being a Jew' has all the qualities I have noticed in Burness' other work, including the wit which saves him from ever seeming pompous. Take for example the wonderful lines:

> I am the Jew
> who knows the Messiah will never come
> Yet keeps the door open for him [18]

It is a brave poem, asserting both the importance of belonging to a tradition but equally the necessity of independence of mind. 'On Being a Jew' is a poem that may offend all sorts of people but it will also inspire and move and energise many more. It is, for me, the real thing: it makes me shiver every time I read it.

If the best compliment you can pay a poet is to admire his later work even more than the earlier, then perhaps that's where I should conclude this brief introduction. But this collection represents only a stage on the long journey; I for one look forward to travelling further with this witty troubadour, this colourful 'bird of many trees', this brave and compassionate

Jew
who composes symphonies
of the Bardie Clan

IMAGINARY CONTINENT: IMAGES OF AFRICA IN MODERN BRITISH POETRY
(A Festival of Voices in Honour of Niyi Osundare)

This essay is an edited version of the Guest Lecture delivered at the University of Ibadan, Nigeria. March 14th 2007 on the occasion of the Celebrations of Niyi Osundare's sixtieth birthday.

1

I have long been a great of admirer of Niyi Osundare as a poet – his qualities and achievements are well known to everyone in this audience.

I have also had the good fortune to come to know him as a friend and a colleague; he spent several months with us at the Centre of West African Studies at the University of Birmingham as a Cadbury Fellow in the mid 1990s and I have worked with him since then when we ran a creative writing workshop together in Wales a few years ago. I have was also working at the University of the West Indies in Barbados when Niyi was a Distinguished Visiting Lecturer there. Indeed having climbed windswept Welsh Mountains with Niyi and swum in the warm waters of the Caribbean with him, I am particularly pleased to be able to complete the triangle as it were and meet him here on his home ground at last.

I should say at this point that I can't help but recall the last time I was in Nigeria speaking at a gathering such as this. That occasion was also in some ways sponsored or facilitated by Niyi. It was in November 1995 and it was the conference of the Nigerian Association of Authors which coincided – gruesomely – with the execution of Ken Saro-Wiwa[1]. That was, to give the word its Jamaican usage, a *dread* occasion and I am very glad to have this occasion of celebration to – not erase – but to overlay that memory.

I was invited to give this lecture "in honour of Niyi Osundare on his 60th birthday". That is quite a challenge: how does one honour a poet of such distinction and accomplishment, one whose praises have been sung many times and in many ways already – and on his home ground? What would he understand by the phrase 'in honour of'? Some writers I can think of would expect – even demand – yet more praise of their personal qualities, an intensification of the spotlight on their life and work to date. After all, who is the star of this show?! But I think I know Niyi well enough to know that he does not think like that and does not does not need or even desire yet more praises to be sung from this particular quarter.

Also, although I'm someone who has taken an interest in – and written about – English language poetry in West Africa for many years now, I don't think that an audience here in Ibadan needs *me* to come and tell *you* about the qualities of *your* poet.

So what should I speak about 'in honour' of the great poet? One characteristic that I particularly associate with Niyi is his intellectual curiosity, his genuine interest in the poets and poetries of other times and other places than his own – particularly places where he has lived or visited. Indeed I would argue that such curiosity has informed and contributed to his own work in various ways – in terms of his often daring notions of craft and form, for example. So perhaps a learned academic disquisition on trends in recent postcolonial poetics would honour that admirable curiosity? But by the time you get to my age – and I am catching Niyi up fast – you should know what you are good at and what not. I'm never going to be someone who gets excited about postcolonial theory or the isms and schisms of contemporary literary criticism. Although I begin as someone who tries to write poems, I am best known as an anthologist, which is not a category of literary scholarship that is particularly well regarded these days. I would argue, however, that one of the most important roles a literary scholar can play is to *spread the word* and make it accessible in places and to people it might not otherwise have reached. That notion chimes with the suggestion of another great African poet, the Ugandan Okot p'Bitek, who believed that the study of literature should be 'a festival of voices',[2] which, it seems to me, is another way of describing an anthology. So the construction of such a 'festival' – on a particular theme lets say for propriety's sake – would seem a fitting way to honour a great poet. Such a project has the additional advantage of allowing some other poets, (in their turn friends of *the* poet) who can't be here in person, to come to the party as it were by having their voices heard among this festival chorus.

So finally to the theme of this festival anthology of poems that reflect Niyi's curiosity and interest in poetic traditions other than his own. For not entirely honourable reasons I have become quite interested in the works of modern British poets (and some English language poets from other parts of the world) who have visited, or more likely lived and worked in Africa for some time. There is a surprisingly large number of them. As someone whose primary academic work has been in African and Caribbean literature, which inevitably involves some engagement with the ways in which – historically – European writers represented Africa, I think it is both interesting and important to observe the ways in which contemporary European and American writers take on that challenge. If I were brave enough I would just read you the poems and let them speak for themselves, but I suspect that might disappoint my sponsors somewhat, so I will try to set these poems in some kind of framework and context. But this is essentially a parade, a masquerade of poems in honour of Niyi Osundare.

2

Writing in the introduction to the first major anthology of creative literature by African authors, Jean Paul Sartre described Africa as being, for the European mind, an *Imaginary Continent*.[3] He meant, I think, that most Europeans had so little factual knowledge of Africa – and were so much a prey to the exotic and barbarous images of the continent circulated through the embellished recollections of the explorers and missionaries, the traders and slavers, and even indeed the early anthropologists, that for his generation Africa was more a construct of fiction than a fact of what is now called Human Geography.

And indeed I'm sorry to say that those images of Africa *persist* in the European popular imagination – notwithstanding the minor industry that has evolved intent on establishing the continent's more complex identity – the histories, the modern anthropological and ethnographic studies, the documentary and feature films, the exhibitions of its art and artifacts, the international prizes its writers' win, despite even (and I say this with some feeling) the best efforts of those who run university departments devoted to the study of Africa in its multitudinous dimensions – still the image that too often persist in the popular media and the popular imagination is that of "Darkest Africa", "the Heart of Darkness", the savage hinterland of cannibals and headhunters beyond that bend in the river where the last glimmer of civilization, of light, penetrates the foliage of omnivorous jungle. These *are* images out of fiction, out of the imagination of the nineteenth century novelists who – with a few notable exceptions – had little or no first hand experience of Africa but invented it as a hell on earth to contrast with the Edenic gentility which their suburban readers liked to think that they inhabited.

The unsavoury mixture of fear and assumed moral superiority which makes up that popular image of Africa constitutes a pocket in the rucksack that contained The White Man's Burden, the Europeans' conception of their civilizing duty in the world they liked to think they had discovered and now controlled. Rudyard Kipling, who might be caricatured as the Poet Laureate of the Empire, captured the mood of the times with typical 'sensitivity' in his famous – or infamous – poem called 'The White Man's Burden',

> Take up the White Man's Burden –
>   And reap his old reward:
> The blame of those ye better,
>   The hate of those ye guard –
> The cry of hosts ye humour
>   (Ah, slowly!) towards the light;–
> "Why brought ye us from bondage,
>   Our loved Egyptian night?"[4]

Some recent revisionist literary scholarship would argue that there was, at least, an ironic subtext to Kipling's poems of Empire, but all I can say is that if it is there at all it is a subtext that lies very deep beneath the surface. However that might be, that same 'Egyptian' darkness that Kipling derides and which engulfed the *imaginary continent* was acknowledged to be primordial, concealing something fundamental about human kind that was as disturbing to the European idea of 'civilisation' as the ubiquitous cartoon image of 'missionary stew' was threatening to the prim Home Counties armchair evangelists. Africa physically repelled the Europeans – its climate, its diseases, its sheer scale meant that although parts of it might be colonized by pale men in *sola toupees* with machine guns and the flag – those pasty pink blotches on Mercator's distorted maps –the continent itself would never be truly conquered. Wasn't Africa the rock on which the other great European Empires of history had foundered?

The British poet and literary historian Robert Gittings was in north Africa during the second World War – when indeed another 'Western Empire' seemed likely to succumb to 'the scorpion's bite' – and his poem 'Stones at Hammamet, Tunisia' turns on that historical understanding of the role of Africa in Classical European history. The poem counterbalances the inherited stereotypes of 'the dark continent' with an evocation of the awe in which more sensitive and informed writers held both the known and the unknown elements of their imaginary Africa

> A fistful of mosaic,
> Seventy rough square stones
> Where Carthage first, then Rome,
> Allied with neutral dust,
> Where even the desert lance
> That founded a holy city
> Broke in the savage drift
> Of a pirate ransomed coast.
> Again, while western empire
> Writhes in the scorpion bite,
> Myself of a dying race,
> I pick these out of the sand,
> And hold the aquiline consul,
> His back towards Africa

Both in my heart and in my hand
While the dark mounts up behind.[5]

A more highly regarded poet - although mostly remembered
now for just one classic war poem[6] – John Pudney was also in
Africa during the second World War, though as a sailor he wouldn't
have ventured much beyond the odd coastal port. All the same
he was conscious, as Gittings was, of the historical relationships
between Africa and Europe, but as he was in West Africa that
consciousness introduced another aspect of the complex mesh
of emotions which go to make up a contemporary European's
feelings about the continent; guilt. His poem 'First Sighting of
West Africa' draws on all the old stereotypes but tries to understand
why, beyond the genuine – if misguided – missionary zeal, and
despite the well deserved reputation of its being 'the white man's
graveyard', Europeans had been so fascinated by the West African
coast over several centuries. The simple, if depressing, answer,
is, of course, greed. Greed for gold, for ivory and most damningly,
for slaves. That history inserts some irony into the British sailor's
excited approach to the continent as an envoy of the self styled
forces of freedom and liberty. Pudney's poem understands that
irony but still manages to convey the excitement of approaching
that 'Land magic with favours....'

> Out of the swelling noon,
> Bursting the eye with tears of heat,
> From the parched sea
> Looms Africa.
>
> O land of lions,
> Of gold guarded by fevers,
> Spinning a drapery of green sierras
> From the sky's side.
> Land, magic with favours,
> Perilous with love,
> Behind the garnish of the noble stance,
> The wonderful ambush.
>
> Travellers bring no peace,
> But thirst and bibles:

Reaching pale medicated hands for more
Favours and gold,
Hard ivory, yielding slaves.
Spoilers for centuries have gained this coast,
Seeking a timeless agony of wealth,
Bright as a fever in the flickering night.[7]

But I am jumping ahead of myself. Kipling and some well-intentioned abolitionist versifiers aside, Africa hardly appears in the English poetry of the century 1840 to 1940, and when it does it is as that simplistic metaphor for evil that the nineteenth century novelist found so useful. In the second half of the twentieth century, however (and indeed on into the present) a surprisingly large number of British poets – and for that matter poets from other English speaking countries – have spent time in Africa. A few in the armed forces like Pudney and Gittings, but more often teaching or working in the media or for NGOs. It is *their* poetic responses to the reality of the continent as they encountered it, written inevitably against the kinds of stereotypes I have described, which is the subject of this talk. There is no particular reason why anyone here should be interested in this body of writing, except to the extent, maybe, that we should all be interested in the ways others see us and our societies. As Edward Said observed when he was formulating his ideas about post-colonialism, there is often something important and valuable about the perspective of the 'outsider' whom is sometimes able to see and say things that might otherwise not be remarked or recorded.[8] His or her versions are, at least, one strand of the story, another contribution to the debate. And if nothing else, they might inspire another generation of outraged young African writers to 'write back' to that old imperial centre.

I say that these poet's responses were to the *reality* of Africa but inevitably they too construct fictions of the place and of their personal situation within the stories they weave. They interpret what they see from the perspective of the particular kind of outsider they are, make sense of it in terms of their own cultural orientation, just as the Victorian explorers did. The Africa that emerges from their work is another, if differently nuanced, imaginary continent.

Perhaps for that reason the sense of being in the footsteps of the early explorers remains a potent force in the contemporary European poet's imagination. The Welsh poet Duncan Bush examines the psychology of the Victorian explorers in his poem 'Days of Empire' to try and understand how, against all reason, those patches of pink got to be on the map at all! The foolhardy, macho single-mindedness of the explorers is all that enabled them to survive, for more intelligently cautious, more calculating, sensitive men, would never have set out. While we may mock their 'Victorian certitude', still, for the European setting out on his first trip to Africa, albeit by Boeing 777 to stay in a ubiquitous Hilton Hotel, unused to the regime of malaria tablets, mosquito nets and injections against unspeakable diseases, the spirit of those intrepid forefathers speaks, mocking in their turn, to the imagination;

> The old African explorers, first
> colonialist, God-fearing, fearless
> men, stayed something of the schoolboy
> all their lives, died
> middle-aged, sick, stricken
> by their knowledge. . . .
>
> Kitted in tropical English bachelorhood –
> moustached, in knee-pants,
> flannel (to prevent chills), capped
> they would have scorned
> the amulet of inoculation,
>
> bet their heart's beat
> on a God
> imperious and imperial as Yahweh,
> read their bibles coverless. .
>
> Armed with Victorian certitude, men
> of hard will,
> they named and slowly moved on, like Aeneas;
> RIPON FALLS, LAKE ALBERT. . .[9]

Even for John Haynes, who, at the time he wrote this next poem, 'Explorer', sometime in the 1980s, had lived almost half his adult life in Zaria, the metaphor of the explorer still seems to resonate with his own sense of the role of the British poet in Africa, sending back images of "what remained strange" to an incredulous public at home. Evoking Livingstone, Stanley and the Nile and that gaggle of Brits – Lander, Clapperton, Mungo Park – who spent so long searching for the source of the Niger – the line and image which starts and ends the poem, 'There's no far source I wanted to get to', claims for its speaker a psychological distance from the attitudes of those historical, self aggrandizing, Livingstonian explorers:

> There's no far source I wanted to get to.
>
> I just journeyed through what remains strange.
> The people here each own a small box
> covered with cowries which they say
> contains their soul. It's detachable.
> No-one looks in it. My notebooks are like that.
> Here, in a waterproof packet, facts
> kinds of face, hut, cloth, gourd – *proof.*
> I want it to go back. It contains nothing of me,
> I've kept away, I've honoured that
> up to the moment now of my soaked bolster
> and shuddering gums, It contains my soul.[10]

But despite the disclaimer, "It contains nothing of me", this is a poem which both exoticises the strange, other place that is this land of cowries, gourds and amulets and intrudes into it. The speaking voice in 'Explorer' may refer to an anonymous imaginary explorer but is also inevitably read as if informed by – at some level – the sensibility of the contemporary narrator poet. Which is interesting because John Haynes' knowledge of – and commitment to – Africa is exceptional among contemporary British poets. I will come back to his most recent, prize winning, work later in this talk.

One echo sounding in that intriguing poem is of that malignant melancholy which overtook so many of the isolated Colonial Officials who followed the explorers into Africa. Such transference of the responsibility for inner pain to outer landscape is characteristic of much of the Western literary response to Africa, perhaps now more than ever. The contemporary expatriate 'expert', is usually little more than a mercenary of technology who hopes, naively, for a cinematic African experience, but the culture shock he or she endures when the reality is not comfortable enough for their cossetted sensibility – the electricity blackouts, the dubious water supply, the strange foods, the incomprehensible and infuriating customs of the people, not to mention the heat, the heat – has spawned quite a volume of sneering poems of bewilderment and resentment. Although this presentation refers particularly to British poets, I should mention in passing that in recent years several interesting young North American writers, who have spent some time in Africa, have written out their frustrations in pained – but also often witty – poems of innocence and experience. Arguably these young Americans arrive in Africa with fewer preconceptions and perhaps more idealism than their more 'culturally burdened' British counterparts. I would refer especially to the work of the Canadian Richard Stevenson, who has published at least two collections of poems focused on his time in Maidugari in the 80s (See for example his 'Expatriate Stories') or the artfully crafted poems reflecting on her time in Kano by the American poet Wendy Bishop, poems like 'Futility Sestina: Getting Housing in Kano, Nigeria':

In the morning when the sky is gray
You return to the Housing Office
Hoping it won't be empty
Again. A secretary
Waves a piece of paper
And tells you Mr. Ojo has gone to Kaduna.

Everyone has gone to Kaduna.
You stride past the gray
Doves that nest in papers
And torn grasses along the ditches. Office
After office and secretary
After secretary, you search

Buildings for Mr Ojo or Sheyshey. Empty
Gesture, for the word *Kaduna*
Comes too easily to the secretaries

Who ignore your gray
And weary face. In their offices
You are no more than a piece of paper

And no less: an illegible paper
On a desk they prefer to keep empty[11]

Amusing and in their ways as 'true' as those poems are (I too pursued Mr Ojo for several months when I first arrived in Kano) these are essentially touristic responses I think. I have written elsewhere,[12] in relation to my own poetry, about categories of poems that reflect the levels of familiarity and knowledge and commitment to a place that an 'outsider' poet might bring to bear on the poem he or she writes and suggested that the categories might be termed Tourist, Traveller and Troublemaker. It is certainly possible for an individual writer to occupy each category at different times and it seems to me that these categories might serve us helpfully in trying to frame the poems I will be discussing in the rest of this talk.

On the one hand Tourist writing may respond excitedly to the ways in which a particular setting is different from places familiar to the poet, or might celebrate the exotic otherness of the people and their culture. But it may as likely record the poet/persona's negative culture shock, explore the trials and tribulations of perceived difference, the disappointments of unfulfilled expectations. Essentially, at the centre of any piece of Tourist writing, the writer/persona's own sensibility is what is being held up for scrutiny and applause. It's the observer's distress or delight which is the real focus of the poem, regardless of the vivid pictures of 'the strange' that may be the ostensible subject matter.

The traveller-as-writer is distinguished from the tourist-writer to some extent just by the seriousness of purpose that they seem to have brought to the enterprise of writing 'about' a place or experience, or it may just be a matter of time spent either travelling *per se* or of staying in a particular place for more than the tourist's fleeting visit. Either way the traveller-as-writer is more self aware, more conscious of his own context, more aware of a heritage – aware particularly of those who have written about the place before.

Those writers works become part of the cultural baggage the traveller inevitably carries with him. The best traveller-writers, I think, manage to convey both a sense of their own 'strangerness' – recognising its consequences in terms of what they see - as well as a real sense of a place observed and 'tasted'. Life there, in the place travelled to or through, is connected with life elsewhere, 'real' life, the life that fixes the writer's identity beyond the role of the tourist or traveller.

It seems to me that the 'African' poems of Tony Harrison, fall into that traveller-writer category. Harrison is, in terms of contemporary British poetry, the most significant poet among this 'interesting crew' of writers who have learnt from and been changed by their encounter with Africa. Born in 1937, Tony Harrison is generally regarded as being among the most accomplished and sophisticated of contemporary British poets as well as being a distinguished playwright. He spent three or four years as a lecturer at Ahmadu Bello University in Zaria in the early 1960s. He is probably best remembered in Nigeria for the his first theatrical piece, *Aikin Mata* (1966), an 'African' version of Aristophanes' *Lysistrata*, which he wrote in collaboration with the Irish poet, James Simmons – who was also at Ahmado Bello at that time – for a student theatre group. In his preface to the 1966 edition Harrison remarks that the combination of music and dance incorporated into the performance highlighted parallels between classical Greek and African dramatic traditions: he said,

'Masquerades like the Yoruba *Engungun* of Oshogbo with their dual sacred and profane functions as ancestor spirits and as comic entertainment seem closer to Greek comedy than anything one has in modern Europe.' [13]

The play was a great success when first performed and – to the best of my knowledge – is still in print and well used both in West Africa and elsewhere.

Harrison's work is characterised by its formality, by its classical associations and, often, by its use of a distinctive northern English voice and dialect. Harrison's background was far from that of

277

the traditional literary or Classics scholar, rather he was the child of more or less illiterate working class parents and subject to the kind of sneering class snobbery that only the English can really exercise. Having won a scholarship to a prestigious grammar school he was made to feel a misfit and described by one of his teachers, because of the dialect he spoke, as "a barbarian", a tag he has explored in creative ways through much of his writing life. He went on to Leeds University where he completed a degree in Classics. The Greek poets would become a model for his English verse: he greatly admired their combination of bawdiness, beauty and craft. Harrison's genius has been to bring those conflicting elements of his background to creative focus in the poetry he has written over the last four decades. His first book, which concerns us today, was *The Loiners*, published in 1970. The collection is in five sections, the first containing poems about 'Loiners' – the local slang term for the citizens of Leeds – and exploring Harrison's own upbringing there. The second section deals with the experience of expatriate Loiners in Africa. Recalling the qualities of some of the Greek verse he so admires, Harrison plays with other associations of the word 'loins' – so there is a definite bawdiness and rough sensuality about many of the poems in the collection, including 'The Songs of the PWD Man' from the 'African' section of the book. 'The Songs of the PWD Man' is a clear attempt at modernising Kipling, to make his jaunty, barrack-room ballad metre a convincing vehicle for the lived colonial experience. The persona, a dissolute and brutish colonial administrator, out of time in all sorts of ways, boasts of the perks and privileges of his position:

> I'll bet you're bloody jealous, you codgers in UK,
> Waiting for your hearses while I'm having it away
> With girls like black Bathshebas who sell their milky curds
> At kerbside markets out of done-up-fancy gourds,
> Black as tar-macadam, skin shining when it's wet
> From washing or from kissing like polished Whitby jet.
> They're lovely, these young lasses. Those colonial DO's
> Knew what they were up to when they upped and chose
> These slender, tall Fulanis like Rowntrees coffee creams
> To keep in wifeless villas. No Boy scout's fleapit dreams
> Of bedding Bridget Bardot could ever better these.[14]

Not exactly politically correct or likely to endear the speaker – or perhaps even the author – to a feminist audience, all the same it is in its way a kind of honouring!

Reading the poem today, forty years after it was written, one thing that strikes us is the thematic connection with so much recent Nigerian poetry lamenting the corruption and abuses of post colonial governments and administrators. Harrison refuses to 'play the game' by pretending that a British administration was all efficiency and probity and draws the Public Works Department man 'warts and all' as the saying goes. Although in some ways an affable and engaging character – reminding me of a pasty faced version Chief Nanga in Achebe's *A Man of the People*[15] he is hardly a model of probity or Christian morality, and he seems to bear the white man's burden very lightly! The ironic tension between the artful measure of the rhyming couplets and the tawdry subject matter maintains both the interest and energy of the poem. It is that crossover of highbrow literary craft and cultural reference with down-to-earth language and subject matter that has marked out Harrison's work in British contemporary letters. And it begins really with 'The Songs of the PWD Man'.

Up to this point you might be forgiven for thinking that this talk has been more about the psychological tribulations of Europeans in Africa than with Africa itself – a conflation and confusion that is still often made. But for the rest of the time I have I want to focus on two poets who have had a deeper and more engaged relationship with Africa and both of them, in different ways, might fit in the category of 'Troublemaker' in my rough and ready hierarchy of modern poets who have written about Africa.

The traveller who stays, who settles and so identifies himself with a place after a significant length of time, is distinguished from the tourist and the traveller in that he gradually does comes to see that place in a different way, and so – if he is a writer – writes about it in a different way. Gradually he sees beyond the glittering or grotesque otherness to understand – to some extent at least – the contexts of what he's seeing. The settler, a kind of convert to the place, becomes sometimes and in some ways 'more native than the natives', feeling himself entitled to make public statements that local people might not – for various social, political or cultural reasons – feel able to make. The settler is both of the place and yet not really bound to accept the consequences of what he might say in terms of whoever he might offend. If push really comes to shove he can (almost) always go home. But the insights that he gains from staying allow him a kind of licence and gives what he says a measure of authority. He may easily become – in the eyes of an offended 'host' government – a certain kind of troublemaker.

That description would certainly apply to Landeg White – a Welshman who taught in various parts of Africa over four decades – who was unceremoniously deported from Hastings Banda's Malawi when he was seen to be too close to other – local – literary troublemakers, in particular his friend and colleague, the poet Jack Mapanje. White went on to lead an international campaign supported by Amnesty International to obtain Mapanje's release from Mikuyu Prison in Zomba where he had been detained for writing poems that offended someone in authority.

I was looking for a way to introduce and summarise Landeg White's career and came upon this paragraph which serves as the Introduction to his autobiography-in-verse *Traveller's Palm* which seems to me to do the job much better than any paraphrase of mine might – he says

All my adult life – my life as a poet in Trinidad, Malawi, Mozambique, Sierra Leone, Zambia, and now Portugal – I have been oppressed with a sense of rich experience, a wealth of poetic material, unused and unusable. For an audience in Britain, anticipating reports on 'the other', there was always so much to explain before the poem could begin. Yet for me, poetry began when I lost my sense of the exotic when – as one poem in the sequence puts it, describing my family surrounded by Kalashnikovs – 'at the time, this all seemed normal'. Added to this, dated as it may now appear, was a Puritan sense of a need to correct colonial misrepresentations by a scrupulous regard for the truth of what I lived and witnessed. No need for clever hyperbole, when the material itself was so strong. So, taking Luis de Camoes – that most literal-minded of poets – as model – I have attempted what I called in The View from the Stockade 'a poetry of fact'. The 'pure', the 'plain', the 'limpid', bordering the 'prosaic': it is the tightrope Wordsworth trod. At whatever different level, I am writing in an honourable tradition, driven by something both Camoes and Wordsworth implicitly recognised, that there is no such person as 'the other'.[16]

Across several collections now Landeg White has tried to carry out that agenda and along the way written some wonderfully evocative and precise poems about the people and places he has known. If there was time I would talk about his poem 'Afternoons Mozambique'[17] in which he catches the lethargic, immemorial aura of hot season afternoons in a small, provincial, frontier town so precisely. The poem also draws a portrait of another kind of expatriate – 'Senhor Santos' – the Portuguese trader who relishes "the yard of freedom" his life in Mozambique allows but knows that the seeming tranquillity may erupt in violence and terror at any moment and has his seat booked on a plane that will take him 'home' when the going gets too tough.

Or I would discuss the beautifully restrained portrait of Emily Makua, drawn in his poem 'The Instinct'[18], a strongly Christian woman whose faith supports her through the tribulations of a life that is, in material terms, 'utterly destitute'. In the face of her humility, faith and dignity the sophisticated, hard nosed, world weary poet is moved to tears. But following through on the 'troublemaker' story I would direct you to his poem 'The New Smiling Bwana' which describe the process of his going to Malawi as an English lecturer to teach what he calls 'the job lot', 'Homer to Naipaul' to students studying English at the university. He arrives fired up for this job but essentially uninformed about the political situation he has entered

The job was the job lot: Homer to Naipaul,
one-third Brit., one-third Europe, one
– third the Third World and all in English.
I embraced such radical immodesty

and I ministered. The platform was
form, about carving the calabash without
spilling a drop of the foaming *masese* beer
– something they knew but had overlooked

till they learned it again through *The Iliad*
Englished. It diverted them back
to their own songs and tales, and sideways
into poems in which I still lay claim

to the odd, exacter epithet. Literary
midwife, Taban called me. The new, smiling
bwana, wrote Chipasula. What's it to me
the best are detained or exiled? Or are dead? [19]

A later scene gives us a sense of the kind of life he lived there
and his growing consciousness of being overheard and monitored
by 'Banda's spies' – and worse, his 'secret' army:

> Banda's
> Spies were attentive, the girl's bored.
>
> Driving back through the deserted township
> We passed three striding in the roadway,
> Sandalled, gowned, rope-waisted,
> Their tonsures glistening in the moonlight.[20]

And then in the final section of the poem the account of his
deportation on 48 hours notice while others were detained without
trial, or worse.

> *What lion spits out,* Jack said, *must be tough.*
> I was flattered. Afterwards, on the VCIO
> banking north-east over the brimming river,
> I saw it in different light as wise counsel.
>
> Once from a dugout on that swift, pewter
> river, I watched the slim jet tilting north.
> Banished, I stared down at the baobabs:
> where snake suns himself must be comfortable.
>
> A country of passive verbs. Deported
> (my 48 hours sentence) or detained
> (Felix was the first of our group to rot):
> when hippo brainy, the pool dries up a little.

Taban was brusque, Okot pre-occupied
with harsher wrongs. It was re-resurrected
Ngugi who talked me through my pain
(active voices, *A Grain of Wheat*).[21]

It's clear that he has become a 'troublemaker' both in terms of his apparent allegiances and his writing. And as I say he went on to create a whole lot more trouble for the Banda regime by focusing attention on the detention of Jack Mapanje.[22]

John Haynes troublemaking was of a different order, although he has also been involved in campaigns to support fellow writers in Nigeria. He settled in one place for an extended period and became involved in the broad political and cultural debates about the values of the society and the direction it should take. He was committed to the life of the country in ways that no short term traveller could begin to understand. One theme that runs through his recent volume, *Letter to Patience*, (which won – against some very distinguished rivals – the Poetry section of the 2007 Costa Prize, one of the UK's major literary awards) is an account of those turbulent political times in Nigeria.

The first thing to say about this book length poem is that it is a magnificent accomplishment, beautifully measured, superbly crafted, by turns lyrical and poignant, informed and visceral, intelligent and angry. A wonderfully sensual, vivid and generally affectionate evocation of a certain kind of African/expatriate life in the last decades of the twentieth century, it is also a powerful indictment of the injustices of colonial history and global politics, of the brutalities and failures of successive Nigerian governments and a moving account of a middle aged son coming to terms with the decline and loss of his parents in 1990s middle England.

The craftsmanship should not be a surprise to anyone who remembers John Haynes first book of poems, *Sabon Gari*,[23] published back in the 1970s. Much of that collection too was set in Nigeria and explored images of life in the (literal and metaphorical) Strangers Quarter – which is how the title translates from Hausa, the dominant language of life in the area of northern Nigeria where John Haynes lived and worked for much of his life. In the three decades between the publication of *Sabon Gari* and *Letter to Patience* John Haynes wrote and published many fine – though often quite oblique and intriguing – individual poems drawn from his engagement with the life around him. Typically, as in his poem 'Tailor', Haynes' cross-cultural embroidery of wit and linguistic sleight becomes a part of the poem's meaning, there is no intrusive self consciousness or mere cleverness about this deft construction, but this is a world known intimately:

> This is how we sew one yard of ignorance
> Into another. My father has died
> And my brass wheel whirs. It is my dazed
> Prayer and my line of straightened stitches.
> So thin a soup we have inherited,
> And a small pencil and an exercise book
> That it is my soul that knows reading
> Instead of me. I study the needles.[24]

Haynes identified so strongly with the region and the political issues that impact on its development that he sometimes adopted the strategy of writing poems using Nigerian pseudonyms. Most significantly, in 1984 he published a pamphlet collection, *First the Desert Came and then the Torturer* under the pseudonym Idi Bukar.[25] Idi Bukar was presented as a radical Marxist poet from Sokoto. Haynes subsequently said of that collection that it was "some sort of humble solidarity with the likes of Ngugi wa Thiong'o and the critics of African dictators and misrulers".[26] As 'Idi Bukar' he clearly felt able to say things in ways that he couldn't as John Haynes, the long stay expatriate friend of Nigeria – if not of Nigerian Governments – whose work, nevertheless, would always and inevitably be consigned to the 'strangers quarter'. Given the sensitivities of the times, and the nature of successive Nigerian regimes, writing under such a pseudonym may also have been a strategy for avoiding the kinds of direct consequences that Landeg White's outspoken troublemaking brought him in Malawi, particularly if he wanted to explore sentiments like those in Idi Bukar's poem 'Revelations':

The generals took power
They went into the bedrooms
and found billions
Ordinary people grabbed up newspapers
Will those thieves get punished?
They asked each other
And forecasted
And debated [27]

Letter to Patience is a reflection back on that Northern Nigerian world from the perspective of a British expatriate teacher who has reluctantly left Nigeria in order to return 'home' to look after his aged and infirm father. In the event, as he relates in the letter he writes to his friend and former colleague, Patience, (a woman in her thirties who now runs a bar just outside the university where they'd both taught) the narrator feels more a stranger in the Britain he returns to than he ever seemed to be in Nigeria, where at least he had a public face and role.

The device of the chatty, episodic letter (52 loosely linked Cantos) allows the poet to pretend a literary informality even while measuring his verse in artful stanzas of mellifluous terza rima. In its formal and linguistic cunning as well as in its setting and to some extent its themes, the poem recalls Tony Harrison's work, but Patience is a much more attractive and convincing character than the debauched PWD man. The letter is written through the course of a single night as the writer attempts both to engage the image/memory of his friend in the cultural world she represents and to come to terms in some way with his sense of displacement and frustration. It is

.... A spell, a selfishness
To try and keep you there, or rather here [28]

The world he now inhabits in "Cowplain, Hants" is of course as far away and exotic a location to her as her bar in Samaru, Zaria, will be to most readers of the poem. One of the interesting things about the poem is the evocation of Patience as not so much the muse and passive recipient of memories and wise words from afar but as an active presence and participant in an imaginary dialogue which brings the spoken pidgin language of her bar into the crafted literary English of the text

Of course I know it isn't *you* I write
to sitting with elbows each side of a beer
chin in your palms and fingers splaying bright

red nails across your cheeks, you who lean near
and slowly close your eyes and then as slowly
open them so that the doubt goes as clear

through mine as through the very ghost of me.
"All dis tok-tok. Na dis, na dat, na dis…!
John? Enh? Wettin now? Me I no sabi!" [29]

The letter ranges widely in terms of the issues it explores and the references it invokes, from the detail of Nigerian radical politics to the scars and tribulations of an English boarding school education, and indeed some of the more arcane details are glossed in notes at the end of the poem. (As with all such notes it is almost as interesting to see what isn't explained and to wonder what that says about the imagined, putative reader.)

In its brilliantly evocative rendering of a Northern Nigerian locale, in its life affirming portrait of Patience and in the thoughtfully turned engagements with Imperial history, *Letter to Patience* is a very long way from Kipling and 'The White Man's Burden'. This is a portrait of a particular African setting and a group of real people – not exotic 'others' – who are known, acknowledged in their complexities and contradictions and respected for their humanity. With John Haynes the list of post war British poets who have spent time in Africa and gone on to write about it makes quite an intriguing squad, including many interesting writers I've not had time to mention in this brief survey, from Ronald Botterel and Alan Ross, through Dawson Jackson and David Sweetman, to John Harley Williams, E. A. Markham and Graham Mort. [30] The more sophisticated among them understood, as John Haynes clearly does, that however deeply they were embedded in the places that they visited or stayed, whatever commitment they made, however skilled and artful their literary representations, what they construct and explore in their poetry is their own *otherness* and their own 'imaginary continent.'

These diverse foreign writers then – several of them personal friends of Niyi's (although not, I don't think, Rudyard Kipling?!) – are brought to this 'Festival of Voices in Honour of Niyi Osundare' to add their congratulations to the praises offered to a great man, a great friend, and most of all a great poet.

FOOTNOTES

1. *Tourist, Traveller, Troublemaker*

1. Jamaica Kincaid, *A Small Place*, London, Virago, 1988. p.3-5.
2. Stewart Brown, 'Zinder' in *Elsewhere:New and Selected Poems*, Leeds, Peepal Tree Press, 1999, p.72.
3. Stewart Brown, *'Elsewhere:New and Selected Poems*, op.cit. p.99.
4. Stewart Brown, *'Elsewhere:New and Selected Poems*, op.cit. p.78.
5. Commenting on the ending of the poem in his Introduction to the *Oxford Book of Travel Verse,* the editor, Kevin Crossley-Holland remarks, "With this allusion to identity and rootlessness, travel poetry engages with one of the main concerns of twentieth century literature..... the idea that through travel people learn not only about other people and places but about themselves is a leitmotif of modern travel verse." (Oxford, OUP, 1986, p. xxxii-xxxiii)
6. Stewart Brown, 'Cricket at Kano' in *Elsewhere:New and Selected Poems*, op.cit., p.78.
7. Stewart Brown, *'Elsewhere:New and Selected Poems*, op.cit. p.13

2. *'Lugard's Bridge': a context*

1. Stewart Brown, 'Lugard's Bridge' in *Elsewhere: New and SelectedPoems*, Leeds, Peepal Tree Press, 1999, p.88-97.
2. Jean Paul Sartre, in *Orphee Noir*, the Introduction to Anthologie de la nouvelle poésie nègre et malgache de langue française [éditée] par Léopold Sédar Senghor. 4e éd. Paris, 1977. (1st edition 1948). The translation is cited in Gerald Moore's essay 'Towards Realism in French African Writing' in Modern African Studies, vol.1. no.1. 1963. p.61-73. (p.66)
3. George Woodcock, *Who Killed the British Empire? An inquest*, London, Jonathan Cape, 1974, p.82.

3. *Finding the Right Words: A Candle for Ken Saro-Wiwa*

1. Ken Saro-Wiwa, *A Forest of Flowers*, Harlow, Longman (African Writers series), 1995; Ken Saro-Wiwa, *Sozaboy: a novel in Rotten English*, Harlow, Longman (African Writers series), 1994
2. See Sanya Osha, *Ken Saro-Wiwa's Shadow: Politics, Nationalism*

and the Ogoni Protest, London, Adonis & Abbey Publishers Ltd, 2007.
3. See 'Literature and Freedom Across Boundaries', essay no. 4 in this collection.
4. Stewart Brown, 'Lugard's Bridge' in *Elsewhere:New and Selected Poems*, op.cit., p.88-97 .

4. Literature and Freedom Across Boundaries

1. Ngugi wa Thiong'o, *Detained: A Writers Prison Diary*, Oxford, Heinemann African Writers Series, 1981
2. Ngugi wa Thiong'o, *Devil on the Cross*, Oxford, Heinemann African Writers Series, 1987.
3. Jack Mapanje in conversation with the journalist Sue Lawley on the BBC radio programme 'Desert Island Discs', 2004.
4. Derek Walcott, 'Forest of Europe' in Collected Poems 1948-1984, New York, Farrar, Straus and Giroux, 1986, p.375.
5. Martin Carter, 'This Is the Dark Time My Love' in Gemma Robinson, ed., *University of Hunger: Collected Poems & Selected Prose*, Tarset, Bloodaxe Books, 2006. p.99.
6. See Gemma Robinson, Ed., *University of Hunger: Collected Poems & Selected Prose*, Tarset, Bloodaxe Books, 2006 for the most complete scholarly edition of Carter's poems. See also Brown and McDonald, Eds., *Martin Carter: Poems*, Oxford, Macmillan Caribbean, 2006, which offers a substantial selection of Carter's poems with less academic apparatus.
7. 'I Clench My Fist', *University of Hunger: Collected Poems & Selected Prose,* op.cit. p.100.
8. John Davies, 'All the Running' in Poetry Wales, Vol.20, no.4.1985, p.41-47.
9. John Davies, *The Visitor's Book*, Bridgend, Poetry Wales Press, 1985.
10. John Davies, 'The visitor's book' in *The Visitor's Book*, op.cit., p.9-14 (p.9)
11. John Davies, 'The white buffalo' in *The Visitor's Book*, op.cit., p.56-67
12. John Davies, 'Regrouping' in the sequence 'The white buffalo' in *The Visitor's Book*, op.cit., p.67.
13. Femi Oyebode, 'Mastering the chaff' in *Wednesday is a Colour*, Birmingham, Ijala Press, 1990. p.1-6 (p.5)

14. Femi Oyebode, 'An Abstracted Space' in *Master of the Leopard Hunt*, Birmingham, Ijala Press, 1995. p.7-16 (p.7)
15. Femi Oyebode, 'Dreamtime' in *Naked to Your Softness and Other Dreams*', Birmingham, Ijala Press, 1989. p.21-31 (p.23)
16. Femi Oyebode, *Forest of Transformation*, Birmingham, Ijala Press, 1991.
17. *The History of the Yorubas from the Earliest Times to the Beginning of the British Protectorate*. By Rev. Samuel Johnson, Ed. By Dr O. Johnson. London, Routledge, 1921.
18. Femi Oyebode, 'Gaha', in *Forest of Transformation*, op.cit., p.39-43.(p.39/40).
19. Femi Oyebode, 'An Abstracted Space' in *Master of the Leopard Hunt*, op.cit., p.7-16 (p.7)

5. Another Music: Poetry in English in West Africa, a preamble

1. For example, Kraft Books, University of Ibadan: Nigeria, Update Communications, Lagos: Heinemann Nigeria, Lagos: Afram Publications, Accra: Woeli Publishing, Accra.

6. Still Daring the Beast: Niyi Osundare and Contemporary Nigerian Poetry

1. Donatus Nwoga, *West African Verse* (London: Longman, 1967), p.17.
2. Christopher Okigbo, *Labyrinths* (London: Heinemann, 1971), p. 68.
3. Since this essay was first published both Ojaide and Osundare have taken up teaching posts in the USA.
4. Nadine Gordimer, 'The Essential Gesture: Writers and Responsibility', in *Granta*, No. 15, 1989, pp. 137-51.
5. Olu Oguibe, *A Song from Exile* (Bayreuth: Boomerang Press, 1990), p. 9.
6. *A Song from Exile*, p. 13.
7. *A Song from Exile*, p. 7.
8. See the discussion of Ofeimun's poem 'A Handle for the Flutist' later in this essay.
9. 'Alter-native' tradition – the term seems to have derived from

Femi Osofison's *Guardian* essay 'The Alternative Tradition: A Survey of Nigerian Literature', but is used by Funso Aiyejina in its broken form in his essay 'Recent Nigerian Poetry in English: an Alter-Native Tradition' (see note 10 below) to draw attention to the alteration of the consciousness in the work of the younger generation of Nigerian poets who are self-consciously *native* – with all the ramifications of that term – in their language, their cultural orientation and their concerns. It has become a reviewers' and critics' shorthand for the writers of that generation.

10. See, for example, the work of Femi Fatoba, Funso Aiyejina, Fred Agdeyegbe, Silas Obadiah, Emerwo Biakolo, Femi Osofisan, Eman Shehu; and see the Association of Nigerian Authors' anthology, edited by Harry Geruba, *Voices from the Fringe* (Lagos: Malthouse Press, 1990).

11. Tanure Ojaide, *The Blood of Peace* (London: Heinemann, 1991), p. 28.

12. Tanure Ojaide, *The Fate of Vultures* (Lagos: Malthouse Press), 1990, p. 9.

13. Tanure Ojaide, 'Song for My Land', *The Fate of Vultures,* p. 41.

14. Funso Aiyejina, 'Recent Nigerian Poetry in English: an Alter-Native Tradition' in *Perspectives on Nigerian Literature: 1700 to the present,* ed. Yemi Ogunbiyi, Vol. 1, (Lagos, Nigeria: Guardian Books, 1988).

15. Onwuchekwa Jemie, 'A Conversation with Odia Ofeimun', in *The Poet Lied* (Lagos: Update Communications Ltd., 1989), pp. 148-76.

16. 'The Poet Lied', *The Poet Lied,* pp. 40-41.

17. 'Our Wild Christian', *The Poet Lied,* p.87.

18. Robert Fraser, *West African Poetry* (Cambridge: Cambridge University Press), 1986.

19. *The Poet Lied,* p. 118.

20. 'A Handle for the Flutist', *The Poet Lied,* p. 119.

21. For a full bibliography of Osundare's work – and a useful bibliographical essay – see Don Burness' essay on Osundare in *The Dictionary of Literary Biography.* See also Biodun Jeyifo's essay 'Niyi Osundare' in volume two of Yemi Ogunbiyi's *Perspectives on Nigerian Literature,* pp. 314-20.

22. Niyi Osundare, *The Eye of the Earth* (Lagos: Heinemann, 1986), p. 14.

23. *The Eye of The Earth,* p. 44.

24. Aderenii Bamikunle, 'Niyi Osundare's Poetry and the Yoruba Oral Artistic Tradition', in *African Literature Today*, No. 18, 1988, pp. 49-61.
25. Unattributed jacket note to *Waiting Laughters* (Lagos: Malthouse Press, 1990).
26. *Waiting Laughter*, p. 25.
27. *Waiting Laughter*, p. 40.
28. Aderemi Bamikunle, 'Niyi Osundare's Poetry and the Yoruba Oral Artistic Tradition', pp. 52-53.
29. *Waiting Laughters*, p.88.
30. *Waiting Laughters*, p.48.
31. *Waiting Laughters*, p. 53.
32. *Waiting Laughters*, pp. 96-97.

7. Niyi Osundare - Crossing the Threshold between Yoruba and English

1. See particularly Aderemi Bamikunle, 'Niyi Osundare's Poetry and the Yoruba Artistic Tradition', in *African Literature Today*, no.18, 1988, pp.49-61.
2. Femi Oyebode, 'Prosody and Literary Texts', in S. Brown, ed., *The Pressures of the Text: Orality, Texts and the Telling of Tales*, Birmingham University African Studies Series, no. 4, 1995, pp.91-95.
3. Niyi Osundare, 'Caliban's Gamble: The Stylistic Repercussions of Writing African Literature in English' in Kola Owolabi, ed. *Language in Nigeria*, Ibadan, 1995, pp.340-363.
4. S. Brown, ed., *Kiss & Quarrel: Yoruba/English: Strategies of Mediation*, BirminghamUniversity African Studies Series, No. 5, 2000.
5 S. Brown, 'Daring the Beast: recent Nigerian Poetry' in Abdulrazak Gurnah, ed. *Essays on African Writing 2: Contemporary Literature*, Oxford, 1995, p.58-72. (See a revised version in this volume.)
6. Stephen H. Arnold, '*Carpe Millennium*: Niyi Osundare's *Seize the Day* and African Literature and the Crisis in Post-Structuralist Theorising', in *Anglophonia/Caliban*, no 7, 2000, pp. 23-32.
7. See S. Brown, *Elsewhere: New and Selected poems*, (Leeds: Peepal Tree, 1999).
8. Abiola Irele, 'Second Language Literatures: An African Perspective', in *Anglophonia/Caliban*, No. 7, 2000, pp. 7-22

9. I understand, from discussion at the conference, that scholars have recently been examining Senghor's work to identify the ways in which his use of the French language was distinctive and reflected his Senegalese situation and heritage. But the point I am trying to make here, that his work in French has been accepted *as* French poetry by many French literary academics and anthologists of modern French poetry, is not really undermined by such recent re-evaluations.

10. Informed reports suggest that Walcott was interested in the possibility of becoming the Laureate. In the event the position was given to Andrew Motion, who is a fine poet but very much part of the English mainstream.

11. I say 'seriously discussed' because when the Oxford Professor of Poetry was to be elected a few years ago several commentators nominated the black British dub poet Benjamin Zephaniah for the post. Their motives for making such a nomination were mostly mischievous, either tweaking the pomposity of the institution or mocking the pretensions of Zephaniah and the wilder claims made for dub poetry. The discussion of Walcott's suitability for the position of Poet Laureate was entirely serious, as far as I could tell, although his nomination gave the debate about the role and meaning of the post a certain edge in terms of a consideration of his eligibility, or otherwise.

12. Niyi Osundare, 'Yoruba Thought, English Words: A Poet's Journey Through The Tunnel Of Two Tongues' in S. Brown, ed., *Kiss & Quarrel: Yoruba/English: Strategies of Mediation, op cit*.pp. 15-31

13. Derek Walcott, 'What the Twilight Says, an Overture', in *Dream on Monkey Mountain and other plays,* (New York: Farrar, Straus and Giroux, 1970), p.31.

14. Karin Barber, *I Could Speak until Tomorrow: Oriki, Women, and the Past in a Yoruba Town*, Edinburgh: Edinburgh University Press, 1991).

15. Niyi Osundare, 'Yoruba Thought, English Words: A Poet's Journey Through The Tunnel Of Two Tongues', *op cit.*

16. Niyi Osundare, *Midlife*, (Ibadan: Heinemann Educational Books, 1993).

17. This quotation is lifted from the longer quotation by Niyi Osundare, below, from his essay 'Yoruba Thought, English Words: A Poet's Journey Through The Tunnel Of Two Tongues'. It is

interesting that Osundare feels that his written English language versions of poems 'thought' in Yoruba become 'lean and competent' English verse, whereas I read the language and style of these same poems as 'florid', 'intensely metaphorical' and 'problematic' in the context of modern English poetry.

18. I am referring really to the Movement poets of the 1950s and 60s and their stylistic successors, who – in the person of poets like Andrew Motion – still effectively dominate the English literary establishment. There are other strands in modern English poetry which might accommodate work like Osundare's more comfortably, 'visionary' poets like Dylan Thomas or – in another way – Peter Redgrove or even the metaphor driven 'Martian' school of the 1980s. His ways of working might also have been more conducive to earlier generations of English poets, in some ways his poetry suggests an 17th century sensibility.

19. 'Lines on a Young Lady's Photograph Album' in *The Less Deceived*, London, 1953.

20. See Karin Barber, 'The Use of English in Yoruba Popular Plays', and Oladejo Okediji, 'Translating AAJo AJE', both in *Kiss & Quarrel: Yoruba/English: Strategies of Mediation, op cit*.pp. 154-171 & 172-181.

21. Niyi Osundare, 'Yoruba Thought, English Words: A Poet's Journey Through The Tunnel Of Two Tongues', *op cit.*

8. Breaking Out of the Dream: Femi Oyebode's 'Black Kites Circling'

1. For discussion of Oyebode's work see *Home and Exile in Femi Oyebode's Poetry*, edited by Obododimma Oha, a special issue of the journal *ASE...*, an interdisciplinary journal for the study of contemporary Nigerian life and literature, published by The Poetry Clubs of the Universities of Calabar and Ibadan, Nigeria, Vol. III, no.III, 1996.

2. Femi Oyebode, Birmingham, Ijala Press: *Naked to Your Softness and Other Dreams'*, 1989; *Wednesday is a Colour*, 1990; *Forest of Transformation*, 1991; *Adagio for Oblong Mirrors,* 1993; *Master of the Leopard Hunt*, 1995; *Indigo, Camwood and Mahogany Red*, 1998; and Femi Oyebode, *Selected Poems*, Ibadan, Kraftgriots, Kraft Books Ltd. 1998.

3. That 'English poetry'/'poetry in English' differentiation raises

the question as to at what point Oyebode becomes 'an English poet'. He has lived longer in England now than he lived in Nigeria...almost all his working life.

4. See Oyebode's essay 'Prosody and Literary Texts' in ed. Stewart Brown, Ed., *The Pressures of the Text: orality, texts and the telling of tales,* Birmingham University African Studies Series, no.4, 1995, p.91-95.

5. In 'The poverty, here, warps and pulls the facial bones' from 'Black Kite's Circling' in *Indigo Camwood and Mahogany Red*, op.cit., p.xxviii.

4. In the case of *Master of the Leopard Hunt*, a book length poem.

5. The phrase is Derek Walcott's in his essay 'The Muse of History' in *What the Twilight Says*, London, Faber and Faber, 1998, p.37.

6. See 'The Metaphysics of Femi Oyebode's Poetry' in *Home and Exile in Femi Oyebode's Poetry, op.cit*, p.26-37.

7. Femi Oyebode, 'Dreamtime' in *Naked to Your Softness and Other Dreams'*, op.cit., p.21-31 (p.23)

8. Femi Oyebode, 'Dreamtime' in *Naked to Your Softness and Other Dreams'*, op.cit., 1989. p.21-31 (p.28)

9. Femi Oyebode, 'Mastering the chaff' in *Wednesday is a Colour*, op.cit., p.1-6 (p.3)

12 Femi Oyebode, 'Karan', in *Forest of Transformation*, op.cit., p.33-35. (p.34).

10. Femi Oyebode, 'Witness', in *Adagio for Oblong Mirrors,* op.cit., p.37-39.(p.38).

11. Femi Oyebode, 'An Abstracted Space' in *Master of the Leopard Hunt*, op.cit., p.7-16 (p.7)

12. Femi Oyebode, 'The names of the principal houses in Ikole' from the sequence 'Black Kites Circling' in *Indigo Camwood and Mahogany Red*, op.cit., p.xxv.

13. Femi Oyebode, 'The names of the principal houses in Ikole' from the sequence 'Black Kites Circling' in *Indigo Camwood and Mahogany Red*, op.cit., p.xxv.

14. Femi Oyebode, 'Lagos, at night, is like a cluster of gems' from the sequence 'Black Kites Circling' in *Indigo Camwood and Mahogany Red*, op.cit., p.xxvii.

15. Femi Oyebode, 'The poverty, here, warps and pulls the facial bones' from the sequence 'Black Kites Circling' in *Indigo Camwood and Mahogany Red*, op.cit., p.xxviii.

16. Given the later identification of that spirit of resistance with Obatala,

perhaps we should recall that Obatala can take female as well as male form and is sometimes depicted as a beautiful woman.

17. Femi Oyebode, 'The poverty, here, warps and pulls the facial bones' from the sequence 'Black Kites Circling' in *Indigo Camwood and Mahogany Red*, op.cit., p.xxix.

18. Femi Oyebode, 'The lagoon is being claimed for land' from the sequence 'Black Kites Circling' in *Indigo Camwood and Mahogany Red*, op.cit., p.xxxii-xxxiii.

19. Femi Oyebode, 'I am yet to write about the agama lizard' from the sequence 'Black Kites Circling' in *Indigo Camwood and Mahogany Red*, op.cit., p.xxxv.

20. Femi Oyebode, 'The names of the principal houses in Ikole' from the sequence 'Black Kites Circling' in *Indigo Camwood and Mahogany Red*, op.cit., p.xxv.

21. Femi Oyebode, 'The lagoon has become even more populated' from the sequence 'Black Kites Circling' in *Indigo Camwood and Mahogany Red*, op.cit., p.xxx.

9: Resisting the Chameleon: the poetry of Jack Mapanje

1. Jack Mapanje, *Of Chameleons and Gods*, London, Heinemann African Writers Series, 1981. Introduction p.xi.

2. Jack Mapanje, *The Last of the Sweet Bananas:New & Selected Poems*, Tarset, Bloodaxe Books, 2004.

3. Jack Mapanje, Introduction to *The Last of the Sweet Bananas:New & Selected Poems*, op.cit., p.xi-xiv. (p.xi)

4. Jack Mapanje, 'Out of Bounds' in *The Last of the Sweet Bananas:New & Selected Poems*, op.cit., p.54.

5. Jack Mapanje, 'Song of Chickens' from the 'Cycles' sequence in *The Last of the Sweet Bananas:New & Selected Poems*, op.cit., p.21.

6. Jack Mapanje, 'Waiting for the Electric Forceps' in *The Last of the Sweet Bananas:New & Selected Poems*, op.cit., p.43.

7. Jack Mapanje, 'Another Fools' Day Touches Down: Shush' in *The Chattering Wagtails of Mikuyu Prison*, London, Heinemann African Writers Series, 1993. p.5.

8. Mapanje's release was to some extent at least a response to the moral and legal pressure generated by an international campaign led by his friend and former colleague, the poet Landeg White.

9. Jack Mapanje, 'The Streak-tease At Mikuyu Prison, 25 Sept. 1987' in *The Last of the Sweet Bananas:New & Selected Poems*, op.cit., p.84.

10. Jack Mapanje, *The Chattering Wagtails of Mikuyu Prison*, Oxford, Heinemann African Writers Series, 1993.

11. Jack Mapanje, *Skipping Without Ropes*, Tarset, Bloodaxe Books, 1998.

12. Jack Mapanje, 'Skipping Without Rope' in *Skipping Without Ropes*, op cit., p.14.

10. The Power to Exclude: Anthologising West Indian Poetry

1. John Figueroa, (ed.) *Caribbean Voices*, London, Evans Bros. 1971.

2. Anne Walmsley, (ed) *The Sun's Eye*, Harlow, Longman, 1968.

3. *NOW,* nos 1-5, St Anne's Bay, Jamiaca, 1972-75.

4. Anne Walmsley, editor of *The Sun's Eye,* op.cit., and, with Nick Caistor, *Facing the Sea,* Oxford, Heinemann Educational, 1986.

5. At the time this essay was written the statement that these multi-national, UK based publishers dominated the publishing of Caribbean literature was true enough. In the years since the influence of the multinationals has declined as their commitment to the region has diminished. West Indian based publishers have emerged and flourished, especially Ian Randle Publications in Jamaica and Imprint Caribbean in Trinidad. The University of the West Indies Press has also developed an extensive list in the field of literature and cultural studies. However the major publisher of new West Indian writing in the last two decades has been the Leeds based Peepal Tree Press.

11. Incest, Assassination and 'The Red Flag': Judging the Guyana Prize

1. As a comparison, Guyana's annual per capita income is approximately US$ 1029, roughly 10% of Trinidad's.

2. Pauline Melville, *The Ventriloquist's Tale*, London, Bloomsbury, 1997.

3. John Agard, 'Coffee in Heaven' in *From the Devil's Pulpit*, Newcastle, Bloodaxe, 1997. p.78.

12. Barbados @ The Crossroads.com: Calypsos in Barbados

1. Spoiler, 'Small Island Carnival', *Mighty Spoiler Unspoilt: Caribbean Classics* (London: Ice Records Ltd., 1995).
2. L'il Rick, *We Surviving* (Barbados: Best Music Ltd., 1997).
3. For more information on Gabby I would commend the interested reader to Curwen Best's *Barbadian Popular Music and the Politics of Caribbean Culture* (New York: Alterations Consultants, 1995).
4. Gabby disdains to record his current calypsos for immediate release so this is transcribed from an off-air recording. The best available collection of Gabby's work is a recent 'selected hits' style CD: *Gabby-till now: Thirty years as a Calypsonian* (Barbados: Blue Wave Records, 1996).
5. *Red plastic @ calypso.com* (Barbados: Bayfield Records Ltd, 1997).
6. Colin Spencer, '10 Points' – not, to my knowledge, available on record.

13. Postscript: a sting 'in de tail'

1. Red Plastic Bag, 'Barbados @ the crossroads.com' on the CD *plastic @ calypso.com*, Barbados, Bayfield Records Ltd, 1996.
2. Buju Banton, *The Early Years: 1990-1995*, New York, Penthouse Records,2001, (B00005NF2K). The text of the controversial lyrics can be found at http://www.lyricskeeper.com/banton_buju-lyrics/209507-boom_bye_bye-lyrics.htm
3. Carolyn Cooper, "'Lyrical Gun': Metaphor and Role Play in Jamaican Dancehall Culture," in *The Massachusetts Review* (Autumn-Winter 1994) p.429-447.See also her book *Sound Clash: Jamaican Dancehall Culture at Large* London, Palgrave Macmillan, 2004.
4. Ian Lumsden, *Machos, Maricones and Gays: Cuba and Homosexuality*, London, Latin America Bureau, 1997.
5. Barry Richard Burg, *Sodomy and the Pirate Tradition: English Sea Rovers in the Seventeenth Century Caribbean*, New York, NYU Press,1995.

14. Nothing about us at all: Olive Senior and West Indian Poetry

1. Derek Walcott, 'Ruins of a Great House' in *Collected Poems 1948-1984*, New York, Farrar, Straus and Giroux, 1986, p.19

2. Olive Senior, 'Birdshooting Season' in *Talking of Trees*, Kingston, Jamaica, Calabash Publications, 1985, p.2

3. Olive Senior, 'Epitaph' in *Talking of Trees*, op.cit., p.6.

4. Olive Senior, 'City Poem' in *Talking of Trees*, op.cit., p.65.

5. Olive Senior, 'Rejected Text for a Tourist Brocure' in *Over the Roofs of the World*, Toronto, Insomniac Press, 2005. p.53.

6. Olive Senior, *Gardening in the Tropics*, Newcastle, Bloodaxe, 1995.

7. Olive Senior, 'Colonial Girls School' in *Talking of Trees*, op.cit., p.26.

8. Olive Senior, 'Shango:God of Thunder' in *Gardening in the Tropics*, op.cit., 1995. p.121-123. (p.121)

9. See particularly Jahan Ramazani, *The Hybrid Muse: Postcolonial Poetry in English*, University of Chicago Press, 2001.

15. Martin Carter: 'The Poems Man'

1. This essay is adapted from a memorial piece, 'No voice in the emptiness: the poetry of Martin Carter' which was first published in *Planet: the Welsh Internationalist*, Aberystwyth, no.129, June 1998. In its current incarnation the essay has benefited greatly from the comments, corrections and creative input of Ian McDonald.

2. Martin Carter, 'They say I am a poet write for them' from the sequence 'Conversations' in *University of Hunger: Collected Poems & Selected Prose*, Tarset, Bloodaxe Books, 2006, p.109.

3. For a writer of such stature and reputation – sustained over so long a period – the serious criticism of Martin Carter's work has been sparse and – until recently – all of it scattered through limited circulation literary magazines and Caribbean academic journals. In 2000 the Leeds based Peepal Tree Press published *All are Involved: the Art of Martin Carter* (ed. S. Brown), a collection of essays and commentaries on Carter's work which draws much of that material together, alongside previously unpublished scholarship. Readers are also directed to two recent editions of the Guyanese literary journal *Kyk-over-al*, edited by Ian McDonald, which focus on aspects of Martin Carter's work: no. 44, May 1993 is a special issue, guest edited by Nigel Westmaas, devoted to Martin Carter's prose; no. 49/50, June 2000, 'The Martin Carter Tribute', which one commentator has described as being effectively "the biography of Martin Carter." It also includes a

supplement to the Martin Carter's prose special issue, no.44.

4. 'University of Hunger' in *University of Hunger: Collected Poems & Selected Prose*, op.cit., p.84.

5. For a full – and brilliant – discussion of Carter's language in this poem see Barbara Lalla's essay 'Conceptual Perspectives on Time and Timelessness in Martin Carter's 'University of Hunger'' in *All are Involved: the Art of Martin Carter*, op.cit.

6. 'Words' in *University of Hunger: Collected Poems & Selected Prose*, op.cit., p.120.

7. Martin Carter, in his essay 'The Location of the Artist' in *Kyk-over- al* 44. May 1993, p.111-112.

8. 'A Mouth is always Muzzled' in *University of Hunger: Collected Poems & Selected Prose*, op.cit., p.124.

9. See Rupert Roopnarine, 'Martin Carter and Politics' in *All are Involved: the Art of Martin Carter*, op.cit. p.48-57.

10. See George Lamming's discussion 'Martin Carter: A Poet of the Americas' in *All are Involved: the Art of Martin Carter*, op.cit., p.311-317.

11. 'Let Every Child Run Wild' in *University of Hunger: Collected Poems & Selected Prose*, op.cit., p.160.

12. In his brief essay 'On Poetry' first published in 1976, Carter suggests that *any* engagement with poetry involves a kind of code breaking exercise, the mutual engagement of minds. See *Kyk-over-al*, no.49/50, June 2000, p.122-3, in the Martin Carter's Prose supplement, edited by Nigel Westmaas.

13. 'Some Kind of Fury' in *University of Hunger: Collected Poems & Selected Prose*, op.cit., p.155.

14. 'Rice' in *University of Hunger: Collected Poems & Selected Prose*, op.cit., p.151.

15. 'Bitter Wood' in *University of Hunger: Collected Poems & Selected Prose*, op.cit., p.167.

16. *'Incalculable Flotsam': The Minor Poetry of Frank Collymore*

1. BIM, the Caribbean literary magazine founded in Barbados in 1942, edited for more than twenty five years by Frank Collymore. Bim played a crucial role in the evolution of West Indian literature, publishing the early work of such writers as Derek Walcott, Kamau Brathwaite and George Lamming.

2. Frank Collymore wrote humorous verse – his 'Rhymed

Ruminations on the Fauna of Barbados' appeared in 1968. Collymore didn't regard these pieces as serious poems, although many people admire and value them still. As far as the avowedly serious poems go, I should say that the poems he published were written in that short period in the 1940s – his notebooks and private papers may reveal other unpublished poems.

3. Obviously I'm not intending to belittle or dismiss such a process of contextualisation, indeed it is self evidently absolutely vital to any informed reading of any body of poetry, but there is also another – perhaps technical – context, in the 'domain of the poem' as it were, where the only criteria that apply are those of poetry itself – in this case I suppose I mean 'the poem in English' but, on a more reckless day, I'd want to argue that there are qualities which good poems share *across* cultural conventions.

4. See footnote 17 below.

5. *The Princeton Encyclopaedia of Poetry and Poetics.*

6. Frank A. Collymore, *Notes for a Glossary of Words and Phrases of Barbadian Dialect,* Barbados National Trust, 1970 (First published 1955)

7. Frank A. Collymore, 'So This Is Love' in *Selected Poems*, Barbados, Private Publication, 1971. p.44.

8. Frank A. Collymore, 'Words are the Poem' in *Selected Poems*, op.cit., p.9.

9. Frank A. Collymore, 'That Day' in *Selected Poems*, op.cit., p.30.

10. Frank A. Collymore, 'Because I have Turned My Back' in *Selected Poems*, op.cit., p.26.

11. Frank A. Collymore, 'Beneath the Casurinas' in *Selected Poems*, op.cit., p.13.

12. Frank A. Collymore, 'Blue Agave' in *Selected Poems*, op.cit., p.14.

13. *Poets of the West Indies, edited by John Figueroa, Caedmon TC1379, 1971.*

14. Frank A. Collymore, 'Voice la Plume de Mon Oncle' in *Selected Poems*, op.cit., p.44.

15. It is interesting that on the *Poets of the West Indies* record of Collymore reading the poem, he reads the second line of the final stanza as 'wondering what about things are' rather than 'wondering about what …', which – given the evidence of the text – is obviously a mistake but which in fact might not have been out of place as a creole inversion of the word order within the sentence.

16. Frank A. Collymore, 'Ballad of an Old Woman' in *Selected Poems*, op.cit., p.14.

17. With these poems one wonders again about the influence Collymore's poems might have had on the young Walcott, who around the same time was writing satirical ballads like the early versions of the poem which finally appeared in his first full collection as 'A Country Club Romance'. In his review of Walcott's early pamphlets Collymore remarks on the apparent influence of W. H. Auden in such pieces, and no doubt Collymore was himself influenced by Auden's poems of social commentary, but it may be that the example of his local mentor was as important to the apprentice Walcott as that of the distant master. There are other echoes too – Walcott's 'Origins' might perhaps owe something to Collymore's poems 'Hymn to the Sea' and 'Words are the Poem'. Inevitably, too, thinking about echoes and possible influences Kamau Brathwaite's long poem 'X/Self' comes to mind, esp. bearing in mind Collymore's line 'Mr X himself: X, as always, the unknown.'

18. Frank A. Collymore, 'Schooner' in *Selected Poems*, op.cit., p.22.

19. Indeed, given the activities of the Creationist movement in the USA and elsewhere, it is still a contentious idea in 2003.

20. See 'The Unspoken Bible' at http://www.usbible.com/usbible/default.htm (See also Genesis 1:2) 'The earth was without form and void, and darkness was upon the face of the deep; and the Spirit of God was moving over the face of the waters.' Leviathan, in the Bible, one of the names of the primeval dragon subdued by God at the outset of creation: 'You crushed Leviathan's heads, gave him as food to the wild animals' (Psalm 74:14)

21. Frank A. Collymore, 'Return' in *Selected Poems*, op.cit., p.13.

22. Frank A. Collymore, 'Hymn to the Sea' in *Selected Poems*, op.cit., p.20.

23. Assuming it is a 'he' – the sea is always addressed as 'she', and as the poem unfolds the poet/speaker is portrayed as its lover and later the sea is described in terms of a muse – but in fact there is nothing to finally establish the gender of the speaking voice in the poem.)

24. Richard Allsopp, *Dictionary of Caribbean English Usage*, Oxford, Oxford University Press, 1996.

17. 'Between me and thee is a great gulf fixed': The Crusoe presence in Walcott's early poetry

All references are by Derek Walcott unless otherwise stated.

1. 'The Muse of History', in O. Coombs Ed., *Is Massa Day Done?* New York, Anchor/Doubleday, 1974, p. 1-27.
2. See Stewart Brown, 'Walcott's Fortunate Traveller: A Patriot in Exile', in *Carib*, no. 5, Kingston, Jamaica, Winter 1989/90 p.1-18; 'Spoiler, Walcott's People's Patriot' in *Wasafiri*, no. 9, Winter 1988, p.10-15; 'The Apprentice' in Stewart Brown, (ed.) *The Art of Derek Walcott*, Bridgend, Seren Books, 1991, p. 13-33.
3. As Hector Mannix 'entered a lion' in 'Mass Man' in *The Gulf*, London: Jonathan Cape, 1970, p.19.
4. 'The Muse of History', *op cit*.
5. See Edward Hirsch, 'An Interview with Derek Walcott', *Contemporary Literature*, vol. 20, no. 3, 1980, 279-92, 282.
6. 'The Figure of Crusoe', unpublished lecture, given at the University of the West Indies, St Augustine, Trinidad, 1965. (Text held in the library.)
7. See *Elogues and Other Poems*, Louis Varese transit, Bollingden Series LV, French text from the *Oeuvre Poetique* (Paris: Librairie Gallimard, 1953).
8. 'The Figure of Crusoe'. *op cit*.
9. *Ibid*.
10. *Ibid*.
11. 'Laventille' in *The Castaway and other Poems*. London, Jonathan Cape, 1965. p. 35.
12. See James Weiland, '"Confronting his Madness": History as Amnesia in The poetry of Derek Walcott', *New Literature Review*, no. 7, 1980, 73-82.
13. 'The Figure of Crusoe', *op cit*.
14. *25 Poems*, private publication, Port of Spain, Trinidad, 1948. p. 18.
15. *The Castaway and Other Poems*, London, Jonathan Cape, 1965. p. 35.
16. See Kevin Ireland, 'Place and Poetic Identity', in *The Journal of Commonwealth Literature*, vol. 1, no. 2, December 1966, 157-60.
17. 'Codicil' in *The Castaway and other Poems*, p. 61.
18. 'Forest of Europe' in *The Star-apple Kingdom* London, Jonathan Cape, 1980, p. 39.

19. *The Gulf*, London, Jonathan Cape, 1970, p. 42.
20. 'A Village Life', in *The Castaway and other Poems*, p. 16.
21. 'God Rest Ye Merry Gentlemen', in *The Castaway and other Poems*, p. 44.
22. 'What the Twilight Says, an Overture' in *Dream on Monkey Mountain and Other Plays*, London, Jonathan Cape, 1972. p. 22.
23. *The Castaway and other Poems*, p. 52.
24. *Ibid*.
25. *Ibid.*, p. 51.
26. *Ibid.*, p. 52.
27. *The Gulf*, op.cit., p.19.
28. 'Crusoe's Island' from *The Castaway and Other Poems*, op.cit., p. 51.
29. Helen Vendler, 'Poet of Two Worlds: The Fortunate Traveller' in Harold Bloom, Ed., *Blooms Modern Critical Views: Derek Walcott*, Broomall, P.A., Chelsea House Publishers, 2003, p.25-33.
30. Kenneth Ramchand, *An Introduction to West Indian Literature*, Sunbury on Thames, Nelson Caribbean, 1976. p. 121.
31. *Remembrance and Pantomime*, New York, Farrar, Strauss & Giroux, 1980, p. 126.
32. *The Castaway and Other Poems*, op.cit., p. 51.
33. 'The Figure of Crusoe'. *op cit*.
34. *Sea Grapes*, London, Jonathan Cape, 1976. p. 93-95.
35. *Midsummer*, New York, Farrar, Strauss & Giroux, 1984. p. 47.
36. 'Sea Grapes', in *Sea Grapes*, op.cit., p. 9.

18. *'Writin in Light': Orality thru typography, Kamau Brathwaite's Sycorax Video style*

1. Kamau Brathwaite, *X/Self*, Oxford, OUP, 1987: pp.84/5 & 87.
2. The full text of the interview is published in *Kyk-over-al*, Georgetown, Guyana, no.40, 1989: pp.84-93.
3. Kamau Brathwaite, *Middle Passages*, Newcastle, Bloodaxe, 1992; *Dreamstories*, Harlow, Longman, 1998: *Barabajan Poems*, New York, Savacou North, 1995.
4. Kamau Brathwaite, *The Arrivants: a New World Trilogy*, Oxford, OUP, 1967: *Ancestors: A Reinvention of Mother Poem, Sun Poem and X/Self*, New York, New Directions, 2001

5. Kamau Brathwaite, *The Development of Creole Society in Jamaica 1770-1820*, Oxford, OUP, 1970: p.17.

6. Kamau Brathwaite, *History of the Voice: The Development of Nation Language in Anglophone Caribbean Poetry*, London, New Beacon Books, 1984.

7. Kamau Brathwaite, *History of the Voice*, op.cit., p.8 & 10.

8. Kamau Brathwaite, 'Caribbean Culture: Two Paradigms' in Jurgen Martini, Ed., *Missile and Capsule*, ed. Bremen, Universitat Bremen, 1983: p.9-54.

9. Kamau Brathwaite, *History of the Voice*, op.cit., p.13.

10. Kamau Brathwaite, *History of the Voice*, op.cit., p.17.

11. Kamau Brathwaite, *History of the Voice*, op.cit., p.49. 'To confine our definitions of literature to written texts in a culture that remains ital in most of its people proceedings is as limiting as its opposite: trying to define Caribbean literature as essentially orature – like eating avocado without its likkle salt.

12. Kamau Brathwaite, *History of the Voice*, op.cit., p.49.

13. Kamau Brathwaite, *History of the Voice*, op.cit., p.9.

14. Donald Hall, *American Poetry*, London, Faber & Faber, 1969. p.12.

15. Kamau Brathwaite, *History of the Voice*, op.cit., p.30.

16. Jerome McGann, *Black Riders: the Visible Language of Modernism*, Princetown, New Jersey, Princetown University Press, 1993, p.77.

17. Jerome McGann, *Black Riders: the Visible Language of Modernism*, p.81.

18. Zukofsky, Louis, Ed. *The 'Objectivist' Anthology*, 1932, cited in McGann, *Black Riders: the Visible Language of Modernism*, op.cit, p.83.

19. I have borrowed the term and much of the substance of the comments in this paragraph from an article by Willie van Peer, 'Typographic foregrounding', in *Language and Literature*, vol.2, No. 1, 1993: pp. 49-59.

20. Willie van Peer, ibid. p.51.

21. There are some grounds for comparison with more literary figures like Ian Hamilton Finlay whose appreciation of the effects of space around 'poetic' statements come to mind when one looks at some of the passages of *Barabajan Poems*.

22. Berjouhi Bowler, *The Word as Image*, London, Studio Vista, 1970, p.14.

23. Edward Brathwaite, Rights of Passage, Oxford, OUP, 1977

24. Kamau Brathwaite, *Ancestors,* New Directions, 2001, p 453.

25. Anthony Easthope, *Poetry as Discourse*, London, Routledge, 1976. p.65.

26. Quoted on the back cover of *DreamStories*, op.cit., (see ref.3)

27. Stewart Brown, 'Interview with Edward Kamau Brathwaite' in *Kyk-over-al*, no.40, 1989: pp.90.

28. Kamau Brathwaite, *The Zea Mexican Diary*, Madison, University of Wisconsin Press, 1993: *Barabajan Poems*, op cit. (see ref. 3); *Middle Passages*, op.cit. (see ref.3)

29. Anne Walmsley argues, rather, in her essay 'Her Stem Singing: Kamau Brathwaite's *Zea-Mexican Diary*', (in *World Literature Today*, vol.68, no.4, Autumn 1994, p.747-749) that *The Zea-Mexican Diary* represents a particularly subtle and appropriate use of the Sycorax video style.

30. Gordon Rohlehr in Kamau Brathwaite, *DreamStories*, p.xviii.

31. Personal discussion with both the poet and the Longman publisher Rosalind Ward.

32. Kamau Brathwaite, *Barabajan Poems*, op.cit. p.282.

19. Postscript to 'Writin' in Light': 'Tidalectics of the Word'

1. The 'Tidalectics' panel consisted of Elaine Savory, Margaret Gill, Silvio Torres-Saillant, Stewart Brown and Gordon Rohlehr. The 'tidalectics' metaphor has been developed by Brathwaite over many years, it is mentioned in passing in *History of the Voice*, (1984) and in more detail in his essay 'The search for a Caribbean Aesthetic' first published in the *Trinidad Express* (November 15th, 1992, p.33-40.) It is explored most fully in his *Barabajan Poems*, New York, Savacou North, 1995. The origins of the metaphor in Brathwaite's imagination is discussed in very insightful ways by his sister, Mary E. Morgan, in her essay 'Highway to vision: this sea our nexus' in *World Literature Today*, vol.68, no. 4. Autumn 1994. p.663-668.

2. Kamau Brathwaite, *The History of the Voice: The Development of Nation Language in Anglophone Caribbean Poetry*, London, New Beacon Books, 1984.

3. Kamau Brathwaite, *Barabajan Poems*, New York, Savacou North, 1995.

4. Kamau Brathwaite, *Dreamstories*, Harlow, Longman, 1998.

5. Raphael Dalleo suggests that in Brathwaite's most recent work, "the computer becomes an almost holy instrument of the process that he describes as Caliban's channeling of Sycorax, the otherwise inaccessible African womb from which he came." in 'Another "Our America"': Rooting a Caribbean Aesthetic in the Work of Jose Marti, Kamau Brathwaite and Edouard Glissant', in the web journal *Anthurium: A Caribbean Studies Journal*, vol. 2, no. 2., Fall 2004. In the notes to his essay Daello remarks, "it is perhaps in 'Namsetoura and the Companion Stranger', published in *Anthurium* on the web, that he (Brathwaite) most fully brings to the reader his vision of poetry "written in light." See http:// scholar.library.miami.edu/anthurium/volume_1/issue_1/brathwaite-namsetoura.htm

20. Celebration Songs: The Poetry of James Berry

1. Chinua Achebe, answering questions after the South Bank lecture, 1990, given at the Royal Society for the Encouragement of the Arts in London. The text of the lecture is published as 'African Literature as Restoration of Celebration', in *Chinua Achebe: A Celebration*, eds. Kirsten Holst Petersen and Anna Rutherford, Oxford, Heinemann, 1991, pp. 1-10.
2. See for example 'Everyday Traveller', *Hot Earth Cold Earth*, Newcastle, Bloodaxe Books, 1995.
3. See for example '3 London Blacks' in *Fractured Circles*, London, New Beacon Books, 1979, p. 48
4. James Berry, *When I Dance*, London: Puffin Books, 1988, p.12.
5. James Berry, *Fractured Circles*, op. cit., p. 12.
6. *Fractured Circles*, p. 13.
7. 'Bluefoot Traveller', *Hot Earth Cold Earth*, op cit., p.25.
8. 'Black Study Students', *Fractured Circles*, p.64.
9. *Chain of Days*, Oxford, Oxford University Press, 1985, p. 12.
10. 'From Lucy: At School' *Lucy's Letters and Loving*, London, New Beacon Books, 1982), p.51.
11. *Lucy's Letters and Loving*, op. cit., p.17.
12. *Fractured Circles*, op. cit., p.26.
13. 'In our Year 1941 My Letter to Mother Africa', in *Hot Earth Cold Earth*, op. cit., p.31
14. 'Chain of Days', in *Chain of Days*, p.5.

15. *Chain of Days*, op. cit., p.5.
16. 'A Schooled Fatherhood' in *Hot Earth Cold Earth*, p.62.
17. 'In our Year 1941 My Letter to Mother Africa' *Hot Earth Cold Earth*, op. cit., p.31.
18. *Chain of Days*, op cit., p.44.
19. 'Faces Around My Father' in *Hot Earth Cold Earth*, p.27.
20. *Chain of Days*, p.49.
21. *Hot Earth Cold Earth*, p.67.
22. *Hot Earth Cold Earth*, p.70.
23. *Chain of Days*, p.70.
24. Ibid.
25. *Chain of Days*, pp. 72-73.
26. Ibid. pp. 31, 34.
27. *Hot Earth Cold Earth*, p.10.
28. *Chain of Days* p.18.
29. *When I Dance*, London, Puffin Books, 1988, p.71.

21. Ian McDonald: A Caribbean Literary Life

1. Ian McDonald, *The Humming-Bird Tree*, Oxford, Macmillan Caribbean, 2005. (First published 1969)
2. Ian McDonald, 'Yusman Ali, Charcoal Seller' in *Jaffo the Calypsonian*, Leeds, Peepal Tree Press, p.47.
3. Ian McDonald, 'God's Work', in *Mercy Ward*, Calstock, Cornwall, Peterloo Press, 1988, p.57.
4. Ian McDonald, 'The Fix', in *Mercy Ward*, op.cit., p.60.
5. Ian McDonald, 'The Sun Parrots Are Late This Year', in *Essequibo*, Calstock, Cornwall, Peterloo Press, 1992, p.60.
6. Ian McDonald, 'Behind the Rib-Cage Lies the Heart' in *Between Silence and Silence*, Leeds, Peepal Tree Press, 2003, p.25.
7. Ian McDonald, 'Middle Age' in *Between Silence and Silence*, op.cit., p.35.
8. Ian McDonald, 'We Don't Stop for Strangers' in *Between Silence and Silence*, op.cit., p.48.
9. Ian McDonald, 'Mr Perfection' in *Between Silence and Silence*, op.cit., p.69.
10. Ian McDonald, 'Spinster Ganteaume and the Birth of Poetry' in *Between Silence and Silence*, op.cit., p.81.
11. Ian McDonald, 'Massa Day Done' in *Between Silence and Silence*, op.cit., p.87.

12. Ian McDonald, 'The Weather in Shanty Town' in *Between Silence and Silence,* op.cit., p.91.
13. Ian McDonald, 'Between Silence and Silence there should be only Praise' in *Between Silence and Silence,* op.cit., p.99.

22: *Straight is not the way: the poetry of Mervyn Morris*

1. Mervyn Morris, 'Behind the Poems' in *Is English we Speaking and other essays*, Kingston, Jamaica, Ian Randle Publishers, 1999, p.162-171. (p.162)
2. Mervyn Morris, 'Data' in *I been there, sort of: New and Selected Poems*, Manchester, Carcanet, 2006, p.90.
3. Mervyn Morris, *Examination Centre*, London, New Beacon Books, 1992. Since this essay was first published Morris has published *I been there, sort of: New and Selected Poems*, 2006. (See note 2 above.)
4. Mervyn Morris, *The Pond*, London, New Beacon Books, 1973. Revised Edition, London, New Beacon Books, 1997.
5. Mervyn Morris, *Shadow Boxing*, London, New Beacon Books, 1979.
6. Mervyn Morris, 'Muse' in *I been there, sort of: New and Selected Poems*, op.cit., p.73.
7. Mervyn Morris, 'To an Expatriate Friend' in *I been there, sort of: New and Selected Poems*, op.cit., p.64.
8. Mervyn Morris, 'I am the Man' in *The Pond*, op. cit. p.15.
9. Mervyn Morris, 'Walk Good' in *I been there, sort of: New and Selected Poems*, op.cit., p.92.
10. Mervyn Morris, 'Valley Prince' in *I been there, sort of: New and Selected Poems*, op.cit., p.63.

23. *Tap Natch Poet: Reading and Listening to Linton Kwesi Johnson*

1. Linton Kwesi Johnson, *Dread Beat and Blood*, London, Bogle-L'Ouverture Publications, 1975. Introduction by Andrew Salkey, p.7-9. (p.8)
2. Linton Kwesi Johnson, 'Dread Beat an Blood' in *Mi Revalueshanary Fren: Selected Poems*, London, Penguin Classics, 2002. p.5.
3. An as yet unpublished interview, read in typescript.
4. Christian Habekost, *Verbal Riddim: The Politics and Aesthetics of African-Caribbean Dub Poetry*, Amsterdam, Rodopi, 1993.

5. Linton Kwesi Johnson, *Tings an Times:Selected Poems*, Newcastle, Bloodaxe, 1991.

6. Christian Habekost, *Verbal Riddim: The Politics and Aesthetics of African-Caribbean Dub Poetry*, op.cit. p.212.

7. An as yet unpublished interview, read in typescript.

8. Linton Kwesi Johnson, *Voices of the Living and the Dead*, London, Race Today Publications, 1974.

9. Fred D'Aguiar, 'Chanting Down Babylon', in Linton Kwesi Johnson, *Mi Revalueshanary Fren:Selected Poems*, op cit. p.ix-xiv. (p.xi)

10. Linton Kwesi Johnson, 'Inglan is a Bitch' in *Mi Revalueshanary Fren: Selected Poems*, op. cit. p.39-41. (p.40)

11. Or maybe not so strangely – for a very interesting discussion of the relevance of Eliot in LKJ's list of 'tap natch poets' see Robert McGill's essay 'Goon poets of the black Atlantic: Linton Kwesi Johnson's imagined canon', in *Textual Practice*, vol.17. no.3. 2003, p.561-574. This is a thoughtful and provocative essay but seems to me to misread and misrepresent the poem at various points. (It also, incidentally, misrepresents my own critical positions by some very partial quotation out of context!)

12. Linton Kwesi Johnson, 'If I Woz a Tap Natch Poet' in *Mi Revalueshanary Fren: Selected Poems*, London, Penguin Classics, 2002. p.94-97. (p.95.)

13. James Berry is quoted by Mario Relich in his entry on Linton Kwesi Johnson in *The Oxford Companion to Twentieth Century Poetry*, edited by Ian Hamilton, Oxford, OUP, 1994, p.258.

14. Linton Kwesi Johnson, 'If I Woz a Tap Natch Poet' in *Mi Revalueshanary Fren: Selected Poems*, London, Penguin Classics, 2002. p.94-97. (p.94.)

15. Linton Kwesi Johnson, *Selected Poems*, London, Penguin Poetry, 2002.

16. Linton Kwesi Johnson, *A Capella*, (CD), Hearne Hill, London, LKJ Records, 2002.

17. Linton Kwesi Johnson, *More Time*, (CD), Hearne Hill, London, LKJ Records, 1998.

24. *Reggae and Requiem: A brief introduction to the work of Kwame Dawes*

1. Kwame Dawes, *Natural Mysticism:Towards a New Reggae Aesthetic in Caribbean Writing*, Leeds, Peepal Tree Press, 1997.

2. Kwame Dawes, *Wheel and Come Again: an anthology of Reggae poetry*, Leeds, Peepal Tree Press, 1999.
3. Kwame Dawes, *Shook Foil*, Leeds, Peepal Tree Press, 1998.
4. Carolyn Cooper, *Noises in the Blood: Orality, Gender and the Vulgar Body of Jamaican Popular Culture*, Basingstoke, Macmillan (Warwick University Caribbean Studies Series), 1993.
5. Kamau Brathwaite, *LX the Love Axe/ L: Developing a Caribbean Aesthetic*, an Account in Fact and Memory of the Cultural Revolution/CR in the *Anglophone Caribbean C.1965-c.1985 and Continuing*, Leeds, Peepal Tree Press, 2008.
6. Antonio Benitez Rojo, *The Repeating Island: The Caribbean and the Postmodern Perspective*, Durham, Duke University Press, 1996.
7. Kwame Dawes, *Requiem*, Leeds, Peepal Tree Press, 1996; Kwame Dawes, *Midland*, Athens, Ohio, Ohio University Press, 2001.
8. Kwame Dawes, 'Family Tree' in *Requiem*, op. cit. p.32.
9. Kwame Dawes, 'Shame' in *Requiem*, op. cit. p.35.
10. Kwame Dawes, 'Crime of Passion' in *Requiem*, op. cit. p.16/17. (p.16)
11. Kwame Dawes, *Bob Marley: Lyrical Genius*, London, Sanctuary Publishing Ltd., 2002.
12. Kwame Dawes, 'Some Tentative Definitions 1' in *Shook Foil*, op cit. p.9.
13. Kwame Dawes, 'I am a Stranger on this Earth' in *Shook Foil*, op cit. p.18-19.
14. Kwame Dawes, *Progeny of Air*, Leeds, Peepal Tree Press, 1994.
15. Kwame Dawes, *Prophets*, Leeds, Peepal Tree Press, 1995.
16. Kwame Dawes, *Jacko Jacobus*, Leeds, Peepal Tree Press, 1997.
17. Kwame Dawes, 'Inheritance' in *Midland*, op. cit., p.3-13. (p.11.)
20. Kwame Dawes, 'Liminal' in *Midland*, op. cit., p.19.

25: Fellow-traveller: A witness in my time and place: the poetry of Don Burness

1. Don Burness, *The Bardie Clan: Selected and New Poems*, Evanston, Troubadour Press, 1998.
2. Don Burness, *Safari*, Evanston, Troubadour Press, 1984.
3. Don Burness, 'The War Never Left Port Harcourt', in *The Bardie Clan: Selected and New Poems*, op. cit. p.3.
4. Don Burness, *Watching the Masquerade*, Rindge, New Hampshire, 1990.

5. Don Burness, 'Along the Elegant Streets of Dakar', in *The Bardie Clan: Selected and New Poems*, op.cit., p.5.
6. Don Burness, 'Safari' in *The Bardie Clan: Selected and New Poems*, op.cit., p.4.
7. Don Burness, 'Yad Vashem' in *The Bardie Clan: Selected and New Poems*, op. cit., p.11.
8. Don Burness, *Il Grido del Corvo/ The Cry of the Crow*, bilingual edition, Naples, Italy, Scrittori Contemporanei no. 6, 1966
9. Don Burness, 'At Elmina Castle' in *The Bardie Clan: Selected and New Poems*, op. cit., p.63
10. Don Burness, 'I Think Of People I Have Not Seen For Years', in *The Bardie Clan: Selected and New Poems*, op.cit., p.24.
11. Don Burness, 'Letter to the Future', in *The Bardie Clan: Selected and New Poems*, op.cit., p.68/9 (p.68).
12. Don Burness, 'At the Conference', in *The Bardie Clan: Selected and New Poems*, op.cit., p.113.
13. Don Burness, 'Epistle To The Critic Russell Hamilton', in *The Bardie Clan: Selected and New Poems*, op.cit., p.103.
14. Don Burness, 'The Rosenburgs: Forty Years Later', in *The Bardie Clan: Selected and New Poems*, op.cit., p.65/6 (p.65).
15. Don Burness, 'Longfellow in Menton', in *The Bardie Clan: Selected and New Poems*, op.cit., p.67.
16. Don Burness, 'I Hear America Crying', in *The Bardie Clan: Selected and New Poems*, op.cit., p.72.
17. Don Burness, 'The Bardie Clan', in *The Bardie Clan: Selected and New Poems*, op.cit., p.90.
18. Don Burness, 'On Being A Jew', in *The Bardie Clan: Selected and New Poems*, op.cit., p.91/2, (p.91.).

26. *Imaginary Continent: Images of Africa in Modern British Poetry*

1. See the essays 'Finding the right words: A Candle for Ken Saro-Wiwa' and 'Literature and Freedom Across Boundaries' elsewhere in this collection.
2. Okot p'Bitek, 'What is Literature'. in his collection of essays, *Africa's Cultural Revolution* Nairobi, Macmillan Books for Africa, 1973, p.15-23. (p.23).
3. Jean Paul Sartre, in *Orphee Noir*, the Introduction to *Anthologie*

de la nouvelle poésie nègre et malgache de langue française edited by Léopold Sédar Senghor. Paris, 1948.

4. Rudyard Kipling, 'The White Man's Burden' first published in the February, 1899 issue of *McClure's Magazine*. Collected in Rudyard Kipling, *Collected Poems*, Ware, Wordsworth Editions, 1994, p.343/4. The poem wasn't actually written about Africa, despite the reference to the 'Egyptian night' but was a response to the American take over of the Phillipines after the Spanish-American War.

5. Robert Gittings 'Stones at Hammamet, Tunisia' in his *Collected Poems*, London, Heinemann, 1976.

6. John Pudney, 'For Johnny' in his *Collected Poems*, London, Putnam, 1957, p.35.

7. John Pudney, 'First Sighting of West Africa' in his *Collected Poems*, London, Putnam, 1957, p.28.

8. Edward Said, see especially his collection of essays *The World, The Text, and the Critic*, London, Faber & Faber, 1984.

9. Duncan Bush, *Days of Empire*. See his collection *The Hook*, Bridgend, Seren Books, 1997.

10. John Haynes, 'Explorer'. As far as I am aware this poem is uncollected. It was included in a group of poems John Haynes read from at a Poetry Workshop at Bayero University, Kano in December 1980. The poems were circulated in a handout to be discussed at the Workshop.

11. Wendy Bishop, 'Futility Sestina: Getting Housing in Kano, Nigeria'. As far as I am aware this poem is uncollected. It was included in a group of poems Wendy Bishop read from at a Poetry Workshop at Bayero University, Kano in 1981. The poems were circulated in a handout to be discussed at the Workshop.

12. See the essay 'Tourist, Traveller, Troublemaker' elsewhere in this collection.

13. T.W. Harrison and James Simmonds, *Aikin Mata: The Lysistrata of Aristophanes,* Ibadan, Oxford University Press, 1966.

14. Tony Harrison, 'The Songs of the PWD Man' in *The Loiners*, London, London Magazine Editions, 1970, p.50-53. (p.50)

15. Chinua Achebe, *A Man of the People*, London, Heinemann, 1966.

16. Landeg White, *Traveller's Tree,* Figuera Da Foz, Portugal, CEMAR, 2002, p.7.

17. Landeg White, 'Afternoons, Mozambique' in *For Captain Steadman*, Liskeard, Harry Chambers/Peterloo Press, 1983, p.9-10.

18. Landeg White, 'The Instinct' in *South*, , Figuera Da Foz, Portugal, CEMAR, 1999, p. 20-23 (p.21).
19. Landeg White, 'Poem 22' in the sequence 'The New Smiling Bwana' in *Traveller's Tree*, Figuera Da Foz, Portugal, CEMAR, 2002, p.21-26. (p.21)
20. Landeg White, 'Poem 23' in the sequence 'The New Smiling Bwana' in *Traveller's Tree*, Figuera Da Foz, Portugal, CEMAR, 2002, p.21-26. (p.21)
21. Landeg White, 'Poem 28' in the sequence 'The New Smiling Bwana' in *Traveller's Tree*, Figuera Da Foz, Portugal, CEMAR, 2002, p.21-26. (p.24)
22. See the essay 'Resisting the Chameleon: the poetry of Jack Mapanje' elsewhere in this collection.
23. John Haynes, *Sabon Gari*, London, London Magazine Editions, 1974.
24. John Haynes, 'Tailor', as far as I'm aware this poem is uncollected.
25. Idi Bukar, *First the Desert Came and then the Torturer*, Zaria, RAG Press, 1984. To further embroider on the identity of Idi Bukar, his work is most seriously discussed in John Haynes' critical study *African Poetry and the English Language*, London, Macmillan, 1987.
26. Cited by Claire Armitstead, January 9, 2007
   http://blogs.guardian.co.uk/books/2007/01/john_haynes_deserves_to_win_1.html
27. Idi Bukar, 'Revelations' from *First the Desert Came and then the Torturer*, Zaria, RAG Press, 1984, p.13.
28. John Haynes, *Letter to Patience*, Bridgend, Seren , 2007 p.17
29. John Haynes, *Letter to Patience*, Bridgend, Seren , 2007 p.66.
30. I might also have cited some African born poets who have migrated to Britain and whose work has become part of the contemporary multi-cultural British poetry scene; Femi Oyebode, Jack Mapanje, John Hendrickse, Ben Okri, etc.

BIBLIOGRAPHY

Chinua Achebe, *A Man of the People*, London, Heinemann, 1966.

Chinua Achebe, 'African Literature as Restoration of Celebration' in Kirsten Holst Peterson and Anna Rutherford, Eds., *Chinua Achebe: A Celebration*, Oxford, Heinemann, 1991, p.1-10.

John Agard, *From the Devil's Pulpit*, Newcastle, Bloodaxe, 1997.

Funso Aiyejina, 'Recent Nigerian Poetry in English: an Alter-Native Tradition' in Yemi Ogunbiyi, Ed., *Perspectives on Nigerian Literature: 1700 to the present*, Vol. 1, Lagos: Guardian Books (Nigeria), 1988.

Richard Allsopp, *Dictionary of Caribbean English Usage*, Oxford, Oxford University Press, 1996.

Stephen H. Arnold, '*Carpe Millennium*: Niyi Osundare's *Seize the Day* and African Literature and the crisis in Post-Structuralist Theorising', in *Anglophonia/Caliban* French Journal of English Studies. Presses Universitaires de Toulouse-Mirail, no. 7, 2000. p.23-32

Aderenii Bamikunle, 'Niyi Osundare's Poetry and the Yoruba Oral Artistic Tradition', in *African Literature Today*, No. 18, 1988, pp. 49-61.

Karin Barber, *I Could Speak until Tomorrow: Oriki, Women, and the Past in a Yoruba Town*, Edinburgh, International African Library, Edinburgh University Press, 1991.

Karin Barber, 'The Use of English in Yoruba Popular Theatre' in Stewart Brown, Ed., *Kiss & Quarrel: Yoruba/English:Strategies of Mediation*, Birmingham, Birmingham University African Studies Series no. 5, 2000, p.154-172.

James Berry, *Fractured Circles,* London, New Beacon Books, 1979

James Berry, *Lucy's Letters and Loving,* London, New Beacon Books, 1982

James Berry, *Chain of Days,* Oxford, Oxford University Press, 1985

James Berry, *When I Dance,* London, Puffin Books, 1988.

James Berry *Hot Earth Cold Earth,* Newcastle, Bloodaxe Books, 1995.

Curwen Best, *Barbadian Popular Music and the Politics of Caribbean Culture*, Alterations Consultants, New York, 1995.

Berjouhi Bowler, *The Word as Image*, London, Studio Vista, 1970.

Stewart Brown, Ed., NOW, nos 1-5, St Anne's Bay, Jamiaca, 1972-74.

Stewart Brown, 'Spoiler, Walcott's People's Patriot' in *Wasafiri*, no. 9, Winter, 1988, p.10-15;

Stewart Brown, 'Interview with Edward Kamau Brathwaite' in *Kyk-over-al*, no.40, 1989: p.84-93.

Stewart Brown, 'Walcott's Fortunate Traveller: A Patriot in Exile', in *Carib*, Kingston, Jamaica, no. 5, Winter 1989/90 1-18;

Stewart Brown, 'The Apprentice' in Stewart Brown, Ed., *The Art of Derek Walcott*, Bridgend, Seren Books, 1991. pp. 13-33.

Stewart Brown, 'Tourist, Traveller, Troublemaker' in *The Works*, Nigel Jenkins, (ed.), Swansea, Welsh Union of Writers,. p.117-128. 1991

Stewart Brown, Ed., *The Art of Derek Walcott*, Bridgend, Seren Books, 1991.

Stewart Brown, Ed., *The Pressures of the Text: Orality Texts and the Telling of Tales*, Birmingham, Birmingham University African Studies Series no.4, 1995.

Stewart Brown, 'Daring the Beast: recent Nigerian Poetry' in Abdulrazak Gurnah, Ed., *Essays on African Writing 2: Contemporary Literature*, Oxford, 1995, p.58-72.

Stewart Brown, 'Between me and thee is a great gulf fixed': The Crusoe Presence in Walcott's early poetry' in *Robinson Crusoe: Myths and Metamorphoses*, eds. Lieve Spaas and Brian Stimpson, Basingstoke, Macmillan, 1996, p.210-224

Stewart Brown, 'Niyi Osundare, Crossing the threshold between Yoruba and English', in *Anglophonia: Journal of English Studies,* no.7, 1998, p.33-41.

Stewart Brown, 'Celebration Songs: the poetry of James Berry', in *Kunapipi*, vol.XX, no.1, 1998, p.45-56.

Stewart Brown, 'No voice in the emptiness: the poetry of Martin Carter' in *Planet: the Welsh Internationalist*, Aberystwyth, no.129, June 1998.

Stewart Brown, *Elsewhere:New and Selected Poems*, Leeds, Peepal Tree Press, 1999

Stewart Brown, Ed., *All are Involved: the Art of Martin Carter,* Leeds, Peepal Tree Press, 2000

Stewart Brown, Ed., *Kiss & Quarrel:Yoruba/English: Strategies of Mediation*, Birmingham, Birmingham University African Studies Series no. 5, 2000.

Stewart Brown, 'Still Daring the Beast: Niyi Osundare and contemporary Nigerian Poetry' in *The People's Poet: Emerging perspectives on Niyi Osundare*, A-R Na'Allah (Editor), Trenton, NJ, Africa World Press, 2003, 97-114.

Stewart Brown, "Incalculable Flotsam": Frank Collymore salvaging poetry from the sea', in *Remembering the Sea: an introduction to Frank A. Collymore*, P.W. Nanton (Editor), Bridgetown, Central Bank of Barbados, 2004, p.54-76.

Stewart Brown and Mark McWatt, Eds., *The Oxford Book of Caribbean Verse*, Oxford, Oxford University Press, 2005.

Stewart Brown and Ian McDonald, Eds., *Martin Carter: Poems*, Oxford, Macmillan Caribbean, 2006.

Edward Brathwaite, *Rights of Passage*, Oxford, OUP, 1967.

Edward Kamau Brathwaite, *The Arrivants: a New World Trilogy*, Oxford, OUP, 1967.

Edward Brathwaite, *The Development of Creole Society in Jamaica 1770-1820*, Oxford, OUP, 1970.

Kamau Brathwaite, 'Caribbean Culture: Two Paradigms' in Jurgen Martini, Ed., *Missile and Capsule*, Bremen, Universitat Bremen, 1983: p.9-54.

Kamau Brathwaite, *History of the Voice: The Development of Nation Language in Anglophone Caribbean Poetry*, London, New Beacon Books, 1984.

Kamau Brathwaite, *X/Self*, Oxford, OUP, 1987.

Kamau Brathwaite, 'Interview' with Stewart Brown, in *Kyk-over-al*, no.40, 1989: p.84-93.

Kamau Brathwaite, *Middle Passages*, Newcastle, Bloodaxe, 1992.

Kamau Brathwaite, *The Zea Mexican Diary*, Madison, University of Wisconsin Press, 1993.

Kamau Brathwaite, *Barabajan Poems*, New York, Savacou North, 1995.

Kamau Brathwaite, *Dreamstories*, Harlow, Longman, 1998.

Kamau Brathwaite, *Ancestors: A Reinvention of Mother Poem, Sun Poem and X/Self*, New York, New Directions, 2001

Kamau Brathwaite, *LX the Love Axe/ L: Developing a Caribbean Aesthetic*, an Account in Fact and Memory of the Cultural Revolution/CR in the *Anglophone Caribbean C.1965-c.1985 and Continuing*, Leeds, Peepal Tree Press, 2008.

Idi Bukar, *First the Desert Came and then the Torturer*, Zaria, RAG Press, 1984.

Barry Richard Burg, *Sodomy and the Pirate Tradition: English Sea Rovers in the Seventeenth Century Caribbean*, New York, NYU Press, 1995.

Don Burness, 'Niyi Osundare' in *The Dictionary of Literary Biography*, vol.157, *(Twentieth Century Caribbean and Black African Writers*, Third Series), Formington Hills, Michigan, Thompson Gale, 1995, p.286-295.

Don Burness, *Il Grido del Corvo/ The Cry of the Crow*, bilingual edition, Naples, Italy, Scrittori Contemporanei no. 6, 1966

Don Burness, *Safari*, Evanston, Troubadour Press, 1984.

Don Burness, *Watching the Masquerade*, Rindge, New Hampshire, 1990.

Don Burness, *The Bardie Clan: Selected and New Poems*, Evanston, Troubadour Press, 1998.

Duncan Bush, *The Hook*, Bridgend, Seren Books, 1997.

Martin Carter, 'The Location of the Artist' in *Kyk-ove-al* 44. May 1993, p.111-112.

Martin Carter, 'On Poetry' in *Kyk-ove-al* 44. May 1993, p.122-3.

Martin Carter, *University of Hunger: Collected Poems & Selected Prose*, Gemma Robinson, ed., Tarset, Bloodaxe Books, 2006.

Martin Carter, *Martin Carter: Poems*, eds. Stewart Brown and Ian McDonald, Oxford, Macmillan Caribbean, 2006.

Frank Collymore, *Rhymed Ruminations on the Fauna of Barbados*, Barbados, Private Publication, 1968.

Frank A. Collymore, *Selected Poems*, Barbados, Private Publication, 1971.

Carolyn Cooper, *Noises in the Blood: Orality, Gender and the Vulgar Body of Jamaican Popular Culture, Basingstoke, Macmillan* (Warwick University, Caribbean Studies Series), 1993.

Carolyn Cooper, 'Lyrical Gun': Metaphor and Role Play in Jamaican Dancehall Culture, in *The Massachusetts Review*, Autumn-Winter 1994, p.429-447

Carolyn Cooper, *Sound Clash: Jamaican Dancehall Culture at Large*, London, Palgrave, Macmillan, 2004.

Kevin Crossley-Holland, ed. *The Oxford Book of Travel Verse*, Oxford, OUP, 1986.

Raphael Dalleo, 'Another "Our America": Rooting a Caribbean Aesthetic in the Work of Jose Marti, Kamau Brathwaite and Edouard Glissant', in *Anthurium: A Caribbean Studies Journal*, vol. 2, no. 2., Fall 2004.

John Davies, 'All the Running' in *Poetry Wales*, vol. 20, no.4, 1985, p.41-47.

John Davies, *The Visitor's Book*, Bridgend, Poetry Wales Press, 1985.

Fred D'Aguiar, 'Chanting Down Babylon', in Linton Kwesi Johnson, *Mi Revalueshanary Fren:Selected Poems*, op cit. p.ix-xiv. (p.xi)

Kwame Dawes, *Progeny of Air*, Leeds, Peepal Tree Press, 1994.

Kwame Dawes, *Prophets*, Leeds, Peepal Tree Press, 1995.

Kwame Dawes, *Requiem*, Leeds, Peepal Tree Press, 1996.

Kwame Dawes, *Natural Mysticism: Towards a New Reggae Aesthetic in Caribbean Writing*, Leeds, Peepal Tree Press, 1997.

Kwame Dawes, *Jacko Jacobus*, Leeds, Peepal Tree Press, 1997.

Kwame Dawes, *Shook Foil*, Leeds, Peepal Tree Press, 1998.

Kwame Dawes, *Wheel and Come Again: an anthology of Reggae poetry*. Leeds, Peepal Tree Press, 1999.

Kwame Dawes, *Midland*, Athens, Ohio, Ohio University Press, 2001.

Kwame Dawes, *Bob Marley: Lyrical Genius*, London, Sanctuary Publishing Ltd., 2002.

Anthony Easthope, *Poetry as Discourse*, London, Routledge, 1976.

John Figueroa, Ed., *Caribbean Voices*, Evans Bros. 1971.

Robert Fraser, *West African Poetry*, Cambridge: Cambridge University Press, 1986.

Harry Geruba, Ed., *Voices from the Fringe*, Lagos: Malthouse Press, 1990.

Robert Gittings, *Collected Poems*, London, Heinemann, 1976.

Nadine Gordimer, 'The Essential Gesture: Writers and Responsibility', in *Granta*, No. 15, 1989, p. 137-51.

Abdulrazak Gurnah, Ed., *Essays on African Writing, 2*, Oxford, Heinemann, 1995.

Christian Habekost, *Verbal Riddim: The Politics and Aesthetics of African-Caribbean Dub Poetry*, Amsterdam, Rodopi, 1993.

Donald Hall, Ed., *American Poetry*, London, Faber & Faber,1969.

Ian Hamilton, Ed., *The Oxford Companion to Twentieth Century Poetry*, Oxford, OUP, 1994,

T.W. Harrison and James Simmonds, *Aikin Mata: The Lysistrata of Aristophanes*, Ibadan, Oxford University Press, 1966.

Tony Harrison, *The Loiners*, London, London Magazine Editions, 1970.

Terrence Hawkes, *Structuralism and Semiotics*, London, Methuen, 1977.

John Haynes, *Sabon Gari*, London, London Magazine Editions, 1974.

John Haynes, (as Idi Bukar) *First the Desert Came and then the Torturer*, Zaria, RAG Press, 1984.

John Haynes, *African Poetry and the English Language*, London, Macmillan, 1987.

John Haynes, *Letter to Patience*, Bridgend, Seren , 2007

Edward Hirsch, 'An Interview with Derek Walcott', *Contemporary Literature*, vol. 20, no. 3, 1980, 279-92.

Kevin Ireland, 'Place and Poetic Identity', in *The Journal of Commonwealth Literature*, vol. 1, no. 2, December 1966, 157-60.

Abiola Irele, 'Second Language Literatures: An African Perspective' in *Anglophonia/Caliban*, no. 7, 2000. p.7-22.

Nigel Jenkins, Ed., *The Works*, Swansea, Welsh Union of Writers, 1991

Onwuchekwa Jemie, 'A Conversation with Odia Ofeimun', in *The Poet Lied*, Lagos: Update Communications Ltd., 1989.

Nigel Jenkins, Ed., *The Works*, Welsh Union of Writers,1991

Rev. Samuel Johnson, *The History of the Yorubas from the Earliest Times to the Beginning of the British Protectorate*. Ed. By Dr O. Johnson. London, Routledge, 1921.

Biodun Jeyifo, 'Niyi Osundare' in Yemi Ogunbiyi, Ed., *Perspectives on Nigerian Literature*, Vol. 2., Lagos: Guardian Books (Nigeria), 1988, p.314-320.

Linton Kwesi Johnson, *Voices of the Living and the Dead*, London, Race Today Publications, 1974.

Linton Kwesi Johnson, *Dread Beat and Blood*, London, Bogle- L'Ouverture Publications, 1975.

Linton Kwesi Johnson, *Tings an Times:Selected Poems*, Newcastle, Bloodaxe, 1991.

Linton Kwesi Johnson, *Mi Revalueshanary Fren: Selected Poems*, London, Penguin Classics, 2002.

Linton Kwesi Johnson, *Selected Poems*, London, Penguin Poetry, 2002.

Jamaica Kincaid, *A Small Place*, London, Virago, 1988.

Rudyard Kipling, *Collected Poems*, Ware, Wordsworth Editions, 1994.

Barbara Lalla, 'Conceptual Perspectives on Time and Timelessness in Martin Carter's 'University of Hunger" in Stewart Brown, Ed., *All are Involved: the Art of Martin Carter*, Leeds, Peepal Tree Press, 2000 p.106-115.

George Lamming, 'Martin Carter: A Poet of the Americas' in *All are Involved: the Art of Martin Carter*, Stewart Brown, ed., Leeds, Peepal Tree Press, 2000, p.311-317.

Philip Larkin, *The Less Deceived*, Hessel, The Marvell Press, 1953.

Ian Lumsden, *Machos, Maricones and Gays: Cuba and Homosexuality*, London, Latin America Bureau, 1997.

Ian McDonald, *Mercy Ward*, Calstock, Cornwall, Peterloo Press, 1988.

Ian McDonald, *Essequibo*, Calstock, Cornwall, Peterloo Press, 1992.

Ian McDonald, (ed.) *Kyk-over-al*, no. 44, May 1993 , a special issue, guest edited by Nigel Westmaas, devoted to Martin Carter's prose.

Ian McDonald, *Jaffo the Calypsonian*, Leeds, Peepal Tree Press. 1994.

Ian McDonald, (ed.) *Kyk-over-al*, no. 49/50, June 2000, 'The Martin Carter Tribute'.

Ian McDonald, *Between Silence and Silence*, Leeds, Peepal Tree Press, 2003.

Ian McDonald, *The Humming-Bird Tree*, Oxford, Macmillan Caribbean, 2005. (First published 1969)

Robert McGill, "Goon poets of the black Atlantic: Linton Kwesi Johnson's imagined canon', in *Textual Practice*, vol.17. no.3. 2003, p.561-574.

Gerald Moore, 'Towards Realism in French African Writing' in *Modern African Studies*, vol.1. no.1. 1963. p.61-73.

Jerome McGann, *Black Riders: the Visible Language of Modernism*, Princetown, New Jersey, Princetown University Press, 1993.

Jack Mapanje, *Of Chameleons and Gods*, London, Heinemann African Writers Series, 1981.

Jack Mapanje, *The Chattering Wagtails of Mikuyu Prison*, London, Heinemann African Writers Series, 1993.

Jack Mapanje, *Skipping Without Ropes*, Tarset, Bloodaxe Books, 1998.

Jack Mapanje, *The Last of the Sweet Bananas:New & Selected Poems*, Tarset, Bloodaxe Books, 2004.

Jurgen Martini, Ed., *Missile and Capsule*, Bremen, Universitat Bremen, 1983

Pauline Melville, *The Ventriloquist's Tale*, London, Bloomsbury, 1997.

Mary E. Morgan, 'Highway to vision: this sea our nexus' in *World Literature Today*, vol.68, no. 4. Autumn 1994. p.663-668.

Mervyn Morris, *The Pond*, London, New Beacon Books, 1973. Revised Edition, London, New Beacon Books, 1997.

Mervyn Morris, *Shadow Boxing*, London, New Beacon Books, 1979.

Mervyn Morris, *Examination Centre*, London, New Beacon Books, 1992.

Mervyn Morris, *Is English we Speaking and other essays*, Kingston, Jamaica, Ian Randle Publishers, 1999.

Mervyn Morris, *I been there, sort of: New and Selected Poems*, Manchester, Carcanet, 2006.

Abdul-Rasheed Na'Allah, Ed., *The People's Poet: Emerging perspectives on Niyi Osundare*, Trenton, NJ, Africa World Press, 2003

P.W. Nanton, Ed., *Remembering the Sea: an introduction to Frank A. Collymore*, Bridgetown, Central Bank of Barbados, 2004.

Ngugi wa Thiong'o, *Detained: A Writers Prison Diary*, Oxford, Heinemann African Writers Series, 1981.

Ngugi wa Thiong'o, *Devil on the Cross*, Oxford, Heinemann African Writers Series, 1987.

Donatus Nwoga, *West African Verse,* London, Longman, 1967.

Obododimma Oha. ed., *Home and Exile in Femi Oyebode's Poetry,* a special issue of the journal <u>ASE...</u>, an interdisciplinary journal for the study of contemporary Nigerian life and literature, published by The Poetry Clubs of the Universities of Calabar and Ibadan, Nigeria, Vol. III, no.III, 1996.

Olu Oguibe, *A Song from Exile,* Bayreuth, Boomerang Press, 1990.

Yemi Ogunbiyi, Ed.,*Perspectives on Nigerian Literature: 1700 to the present,* Vol. 1, Lagos: Guardian Books (Nigeria), 1988.

Yemi Ogunbiyi, Ed.,*Perspectives on Nigerian Literature: 1700 to the present,* Vol. 2, Lagos: Guardian Books (Nigeria), 1988.

Tanure Ojaide, *The Fate of Vultures,* Lagos: Malthouse Press, 1990.

Tanure Ojaide, *The Blood of Peace,* London: Heinemann, 1991.

Oladejo Okediji, 'Translating AAJO AJE' in Stewart Brown, Ed., *Kiss & Quarrel:Yoruba/English: Strategies of Mediation,* Birmingham, Birmingham University African Studies Series no. 5, 2000, p.172-181.

Christopher Okigbo, *Labyrinths,* London: Heinemann, 1971.

Sanya Osha, *Ken Saro-Wiwa's Shadow: Politics,Nationalism and the Ogoni Protest,* London, Adonis & Abbey Publishers Ltd, 2007.

Oshita O. Oshita, 'The Metaphysics of Femi Oyebode's Poetry' in *Home and Exile in Femi Oyebode's Poetry,* Ed., Obododimma Oha, a special issue of the journal ASE..., an interdisciplinary journal for the study of contemporary Nigerian life and literature, published by The Poetry Clubs of the Universities of Calabar and Ibadan, Nigeria, Vol. III, no.III, 1996, p.26-37.

Femi Osofisan, 'The Alternative Tradition: A Survey of Nigerian Literature in English After the Civil War', *Presence Africane, no.139, 1986, p.162-184*

Niyi Osundare, *The Eye of the Earth,* Lagos: Heinemann, 1986.

Niyi Osundare, *Waiting Laughters,* Lagos: Malthouse Press, 1990.

Niyi Osundare, *Midlife,* Ibadan, Heinemann Educational Books, 1993.

Niyi Osundare, 'Caliban's Gamble: The Stylistic Repercussions of Writing African Literature in English' in Kola Owolabi, ed. *Language in Nigeria,* Group Publishers, Ibadan, 1995, p.340-363.

Niyi Osundare, 'Yoruba Thought, English Words: A Poet's Journey Through The Tunnel Of Two Tongues' in Stewart Brown, Ed., *Kiss & Quarrel: Yoruba/English: Strategies of Mediation,* op cit. 2000, p.15-31.

Kola Owolabi, ed., *Language in Nigeria,* Ibadan, Group Publishers, 1995.

Femi Oyebode, *Naked to Your Softness and Other Dreams',* Birmingham, Ijala Press, 1989.

Femi Oyebode, *Wednesday is a Colour,* Birmingham, Ijala Press, 1990.

Femi Oyebode, *Forest of Transformation,* Birmingham, Ijala Press, 1991.

Femi Oyebode, *Adagio for Oblong Mirrors,* Birmingham, Ijala Press,1993

Femi Oyebode, *Master of the Leopard Hunt,* Birmingham, Ijala Press, 1995.

Femi Oyebode, 'Prosody and Literary Texts' in Stewart Brown, Ed., *The Pressures of the Text: orality, texts and the telling of tales,* Birmingham University African Studies Series, no.4, 1995, p.91-95.

Femi Oyebode, *Indigo, Camwood and Mahogany Red,* Birmingham, Ijala Press, 1998

Femi Oyebode, *Selected Poems,* Ibadan, Kraftgriots, Kraft Books Ltd., 1998.

Okot p'Bitek, 'What is Literature' in his collection of essays, *Africa's Cultural*

Revolution Nairobi, Macmillan Books for Africa, 1973, p.15-23.

Okot p'Bitek, *Africa's Cultural Revolution* Nairobi, Macmillan Books for Africa, 1973, Kirsten Holst Peterson and Anna Rutherford, Eds., *Chinua Achebe: A Celebration*, Oxford, Heinemann, 1991.

Alex Preminger, Frank Joseph Warnke, Eds., *The Princeton Encyclopaedia of Poetry and Poetics*, London, Palgrave Macmillan, 1975.

John Pudney, *Collected Poems*, London, Putnam, 1957.

Jahan Ramazani, *The Hybrid Muse: Postcolonial Poetry in English*, University of Chicago Press, 2001.

Kenneth Ramchand, *An Introduction to West Indian Literature,* Sunbury on Thames, Nelson Caribbean, 1976.

Gemma Robinson, Ed., *University of Hunger: Martin Carter, Collected Poems & Selected Prose*, Tarset, Bloodaxe Books, 2006

Rupert Roopnarine, 'Martin Carter and Politics' in *All are Involved: the Art of Martin Carter,* Stewart Brown, ed., Leeds, Peepal Tree Press, 2000, p.48-57.

Gordon Rohlehr, 'Dream Journeys', the Introduction to Kamau Brathwaite, *DreamStories*, op.cit. p.iii-xvi.

Antonio Benitez Rojo, *The Repeating Island: The Caribbean and the Postmodern Perspective*, Durham, Duke University Press, 1996.

Edward W. Said, *The World, The Text, and the Critic*, London, Faber & Faber, 1984.

Ken Saro-Wiwa, *Sozaboy: a novel in Rotten English*, Harlow, Longman (African Writers series), 1994

Ken Saro-Wiwa, *A Forest of Flowers*, Harlow, Longman (African Writers series), 1995

Jean Paul Sartre, 'Orphee Noir', the Introduction to *Anthologie de la nouvelle poésie nègre et malgache de langue française* [éditée] par Léopold Sédar Senghor. 4e éd. Paris, 1977. (1st edition 1948).

Léopold Sédar Senghor, ed., Anthologie de la nouvelle poésie nègre et malgache de langue française, Paris, 1977. 4e éd. (1st edition 1948).

Olive Senior, *Talking of Trees*, Kingston, Jamaica, Calabash Publications, 1985.

Olive Senior, *Gardening in the Tropics*, Newcastle, Bloodaxe, 1995.

Olive Senior, *Over the Roofs of the World,* Toronto, Insomniac Press, 2005.

Lieve Spaas and Brian Stimpson, Eds., *Robinson Crusoe: Myths and Metamorphoses,* Basingstoke, Macmillan, 1996,

St. John Pearse, *Elogues and Other Poems*, Louis Varese transit, Bollingden Series LV, French text from the *Oeuvre Poetique,* Paris: Librairie Gallimard, 1953.

Willie van Peer, 'Typographic foregrounding', in *Language and Literature*, vol.2, No. 1, 1993: pp. 49-59.

Helen Vendler, 'Poet of Two Worlds: The Fortunate Traveller' in Harold Bloom, Ed., Bloom's Modern Critical Views: Derek Walcott, Broomall, P.A., Chelsea House Publishers, 2003, p.25-33.

Derek Walcott, *25 Poems*, private publication, Port of Spain, Trinidad, 1948.

Derek Walcott, *The Castaway and other Poems*, London, Jonathan Cape, 1965

Derek Walcott, *The Gulf*, London, Jonathan Cape, 1970.

Derek Walcott, 'What the Twilight Says, an Overture', in *Dream on Monkey Mountain and other plays*, New York, 1970.

Derek Walcott, *Dream on Monky Mountain and Other Plays*, London, Jonathan Cape, 1972.

Derek Walcott, 'The Muse of History', in O. Coombs (ed.) *Is Massa Day Done?* New York: Anchor/Doubleday, 1974

Derek Walcott, *Sea Grapes*, London, Jonathan Cape, 1976.

Derek Walcott, *The Star-apple Kingdom*, London: Jonathan Cape, 1980.

Derek Walcott, *Remembrance and Pantomime*, New York, Farrar, Strauss & Giroux, 1980.

Derek Walcott, 'An Interview with Derek Walcott', (Edward Hirsch,) *Contemporary Literature*, vol. 20, no. 3, 1980, 279-92,

Derek Walcott, *Midsummer*, New York, Farrar, Strauss & Giroux, 1984.

Derek Walcott, *Collected Poems 1948-1984*, New York, Farrar, Straus and Giroux, 1986,

Derek Walcott, 'The Muse of History' in *What the Twilight Says*, London Faber and Faber, 1998, p.37.

Anne Walmsley, Ed., *The Sun's Eye*, Harlow, Longman, 1968.

Anne Walmsley, 'Her Stem Singing: Kamau Brathwaite's *Zea-Mexican Diary*', in *World Literature Today*, vol.68, no.4, Autumn 1994, p.747-749.

Anne Walmsley and Nick Caistor, Eds., *Facing the Sea*, London, Heinemann, 1986.

James Weiland, '"Confronting his Madness": History as Amnesia in the poetry of Derek Walcott, ' *New Literature Review*, no. 7, 1980, 73-82.

Nigel Westmas, ed. *Kyk-over-al*, no. 44, May 1993 , a special issue, devoted to Martin Carter's prose.

Landeg White, 'Afternoons, Mozambique' in *For Captain Steadman*, Liskeard, Harry Chambers/Peterloo Press, 1983.

Landeg White, *South*, Figuera Da Foz, Portugal, CEMAR, 1999.

Landeg White, *Traveller's Tree,* Figuera Da Foz, Portugal, CEMAR, 2002.

George Woodcock, *Who killed the British Empire? An Inquest*, London, Cape, 1974.

Zukofsky, Louis, ed. *An 'Objectivist' Anthology*, Paris, To, Publishers, 1932.

Discography

Red Plastic Bag, *plastic @ calypso.com*, BF-CD 047 (CD) Bayfield Records Ltd, Barbados, 1996.

Buju Banton, *The Early Years: 1990-1995*, New York, Penthouse Records,2001, (B00005NF2K).

John Figueroa, Ed., *Poets of the West Indies*, Caedmon TC1379, 1971.

Gabby, *Gabby – till now, (Thirty years as a Calypsonian)* Caribbean Classic 961702, Blue Wave Records, Barbados, 1996.

Linton Kwesi Johnson, *A Capella*, (CD), Hearne Hill, London, LKJ Records, 2002.

Linton Kwesi Johnson, *More Time*, (CD), Hearne Hill, London, LKJ Records, 1998.

The Mighty Spoiler, *Mighty Spoiler Unspoilt*, Caribbean Classics 950502 (CD), Ice Records Ltd., London, 1995.

poetry to critical discussion of other poets, 9-10; poems discussed: 'Zinder', 16-18; 'Tourist Guide, West Africa', 18-19, 292, 'Cricket at Kano', 20-22; 'Whales', 22-24; 'Lugard's Bridge', 25-40, 49-50, 55; founding of Caribbean literary magazine, *NOW*, 117; work as anthologist/editor, for Longman African and Caribbean Writers imprint, 43, 118-119, 212-213; self-reflections on outsider status, 119; role as judge of Caribbean literary prize, 122-133;

Brown, Wayne, 117

Bukar, Idi (alias John Haynes), 284-285, 314

Burg, B.R., 147-148: *Sodomy and the Pirate Tradition: English sea rovers in the Seventeenth Century*, 147-148, 298

Burness, Don, 13, **257-265**, 311-312; definitions of the traveller in Burness's work, 257-258; involvement with Nigeria, 258; observation and meditation, 259-260; humour, 262; on Jewish inheritance, 264-265; work discussed: *Safari*, 257; *Watching the Masquerade*, 258; *The Cry of the Crow*, 260; *The Bardie Clan*, 257: 'The War Never Left Port Harcourt', 258, 'Along the Elegant Streets of Dakar', 258-259, 'Safari', 259, 'Yad Vashem', 260, 'At Elmina Castle', 260, 'I think of people I have not seen for years', 261, 'Praise Song for Hilda Leach', 261, 'Letter to the Future', 261, 'Modern Love', 262, 'Couplets', 262, 'Epistle to the Critic Russell Hamilton', 262, 'The Rosenbergs: Forty Years Later', 263, 'Longfellow in Menton', 263, 'I Hear America Crying', 263, 'The House on Griswold Drive', 264, 'The Bardie

Clan', 264, 'On Being a Jew', 264-265

Burnham, Forbes, 122, 159

Burrows, E.R., 172

Bush, Duncan, 273, 313

'Caliban's Gamble [essay] (Osundare), 87

Canon-formation, West Indian poetry, 118-120

Carew, Jan, 124

'Caribbean Culture: Two Paradigms' (Brathwaite), 198

Caribbean New Wave (ed. Brown), 118

Caribbean Poetry Now (ed. Brown), 117, 118

Caribbean Voices (ed. Figueroa), 116, 174

Carter, Martin, 12, 47, 55, **56-58**, 77, 124, 125, 130, 150, **156-162**, 164, 237, 289, 299-300; poems discussed: 'This is the Dark Time My Love', **56**, 157, 'I Clench My Fist', **57-58**, 'University of Hunger', 156-157, 'Words', 157, 'I Come from the Nigger Yard', 157, 'A Mouth is Always Muzzled', 159, 'Let Every Child Run Wild', 160, 'Some Kind of Fury', 161, 'Rice', 162, 'Bitter Wood', 162

Castaway, The (Walcott), 186; 'The Castaway', 189

Césaire, Aimé, 156

Chain of Days (Berry), 217

'Chanting Down Babylon' (essay, D'Aguiar), 247

Chattering Wagtails of Mikuyu Prison, The (Mapanje), 114

'City Poem' (Senior), 153

Clarke, J.P., 71

Collins, Merle, 151

Collymore, Frank, 12, **163-181**, 300-302; editorship of *Bim* and mentoring of younger poets, 165; range of themes in *Selected Poems*, (poems of spirit, satires, poems of place, love poems, memorials) 167; humorous verse, 300-301; work discussed: 'Hymn to the Sea', 165, **176-181**; *Notes for a Glossary of Words and Phrases of Barbadian Dialect*, 167; 'Amanda – the negress', 167, 'So this is Love', 168, 'Beneath the Casuarinas',168, 170, **171-172**, 'Because I have Turned my Back', 168, **171**, 'That Day', 168, **170-171**, 'Words are the poem', 168, **169-170**, 'Blue Agave', 168, 170, **173**, 'Voici la plume de mon oncle', **173-174**, 175, 'Ballad of an Old Woman', 175, 'Portrait of Mr X', 175, 'Schooner', 176, 'Return' 177-180; 'Rhymed Ruminations on the Fauna of Barbados', 300-301.

Colonialism, and writing in English, 66-67, 165-166

Commonwealth Writers Prize, 125

Cooper, Carolyn, 142, 146, 252, 298, 311

'Couplets' (Burness), 262

Creighton, Al, 127, 129

'Cricket at Kano' (Brown), 20-22

'Crime of Passion' (Dawes), 254

Crop-Over Festival, Barbados, 134-135

Crossley-Holland, Kevin, 288

'Crusoe's Journal' (Walcott), 185, 189, 192-193

Cullen, Countee, 201

Dabydeen, David, 124

D'Aguiar, Fred, 124, 237, 247, 310

Dalleo, Raphael, 306

Dann, Graham, 145

Darker Side of Black, The (film, Isaac Julian), 146

Das, Mahadai, 151

'Data' (Morris), 239

Davies, John, 47, 56, **58-61**, 289; work discussed: 'All the Running', 59, 'The Visitor's Book', 59-60, 'The White Buffalo', 60-61

Dawes, Kwame, 13, 246, 247, **251-256**, 310-311; reggae aesthetic, 251-252; relationship to Brathwaite and Walcott, 252-253; work discussed: *Natural Mysticism: Towards a Reggae Aesthetic*, 251-252; *Wheel and Come Again*, 251; *Requiem*, **252-254**: 'Family Tree', 253, 'Shame', 253, 'Crime of Passion' 254; *Shook Foil*, 252, **254-255**: 'Some Tentative Definitions 1', 254, 'I am a Stranger on Earth', 255; *Midland*, 252, 255-256: 'Inheritance', 255-256, 'Ska Memory', 256, 'Liminal', 256; *Progeny of Air*, 255; *Prophets*, 255; *Jacko Jacobus*, 255

Dawes, Neville, 117, 256

'Days of Empire' (Bush), 273

Detained (Ngugi), 53

Development of Creole Society in Jamaica 1770-1820, The (Brathwaite), 197-198

Devil on the Cross (Ngugi), 53

'Dialogue Between Two Large Village Women' (Berry), 220-221

Dread Beat and Blood (Johnson), 245-246

Dream Stories (Brathwaite), 206-207, 209, 212-213, 'Dream Chad', 207

'Dreamtime' (Oyebode), 63

Diop, David, 74

Dub poetry (see Johnson), 246-250

Duenne (Mohammed), 132

Easthope, Anthony, 205, 305

Eliot, T.S., 166, 200

'Epistle to the Critic Russell Hamilton' (Burness), 262

'Epitaph' (Senior), 152-153

Homophobia, in popular culture, 142-148; in reggae, 142; in Barbadian calypso, 142-148
Homosexuality, discourse on in Barbados, 144-145
'Homer to Naipaul' (White), 281-282
Horses of Memory (Osundare), 79
Hot Earth Cold Earth (Berry), 223, 224
'Howl' (Ginsberg), 263
Hummingbird Tree, The (McDonald), 229
Hybrid Muse: Postcolonial Poetry in English, The (Ramazani), 155, 299
'Hymn to the Sea' (Collymore), 165, **176-181**
Hughes, Langston, 201
Hughes, Ted, 92

'I am Racism' (Berry), 218-219
'I am a Stranger on Earth' (Dawes), 255
'I am The Man' (Morris), 242-243
Ian Randle Publications, 297
I Been There, sort of: New and Selected Poems (Morris), 239
'I Come from the Nigger Yard' (Carter), 157
'If I Woz a Tap Natch Poet' (Johnson), 248
'I Hear America Crying' (Burness), 263
Immigration, West Indian, to Britain, 214-215
Imprint Caribbean, 297
Indigo Camwood and Mahogany Red (Oyebode), 103
'Inglan is a Bitch' (Johnson), 247
'Inheritance' (Dawes), 255-256
'In our Year 1941 My Letter to you Mother Africa' (Berry), 225-226
'I think of people I have not seen for years' (Burness), 261

Irele, Abiola, 90
Is English We Speaking (criticism, Morris), 239

Jacko Jacobus (Dawes), 255
Jackson, Dawson, 286
Jaffo the Calypsonian (McDonald), 231, 233; 'Jaffo the Calypsonian', 229
Jagan, Cheddi, 159
Jagan, Janet, 130
Jakobson, Roman, 11
Jamaican Sunday Gleaner, 24
Jemie, Onwuchekwu, 77, 291
Johnson, Linton Kwesi, 13, **245-250**, 310; frustration within public mode, 247; poetry on the page and in performance, 248-250; work discussed: *Dread Beat and Blood*, 245-246: 'Five Nights of Bleeding', 245, 'All Wi Doin is Defendin', 245, 'Inglan is a Bitch', 247; *Tings and Times*, 246; *Voices of the Living and the Dead*, 247; *Mi Revalueshanary Fren*, 247: 'If I Waz a Tap Natch Poet', 248; *Selected Poems*, 250; CDs: *A Capella*, 250, *More Time*, 250
Johnson, Rev. Samuel, 63, 102, 290
Julian, Isaac, 146, 147

Keats, John, 66, 180
Kincaid, Jamaica, 14-15, 16
Kipling, Rudyard, 13, 28, 93, 269-270, 272, 287, 312
Kuti, Fela, 50

Lalla, Barbara (see Carter), 300
Lamming, George, 300
Larkin, Philip, 96, 294
Last of the Sweet Bananas, The (Mapanje), 111, 114-115
'Laventille' (Walcott), 185, 186
'Let Earth's Pain be Soothed' (Osundare), 81

McNeill, Anthony, 117

'Meeting Mr Cargill on my Village Road' (Berry), 224

Melville, Pauline, 124, 131, 237, 297

Mercy Ward (McDonald), 231

'Middle Age' (McDonald), 235

Middle Passages (Brathwaite), 197, 203

Midland (Dawes), 252, 255-256

Midlife (Osundare), 95

Midsummer, 'XXXIV' (Walcott), 194

'Migrant in London' (Berry), 216-217

Milton, John

Minor poetry, discussion of term, 163-164

Mi Revalueshanary Fren (Johnson), 247

Mittelholzer, Edgar, 124

Mnthali, Felix, 113

'Modern Love' (Burness), 262

Mohamed, Paloma, 132

Moore, Philip, 124

Morgan, Mary E., 306

Morris, Mervyn, 119, **239-244**, 309, influences, 240, 242, 244; relationship to social ferment of post-independence period, 241: work discussed: *Is English We Speaking* (criticism), 239; *Examination Centre*, 240: 'Data', 239, 'Walk Good', 243; *The Pond*, 240, 241: 'Stripper', 240, 'To an Expatriate Friend', 241-242, 'I am The Man', 242-243, 'Valley Prince', 110, 243-244; *Shadow Boxing*, 240: 'Muse', 240; *On Holy Week*, 240; *I Been There, sort of: New and Selected Poems*, 239

Morris, William, 201

Mort, Graham, 286

Motion, Andrew, 293, 294

'Mr Perfection' (McDonald), 236

'Muse' (Morris), 240

'Mystery: African Gods of the New World' (Senior), 154

Naked to Your Softness, (dream sequence) (Oyebode), 62-63, 101-102

Natural Mysticism: Towards a Reggae Aesthetic, (Dawes) 251-252

Neruda, Pablo, 74, 160

New Negro, The (ed. Locke), 201

News for Babylon (ed. Berry), 227

'New World Colonial Childhood' (Berry), 223

Nichols, Grace, 125, 151

Noises in the Blood (Cooper), 252

NOMA Award, 125

Notes for a Glossary of Words and Phrases of Barbadian Dialect (Collymore), 167

NOW (ed. S. Brown), 117

Ngugi, wa Thiongo, 53, 289

Nwoga, Donatus, 290

Of Chameleons and Gods (Mapanje), 110-112

Ofeimun, Odia, 43, 45, 46, 48, **76-79**; work discussed: *The Poet Lied*, 76, **77**; *A Handle for the Flutist*, 76-77, 'Our Wild Christian', 79

Oguibe, Olu, **72-73**, 84, 290-291; work discussed: *A Song from Exile*, 72-73, 'The Emperor and the Poet', 72-73

Ojaide, Tanure, 72, **74-76**, 84, 291; poems discussed: 'Before Our God', 74, 'What Poets do our Leaders Read?', 74, 'When soldiers are diplomats', 74, 'Song for my Land', 74-75

Okigbo, Christopher, 71, 258, 290

'On Being a Jew' (Burness), 264-265

'On his Royal Blindness Paramount Chief Kwangala' (Mapanje), 113

On Holy Week (Morris), 240

Orphée Noir (Sartre), 25, 312

Osadebay, Dennis, 71

ALSO BY STEWART BROWN

Elsewhere
ISBN: 9781900715324; pp. 118, pub. 1999; £7.99

Stewart Brown has been described as 'one of the most exciting and original poets currently writing' and praised by Fred D'Aguiar for the 'peculiar chameleon-like power of his imagination to belong anywhere and to any experience without becoming compromised'. The poems in this collection encompass Africa, the Caribbean, Wales and England; and range from the sweep of imperial history and its painful aftermath, to the intimacies of domestic life. He writes of Africa and the Caribbean with a rare combination of sympathy, honesty and inwardness, while never pretending to be other than an Englishman abroad. He writes affectionately but without sentiment of 'ordinary' English life from the perspective of one who has been elsewhere, in ways which allow us to see it afresh.

But if these poems have a passionate concern with love, politics, history and the natural world, they are no less concerned with the shaping power of art, both as a subject and in the poems' own formation.

Elsewhere brings together, frequently in much revised form, the best work from his earlier much praised collections (*Mekin Foolishness*, *Zinder* and *Lugard's Bridge*) with many new poems. The long sequence 'Elsewhere', which brings Brown's painterly eye and witty humanity to the experience of living in the Caribbean, and 'Elmina', a moving and imaginative meditation on an Englishman's sense of complicity in the history of the slave trade, will further enhance his reputation.

Adele Newson writes in *World Literature Today*: 'Stewart Brown's volume of poetry *Elsewhere* is reminiscent of Jamaica Kincaid's *A Small Place* set to verse. The personas adopted by the poets in various parts of the Caribbean, Great Britain, and Africa speak to an ever-present awareness of "exiles, strangers, parasites." The world of the poet fashioned by Brown is collaborative, thought-provoking, and startling. In sum, the poems provide a response from a pensive citizen of the metropolis to the wreckage to be found in modern-day, former colonies.'

Laurence A. Breiner
Black Yeats: Eric Roach and the Politics of Caribbean Poetry
ISBN 13: 9781845230470; pp. 312; Jan. 2008; £17.99

For readers of West Indian literature, a study of Eric Roach requires no justification. He is the most significant poet in the English-speaking Caribbean between Claude McKay (who spent nearly all of his life abroad) and Derek Walcott. Roach began publishing in the late 1930s and continued, with a few interruptions, until 1974, the year of his suicide. His career thus spans an extraordinary period of Anglophone Caribbean history, from the era of violent strikes that led to the formation of most of the region's political parties, through the process of decolonization, the founding and subsequent failure of the Federation of the West Indies (1958-1962), and the coming of Independence in the 1960s. This book presents a critical analysis of all of Roach's published poetry, but it presents that interpretation as part of a broader study of the relations between his poetic activity, the political events he experienced (especially West Indian Federation, Independence, the Black Power movement, the 'February Revolution' of 1970 Trinidad), and the seminal debates about art and culture in which he participated.

By exploring Roach's work within its conditions, this book aims above all to confirm Roach's rightful place among West Indian and metropolitan poets of comparable gifts and accomplishments.

All Peepal Tree titles are available from our website: www.peepaltreepress.com; email hannah@peepaltreepress.com Or you can contact us at Peepal Tree Press, 17 Kings Avenue, Leeds LS6 1QS, UK (Tel +44 113 245 1703)

A	B	C	D	E	F	G	H

IAKER:

I	J	K	L	M	N	P	Q

ALSO BY STEWART BROWN